Beginning Power BI

A Practical Guide to Self-Service
Data Analytics with Excel 2016 and
Power BI Desktop

Second Edition

Dan Clark

Apress®

Beginning Power BI: A Practical Guide to Self-Service Data Analytics with Excel 2016 and Power BI Desktop

Dan Clark
Camp Hill, Pennsylvania, USA

ISBN-13 (pbk): 978-1-4842-2576-9   ISBN-13 (electronic): 978-1-4842-2577-6
DOI 10.1007/978-1-4842-2577-6

Library of Congress Control Number: 2017934876

Managing Director: Welmoed Spahr
Editorial Director: Todd Green
Acquisitions Editor: Gwenan Spearing
Development Editor: Laura Berendson
Technical Reviewer: Massimo Nardone
Coordinating Editor: Nancy Chen
Copy Editor: Corbin Collins
Compositor: SPi Global
Indexer: SPi Global
Artist: SPi Global
Cover image designed by FreePik

Distributed to the book trade worldwide by Springer Science+Business Media New York, 233 Spring Street, 6th Floor, New York, NY 10013. Phone 1-800-SPRINGER, fax (201) 348-4505, e-mail orders-ny@springer-sbm.com, or visit www.springeronline.com. Apress Media, LLC is a California LLC and the sole member (owner) is Springer Science + Business Media Finance Inc (SSBM Finance Inc). SSBM Finance Inc is a **Delaware** corporation.

For information on translations, please e-mail rights@apress.com, or visit http://www.apress.com/rights-permissions.

Apress titles may be purchased in bulk for academic, corporate, or promotional use. eBook versions and licenses are also available for most titles. For more information, reference our Print and eBook Bulk Sales web page at www.apress.com/bulk-sales.

Any source code or other supplementary material referenced by the author in this book is available to readers on GitHub via the book's product page, located at www.apress.com/9781484225769. For more detailed information, please visit http://www.apress.com/source-code.

Contents at a Glance

Contents

About the Author

Dan Clark is a senior business intelligence (BI)/programming consultant specializing in Microsoft technologies. He is focused on learning new BI/data technologies and on training others how to best implement the technology. Dan has published several books and numerous articles on .NET programming and BI development. He is a regular speaker at various developer/database conferences and user group meetings and enjoys interacting with the Microsoft developer and database communities. In a previous life, he was a physics teacher; he is still inspired by the wonder and awe of studying the universe and figuring out why things behave the way they do. Dan can be reached at Clark.drc@gmail.com.

About the Technical Reviewer

Massimo Nardone has more than 22 years of experiences in security, web/mobile development, cloud, and IT architecture. His true IT passions are security and Android. He has been programming and teaching programming with Android, Perl, PHP, Java, VB, Python, C/C++, and MySQL for more than 20 years. He holds a Master of Science degree in computing science from the University of Salerno, Italy. He has worked as a project manager, software engineer, research engineer, chief security architect, information security manager, PCI/SCADA auditor, and senior lead IT security/cloud/SCADA architect for many years. His technical skills include: security, Android, cloud, Java, MySQL, Drupal, Cobol, Perl, web and mobile development, MongoDB, D3, Joomla, Couchbase, C/C++, WebGL, Python, Pro Rails, Django CMS, Jekyll, Scratch, and others. He currently works as chief information security office (CISO) for Cargotec Oyj. He has worked as visiting lecturer and supervisor for exercises at the Networking Laboratory of the Helsinki University of Technology (Aalto University). He holds four international patents (PKI, SIP, SAML, and Proxy areas). Massimo has reviewed more than 40 IT books for different publishing companies and is the coauthor of *Pro Android Games* (Apress, 2015).

Acknowledgments

Once again, thanks to the team at Apress for making the writing of this book an enjoyable experience. A special thanks goes to my technical reviewer, Massimo—thank you for your attention to detail and excellent suggestions while reviewing this book.

—Dan Clark

Introduction

Self-service business intelligence (BI)—you have heard the hype, seen the sales demos, and are ready to give it a try. Now what? You have probably checked out a few web sites for examples, given them a try, and learned a thing or two, but you are probably still left wondering how all the pieces fit together and how you go about creating a complete solution. If so, this book is for you. It takes you step by step through the process of analyzing data using the tools that are at the core of Microsoft's self-service BI offering: Power Query, Power Pivot, and Power BI.

Quite often, you need to take your raw data and transform it in some way before you load it into the data model. You may need to filter, aggregate, or clean the raw data. I show you how Power Query allows you to easily transform and refine data before incorporating it into your data model. Next, I show you how to create robust, scalable data models using Power Pivot. Because Power Pivot is the core tool you will use to create self-service BI solutions, I cover it extensively in this book. Next up, I show you how to use Power BI Desktop to easily build interactive visualizations that allow you to explore your data to discover trends and gain insight. Finally, I show you how to deploy your solution to the Power BI Service for your colleagues to use.

I strongly believe that one of the most important aspects of learning is doing. You can't learn how to ride a bike without jumping on a bike, and you can't learn to use the BI tools without actually interacting with them. Any successful training program includes both theory and hands-on activities. For this reason, I have included a hands-on activity at the end of every chapter designed to solidify the concepts covered in the chapter. I encourage you to work through these activities diligently. It is well worth the effort.

PART I

Building Models in Power Pivot

CHAPTER 1

■ ■ ■

Introducing Power Pivot

The core of Microsoft's self-service business intelligence (BI) toolset is Power Pivot. It is integrated into both Excel 2016 and Power BI and forms the foundation on top of which you will build your analytical reports and dashboards. This chapter provides you with some background information on why Power Pivot is such an important tool and what makes it perform so well. The chapter also provides you with an overview of the Power Pivot interface in Excel 2016 and gives you with some experience using the different areas of the interface.

After reading this chapter you will be familiar with the following:

- Why you should use Power Pivot
- The xVelocity in-memory analytics engine
- Exploring the Data Model Management interface
- Analyzing data using a pivot table

Why Use Power Pivot?

You may have been involved in a traditional BI project consisting of a centralized data warehouse where the various data stores of the organization are loaded, scrubbed, and then moved to an online analytical processing (OLAP) database for reporting and analysis. Some goals of this approach are to create a data repository for historical data, create one version of the truth, reduce silos of data, clean the company data and make sure it conforms to standards, and provide insight into data trends through dashboards. Although these are admirable goals and are great reasons to provide a centralized data warehouse, there are some downsides to this approach. The most notable is the complexity of building the system and implementing change. Ask anyone who has tried to get new fields or measures added to an enterprise-wide data warehouse. Typically, this is a long, drawn-out process requiring IT involvement along with data steward committee reviews, development, and testing cycles.

What is needed is a solution that allows for agile data analysis without so much reliance on IT and formalized processes. To solve these problems, many business analysts have used Excel to create pivot tables and perform ad hoc analysis on sets of data gleaned from various data sources. Some problems with using isolated Excel workbooks for analysis are conflicting versions of the truth, silos of data, and data security.

So how can you solve this dilemma of the centralized data warehouse being too rigid while the Excel solution is too loose? This is where Microsoft's self-service BI toolset comes in. These tools do not replace your centralized data warehouse solution but rather augment it to promote agile data analysis. Using Power Pivot, you can pull data from the data warehouse, extend it with other sources of data such as text files or web data feeds, build custom measures, and analyze the data using pivot tables and pivot charts. You can create quick proofs of concepts that can be easily promoted to become part of the enterprise-wide solution. Power Pivot also promotes one-off data analysis projects without the overhead of a drawn-out development

© Dan Clark 2017
D. Clark, *Beginning Power BI*, DOI 10.1007/978-1-4842-2577-6_1

cycle. When combined with SharePoint 2016, SQL Server Reporting Services 2016, and/or One Drive, workbooks can be shared, secured, and managed. This goes a long way to satisfying IT's need for governance without impeding the business user's need for agility.

Here are some of the benefits of Power Pivot:

- Functions as a free add-in to Excel

- Easily integrates data from a variety of sources

- Handles large amounts of data, upward of tens to hundreds of millions of rows

- Uses familiar Excel pivot tables and pivot charts for data analysis

- Includes a powerful Data Analysis Expressions (DAX) language

- Has data in the model that is read only, which increases security and integrity

When Excel Power Pivot workbooks are hosted in SharePoint, Reporting Services, and/or One Drive, here are some of its added benefits:

- Enables the sharing and collaboration of Excel Power Pivot solutions

- Can schedule and automate data refresh

- Can audit changes through version management

- Can secure users for read-only and updateable access

Now that you know some of the benefits of Power Pivot, let's see what makes it tick.

The xVelocity In-memory Analytics Engine

The special sauce behind Power Pivot is the xVelocity in-memory analytics engine (yes, that is really the name). xVelocity allows Power Pivot to provide fast performance on large amounts of data. One of the keys to this is it uses a columnar database to store the data. Traditional row-based data storage stores all the data in the row together and is efficient at retrieving and updating data based on the row key, for example, updating or retrieving an order based on an order ID. This is great for the order-entry system but not so great when you want to perform analysis on historical orders (say you want to look at trends for the past year to determine how products are selling, for example). Row-based storage also takes up more space by repeating values for each row; if you have a large number of customers, common names like John or Smith are repeated many times. A columnar database stores only the distinct values for each column and then stores the row as a set of pointers back to the column values. This built-in indexing saves a lot of space and allows for significant optimization when coupled with data-compression techniques that are built into the xVelocity engine. It also means that data aggregations (like those used in typical data analysis) of the column values are extremely fast.

Another benefit provided by the xVelocity engine is the in-memory analytics. Most processing bottlenecks associated with querying data occur when data is read from or written to a disk. With in-memory analytics, the data is loaded into the RAM memory of the computer and then queried. This results in much faster processing times and limits the need to store pre-aggregated values on disk. This advantage is especially apparent when you move from 32-bit to 64-bit operating systems and applications, which are becoming the norm these days.

Another benefit worth mentioning is the tabular structure of the Power Pivot model. The model consists of tables and table relationships. This tabular model is familiar to most business analysts and database developers. Traditional OLAP databases such as SQL Server Analysis Server (SSAS) present the data model as a three-dimensional cube structure that is difficult to work with and requires a complex query language called Multidimensional Expressions (MDX). I find that in most cases (but not all), it is easier to work with tabular models and DAX than OLAP cubes and MDX.

Enabling Power Pivot for Excel

Power Pivot is a free add-in to Excel and has been available since Excel 2010. If you are using Excel 2010, you have to download and install the add-in from the Microsoft Office website. If you are using Excel 2013, the add-in is already installed and you just have to enable it. If you are using Excel 2016 (the version covered in this book), it is already installed and enabled for you. To check what edition you have installed, click the File menu in Excel and select the Account tab, as shown in Figure 1-1.

Figure 1-1. *Checking for the Excel version*

On the Account tab, click the About Excel button. You are presented with a screen showing version details, as shown in Figure 1-2. Take note of the edition and the version. Although the 32-bit version will work fine for smaller data sets, to get the optimal performance and experience from Power Pivot you should use the 64-bit version running on a 64-bit version of Windows with at least 8 GB of RAM.

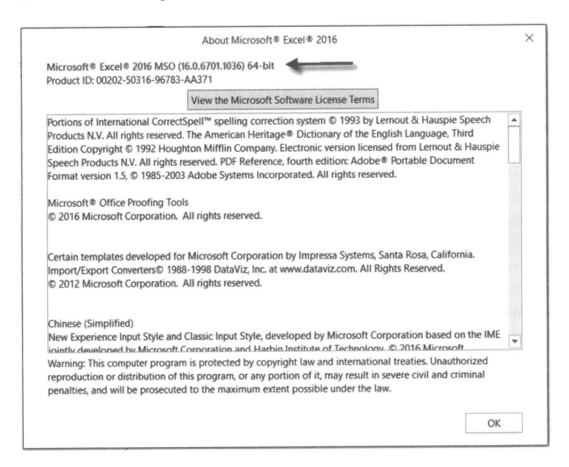

Figure 1-2. Checking the Excel edition and version

Once you have determined that you are running the correct version, you can enable/disable the Power Pivot add-in by clicking the File menu and selecting the Options tab. In the Excel Options window, click the Add-Ins tab. In the Manage drop-down select COM Add-ins and click the Go button (see Figure 1-3).

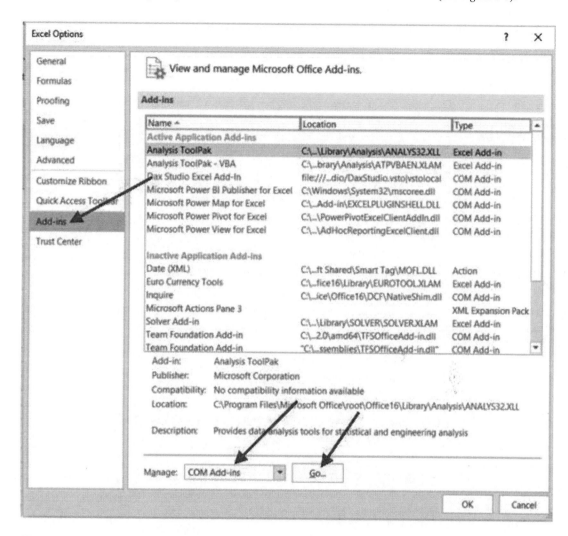

Figure 1-3. Managing COM add-ins

You are presented with the COM Add-ins window (see Figure 1-4). Make sure Microsoft Power Pivot for Excel is checked and click OK.

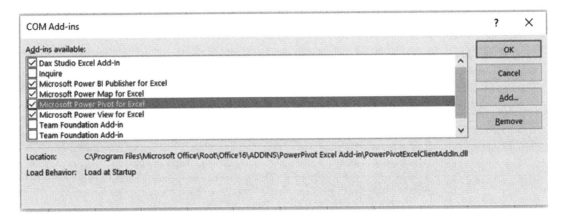

Figure 1-4. *Selecting the Power Pivot add-in*

Now that you have ensured that the Power Pivot add-in for Excel is enabled, it is time to explore the Data Model Manager.

Exploring the Data Model Manager Interface

If Power Pivot is enabled, you should see a Power Pivot tab in Excel (see Figure 1-5). Clicking the Manage button launches the Data Model Management interface.

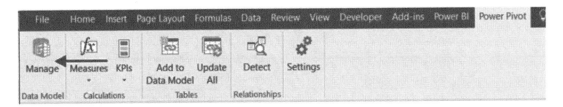

Figure 1-5. *Launching the Data Model Manager*

When the Data Model Manager launches, you will have two separate but connected interfaces. You can switch back and forth between the normal Excel interface and the Data Model Management interface. This can be quite confusing for new Power Pivot users. Remember, the Data Model Manager (Figure 1-6) is where you define the model including tables, table relationships, measures, calculated columns, and hierarchies. The Excel interface (Figure 1-7) is where you analyze the data using pivot tables and pivot charts.

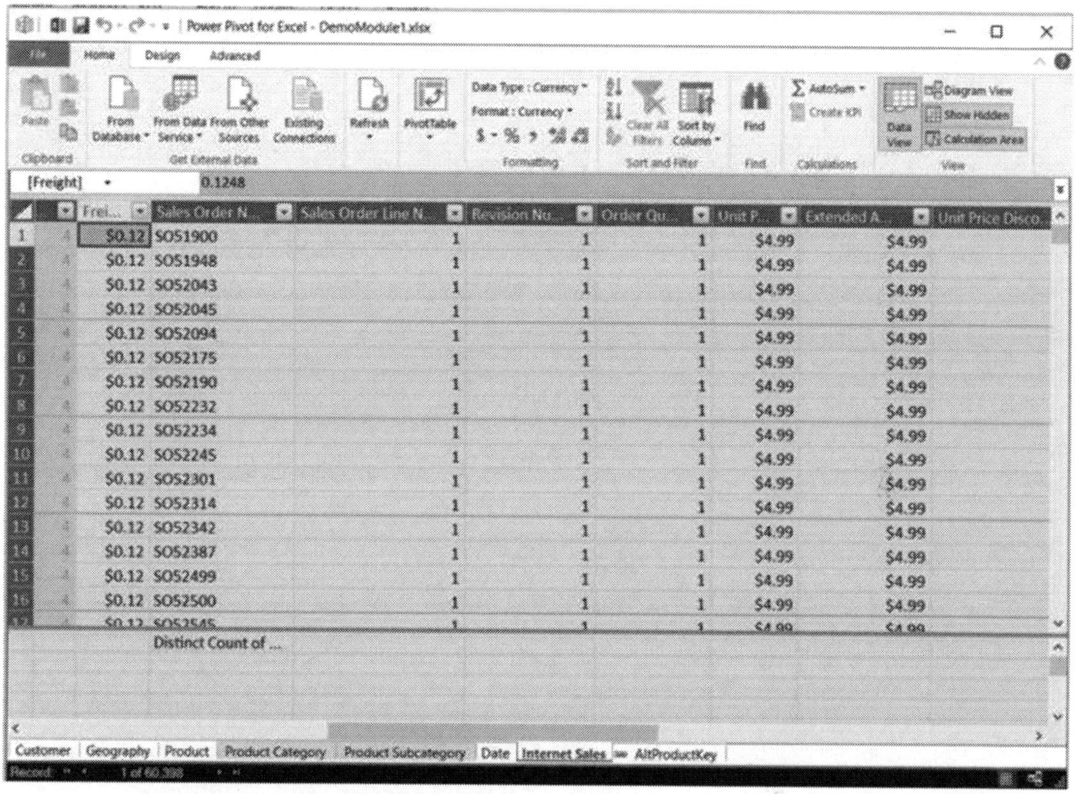

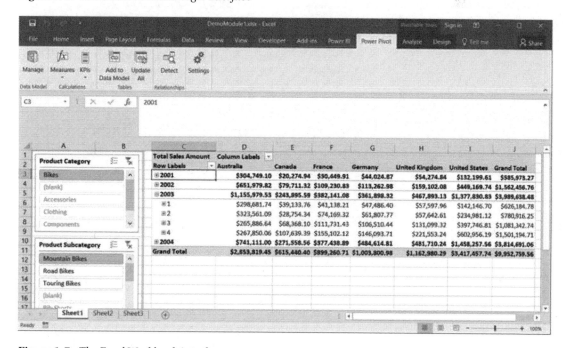

Figure 1-6. *The Data Model Manager interface*

Figure 1-7. *The Excel Workbook interface*

There are two views of the data model in the Data Model Manager: the data view and the diagram view. When it first comes up, it is in the data view mode. In data view mode, you can see the data contained in the model. Each table in the model has its own tab in the view. Tables can include columns of data retrieved from a data source and also columns that are calculated using DAX. The calculated columns appear a little darker and have a different-colored header than the other columns. Figure 1-8 shows the Full Name column, which is derived by concatenating the First Name and Last Name columns.

	First Name	Middle Name	Last Name	Full Name	Birth ...
1	Latasha		Suarez	Latasha Suarez	9/25/197...
2	Larry		Gill	Larry Gill	4/13/197...
3	Edgar		Sanchez	Edgar Sanchez	6/3/1977...
4	Shelby		Bailey	Shelby Bailey	6/3/1977...
5	Alexa		Watson	Alexa Watson	8/25/197...
6	Jacquelyn		Dominguez	Jacquelyn Dominguez	9/27/197...
7	Kate		Shan	Kate Shan	1/24/197...
8	Colleen		Lu	Colleen Lu	7/17/197...
9	Dale		Shen	Dale Shen	3/16/197...
10	Tammy		Sai	Tammy Sai	11/14/19...
11	Leah		Li	Leah Li	10/6/197...
12	Andrea		Cox	Andrea Cox	8/3/1977...
13	Alyssa		Lee	Alyssa Lee	8/13/197...
14	Jill		Rubio	Jill Rubio	6/27/197...
15	Dennis		Li	Dennis Li	7/17/197...
16	Natasha		Sanz	Natasha Sanz	5/18/197...
17	Autumn		Zhu	Autumn Zhu	10/23/19

Figure 1-8. *A calculated column in the Data Model Manager*

Each tab also contains a grid area below the column data. The grid area is where you define measures in the model. The measures usually consist of some sort of aggregation function. For example, you may want to look at sales rolled up by month or by products. Figure 1-9 shows some measures associated with the Internet Sales table.

[Sales Am... ▾	f_x Total Sales Amount:=SUM([Sales Amount])	
Total Produc... ▼	Sales Amount ▼	Margin ▼
1	$1.87	$4.99	$3.12
2	$1.87	$4.99	$3.12
3	$1.87	$4.99	$3.12
4	$1.87	$4.99	$3.12
5	$1.87	$4.99	$3.12
6	$1.87	$4.99	$3.12
	Total Sales Amount: $29,358,677.22	Total Margin: $12,080,883.65

Figure 1-9. The measures grid area in the Data Model Manager

There are four menu tabs at the top of the designer: File, Home, Design, and Advanced. If you don't see the Advanced tab, you can show it by clicking the File menu tab and selecting Switch To Advanced Mode. You will become intimately familiar with the menus in the designer as you progress through this book. For now, suffice it to say that this is where you initiate various actions such as connecting to data sources, creating data queries, formatting data, setting default properties, and creating key performance indicators (KPIs). Figure 1-10 shows the Home menu in the Data Model Manager.

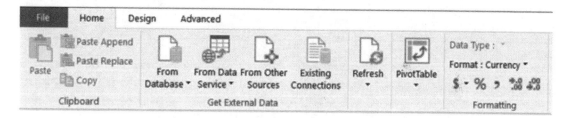

Figure 1-10. The Home menu tab in the Data Model Manager

On the right side of the Home menu you can switch from the data view mode to the diagram view mode. The diagram view shown in Figure 1-11 illustrates the tables and the relationships between the tables. This is where you generally go to establish relationships between tables and create hierarchies for drilling through the model. The menus are much the same in both the data view and the diagram view. You will find, however, that some things can only be done in the data view, and some things can only be done in the diagram view.

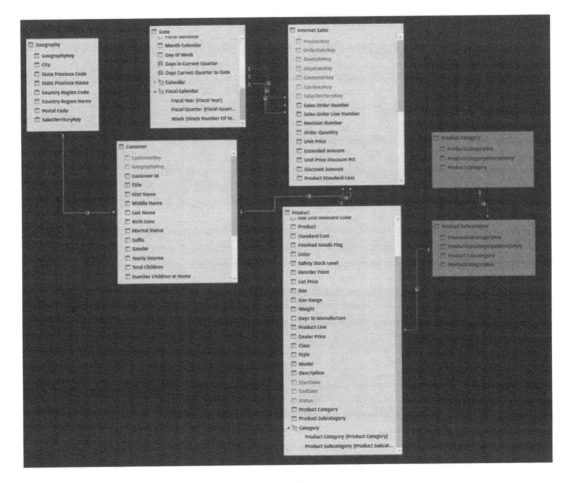

Figure 1-11. *Using the diagram view in the Data Model Manager*

Now that you are familiar with the various parts of the Data Model Manager, it's time to get your hands dirty and complete the following hands-on lab. This lab will help you become familiar with working in the Data Model Manager.

■ **Note**   To complete the labs in this book, make sure you download the starter files from `https://github.com/Apress/beginning-power-bi-2ed`.

HANDS-ON LAB: EXPLORING POWER PIVOT

In this following lab you will

- Verify that the Power Pivot add-in is enabled.

- Analyze data using pivot tables.

- Explore the Data Model Manager.

1. Open Excel 2016.

2. On the File menu, select Account (refer to Figure 1-1).

3. Click About Excel and check the version (32-bit or 64-bit) you are using.

4. On the File menu select Options and then click the Add-Ins tab. In the Manage drop-down, select COM Add-ins and click Go.

5. In the COM Add-ins window, make sure the Power Pivot add-in (refer to Figure 1-4) is checked.

6. Open the Chapter1Lab1.xlsx file located in the LabStarterFiles folder.

7. Click Sheet1. You should see a basic pivot table showing sales by year and country, as shown in Figure 1-12.

Total Sales Amount	Column Labels						
Row Labels	Australia	Canada	France	Germany	United Kingdom	United States	Grand Total
⊞2001	$1,309,047.20	$146,829.81	$180,571.69	$237,784.99	$291,590.52	$1,100,549.45	$3,266,373.66
⊞2002	$2,154,284.88	$621,602.38	$514,942.01	$521,230.85	$591,586.85	$2,126,696.55	$6,530,343.53
⊞2003	$3,033,784.21	$535,784.46	$1,026,324.97	$1,058,405.73	$1,298,248.57	$2,838,512.36	$9,791,060.30
⊞2004	$2,563,884.29	$673,628.21	$922,179.04	$1,076,890.77	$1,210,286.27	$3,324,031.16	$9,770,899.74
Grand Total	$9,061,000.58	$1,977,844.86	$2,644,017.71	$2,894,312.34	$3,391,712.21	$9,389,789.51	$29,358,677.22

Figure 1-12. *Using a pivot table*

8. Click anywhere in the pivot table. You should see the field list on the right side, as shown in Figure 1-13.

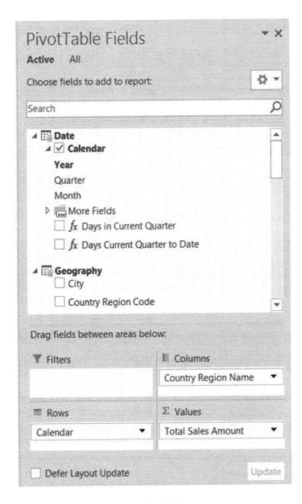

Figure 1-13. The pivot table field list

9. Below the field list are the drop areas for the filters, rows, columns, and values. You drag and drop the fields into these areas to create the pivot table.

10. Click the All tab at the top of the PivotTable Fields window. Expand the Product table in the field list. Find the Product Category field and drag it to the Report Filter drop zone.

11. A filter drop-down appears above the pivot table. Click the drop-down filter icon. You should see Product Categories.

12. Change the filter to Bikes and notice the values changing in the pivot table.

13. When you select multiple items from a filter, it's hard to tell what is being filtered on. Filter on Bikes and Clothing. Notice that when the filter drop-down closes, it just shows (Multiple Items). Remove the Product Category field from the Report Filter drop zone.

14. Slicers act as filters but they give you a visual to easily determine what is selected. On the Insert menu, click the Slicer. In the pop-up window that appears, select the All tab and then select the Category hierarchy under the Product table, as shown in Figure 1-14.

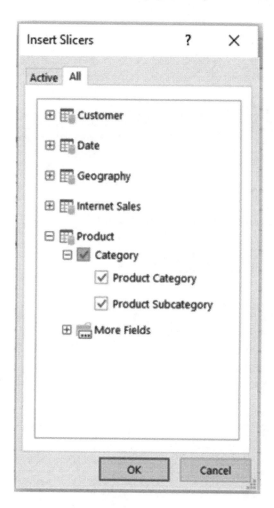

Figure 1-14. *Selecting slicer fields*

15. Product Category and Product Subcategory slicers are inserted and are used to filter the pivot table. To filter by a value, click the value button. To select multiple buttons, hold down the Ctrl key while clicking (see Figure 1-15). Notice that because these fields were set up as a hierarchy, selecting a product category automatically filters to the related subcategories in the Product Subcategory slicer.

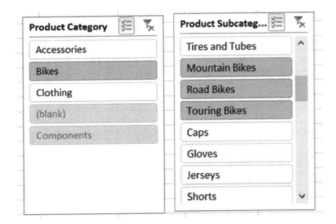

Figure 1-15. *Using slicers to filter a pivot table*

16. Hierarchies are groups of columns arranged in levels that make it easier to navigate the data. For example, if you expand the Date table in the field list, you can see the Calendar hierarchy, as shown in Figure 1-16. This hierarchy consists of the Year, Quarter, and Month fields and represents a natural way to drill down into the data.

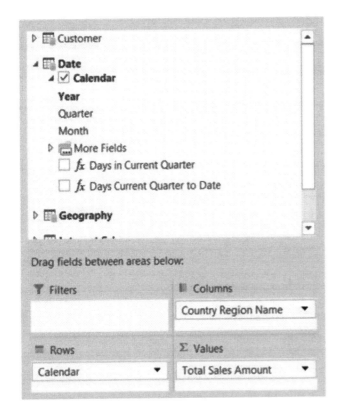

Figure 1-16. *Using hierarchies in a pivot table*

17. If you expand the Internet Sales table in the field list, you will see a traffic light icon. This icon represents a KPI. KPIs are used to gauge the performance of a value. They are usually represented by a visual indicator to quickly determine performance.

18. Under the Power Pivot menu, click the Manage Data Model button.

19. In the Data Model Manager, select the different tabs at the bottom to switch between the different tables.

20. Go to the ProductAlternateKey column in the Product table. Notice that it's grayed out. This means it's hidden from any client tool. You can verify this by switching back to the Excel pivot table on sheet 1 and verifying that you cannot see the field in the field list.

21. In the Internet Sales table, click the Margin column. Notice this is a calculated column. It has also been formatted as currency.

22. Below the Sales Amount column in the Internet Sales table, there is a measure called Total Sales Amount. Click the measure and note that in the formula bar above the table is the DAX code used to calculate the measure.

23. On the left side of the Home tab of the Data Model Manager, switch to the diagram view. Observe the relationships between the tables.

24. If you hover over the relationship with the mouse pointer, you can see the fields involved in the relationship, as shown in Figure 1-17.

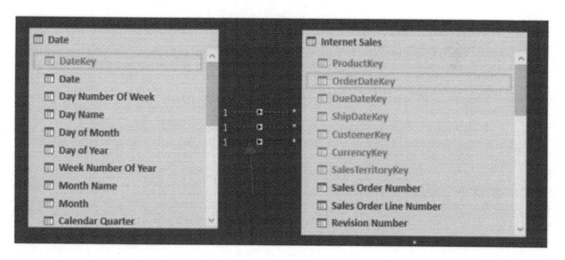

Figure 1-17. Exploring relationships

25. Click the Date table in the diagram view. Note the Create Hierarchy button in the upper right corner of the table (see Figure 1-18). This is how you define hierarchies for a table.

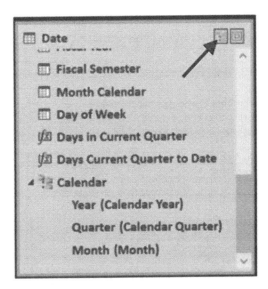

Figure 1-18. Creating a hierarchy

26. Take some time to explore the model and the pivot table. (Feel free to try to break things!) When you're done, close the file.

Summary

This chapter introduced you to the Power Pivot add-in to Excel. You got a little background into why Power Pivot can handle large amounts of data through the use of the xVelocity engine and columnar data storage. You also got to investigate and gain some experience with the Power Pivot Data Model Manager. Don't worry about the details of how you develop the various parts of the model just yet. That will be explained in detail as you progress through the book. In the next chapter, you will learn how to get data into the model from various kinds of data sources.

CHAPTER 2

▉ ▉ ▉

Importing Data into Power Pivot

One of the first steps in creating the Power Pivot model is importing data. Traditionally, when creating a BI solution based on an OLAP cube, you need to import the data into the data warehouse and then load it into the cube. It can take quite a while to get the data incorporated into the cube and available for your consumption. This is one of the greatest strengths of the Power Pivot model. You can easily and quickly combine data from a variety of sources into your model. The data sources can be from relational databases, text files, web services, and OLAP cubes, just to name a few. This chapter shows you how to incorporate data from a variety of these sources into a Power Pivot model.

After completing this chapter, you will be able to

- Import data from relational databases.

- Import data from text files.

- Import data from a data feed.

- Import data from an OLAP cube.

- Reuse existing connections to update the model.

Importing Data from Relational Databases

One of the most common types of data sources you will run into is a relational database. Relational database management systems (RDMS) such as SQL Server, Oracle, DB2, and Access consist of tables and relationships between the tables based on keys. For example, Figure 2-1 shows a purchase order detail table and a product table. They are related by the ProductID column. This is an example of a one-to-many relationship. For every one row in the product table there are many rows in the purchase order detail table. The keys in a table are referred to as primary and foreign keys. Every table needs a primary key that uniquely identifies a row in the table. For example, the ProductID is the primary key in the product table. The ProductID is considered a foreign key in the purchase order detail table. Foreign keys point back to a primary key in a related table. Note that a primary key can consist of a combination of columns; for example, the primary key of the purchase order detail table is the combination of the PurchaseOrderID and the PurchaseOrderDetailID.

© Dan Clark 2017

D. Clark, *Beginning Power BI*, DOI 10.1007/978-1-4842-2577-6_2

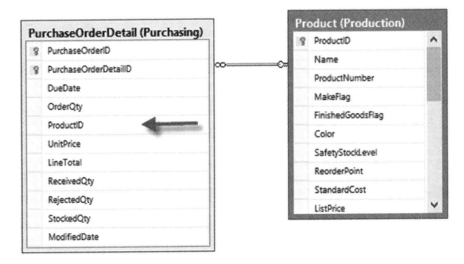

Figure 2-1. *A one-to-many relationship*

Although one-to-many relationships are the most common, you will run into another type of relationship that is fairly prevalent: the many-to-many. Figure 2-2 shows an example of a many-to-many relationship. A person may have multiple phone numbers of different types. For example, they may have two fax numbers. You can't relate these tables directly. Instead you need to use a *junction* table that contains the primary keys from the tables. The combination of the keys in the junction table must be unique.

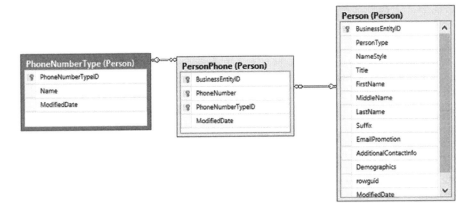

Figure 2-2. *A many-to-many relationship*

Notice that the junction table can contain information related to the association; for example, the PhoneNumber is associated with the customer and phone number type. A customer cannot have the same phone number listed as two different types.

One nice aspect of obtaining data from a relational database is that the model is very similar to a model you create in Power Pivot. In fact, if the relationships are defined in the database, the Power Pivot import wizard can detect these and set them up in the model for you.

The first step to getting data from a relational database is to create a connection. On the Home tab of the Model Designer there is a Get External Data grouping (see Figure 2-3).

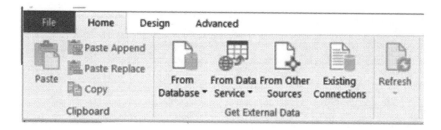

Figure 2-3. *Setting up a connection*

The From Database drop-down allows you to connect to SQL Server, Access, Analysis Services, or from another Power Pivot model. If you click the From Other Sources button, you can see all the various data sources available to connect to (see Figure 2-4). As you can see, you can connect to quite a few relational databases. If you need to connect to one that's not listed, you may be able to install a driver from the database provider to connect to it. Chances are, you may also be able to use the generic ODBC (Open Database Connectivity) driver to connect to it.

Connect to a Data Source

You can either create a connection to a data source, or you can use one that already exists.

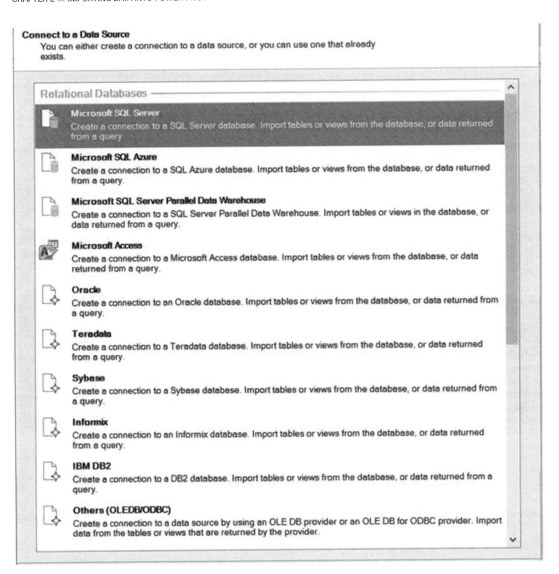

Figure 2-4. *Selecting a data source*

After selecting a data source, you are presented with a window to enter the connection information. The connection information depends on the data source you are connecting to. For most relational databases, the information needed is very similar. Figure 2-5 shows the connection information for connecting to a SQL Server. Remember to click the Test Connection button to make sure everything is entered correctly.

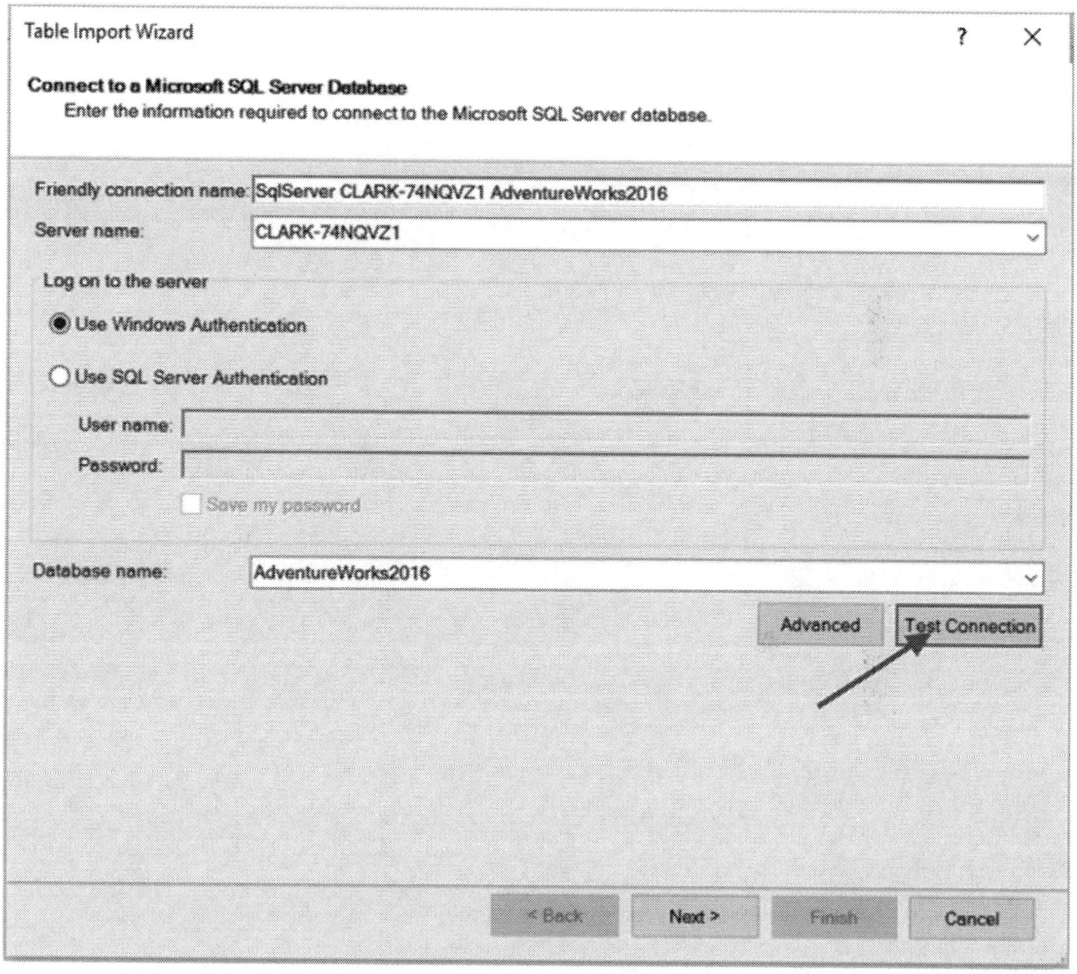

Figure 2-5. *Setting up a connection to a database*

After setting up the connection, the next step is to query the database to retrieve the data. You have two choices at this point: you can choose to import the data from a list of tables and views or you can write a query to import the data (see Figure 2-6). Even if you choose to import the data from a table or view under the covers, a query is created and sent to the database to retrieve the data.

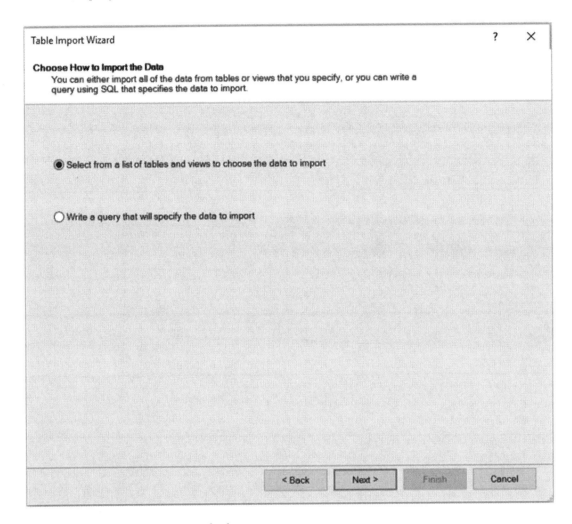

Figure 2-6. *Choosing how to retrieve the data*

If you choose to get the data from a list of tables and views, you are presented with the list in the next screen. From your perspective, a view and a table look the same. In reality, a *view* is really a stored query in the database that masks the complexity of the query from you. Views are often used to show a simpler conceptual model of the database than the actual physical model. For example, you may need a customer's address. Figure 2-7 shows the tables you need to include in a query to get the information. Instead of writing a complex query to retrieve the information, you can select from a view that combines the information in a virtual Customer Address table for you. Another common use of a view is to secure columns of the underlying table. Through the use of a view, the database administrator can hide columns from various users.

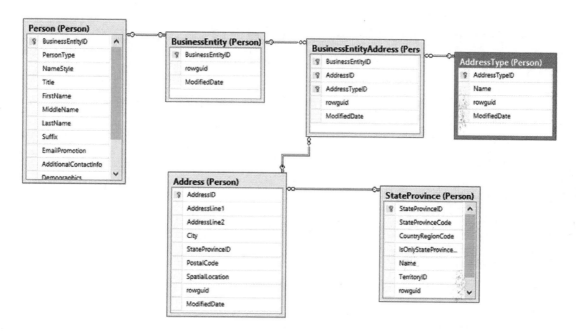

Figure 2-7. *Tables needed to get a customer address*

By selecting a table and clicking the Preview & Filter button (see Figure 2-8), you can preview the data in the table and filter the data selected.

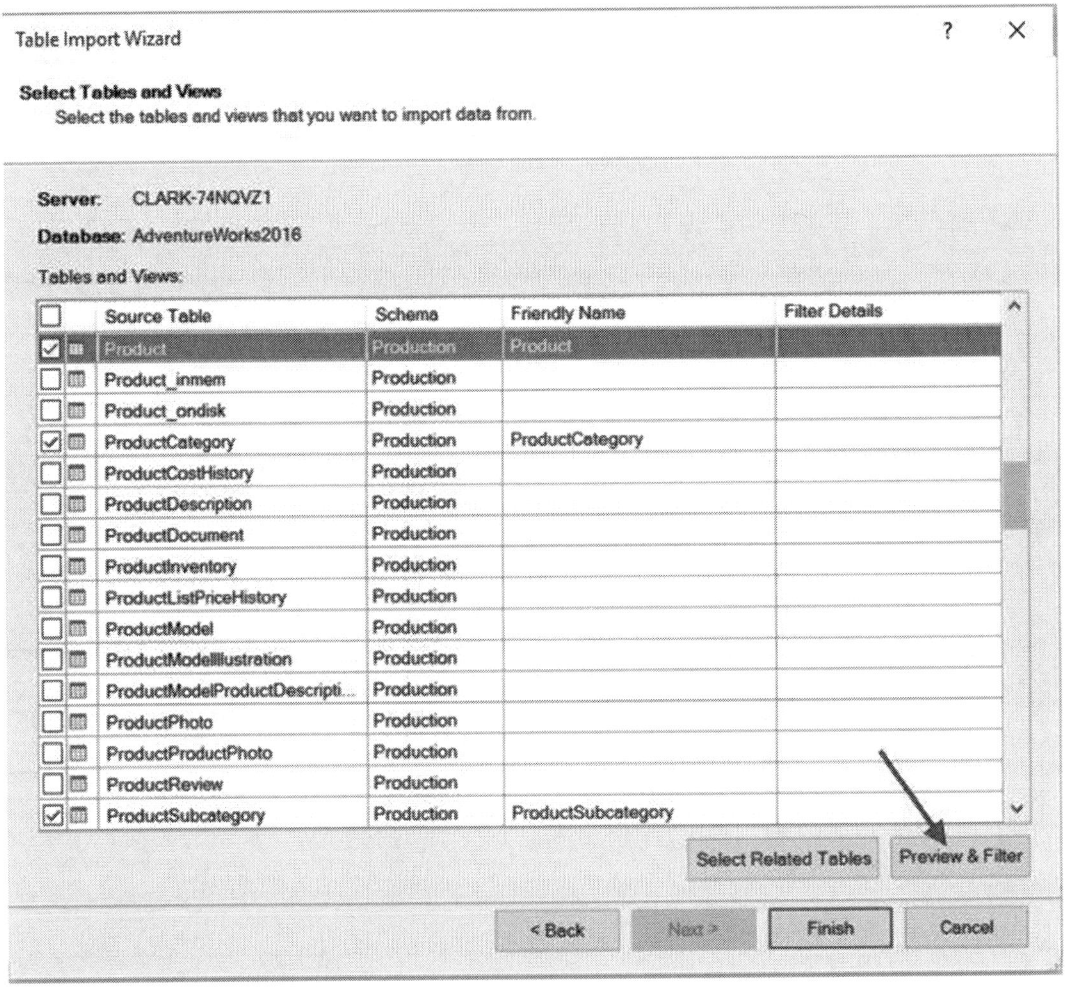

Figure 2-8. Selecting tables and views

In Figure 2-9 you can see the preview and filter screen.

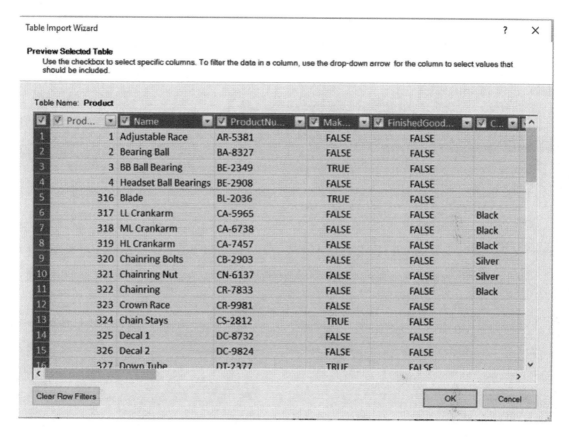

Figure 2-9. *Previewing and filtering the data*

One way you can filter a table is by selecting only the columns you are interested in. The other way is to limit the number of rows by placing a filter condition on the column. For example, you may only want sales after a certain year. Clicking the drop-down next to a column allows you to enter a filter to limit the rows. Figure 2-10 shows the SalesOrderHeader table being filtered by order date.

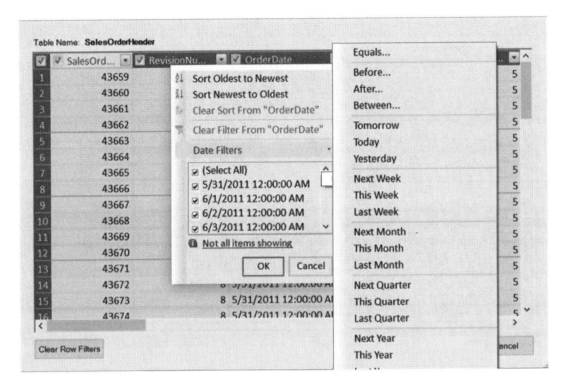

Figure 2-10. *Filtering rows*

When working with large data sets it is a good idea, for performance reasons, to only import the data you are interested in. There is a lot of overhead in bringing in all the columns of a table if you are only interested in a few. Likewise, if you are only interested in the last 3 years of sales, don't bring in the entire 20 years of sales data. You can always go back and update the data import to bring in more data if you find a need for it.

After filtering the data, click Finish on the Select Tables And Views screen (see Figure 2-8). At this point the data is brought into the model, and you see a screen reporting the progress (see Figure 2-11). If there are no errors, you can close the Table Import Wizard.

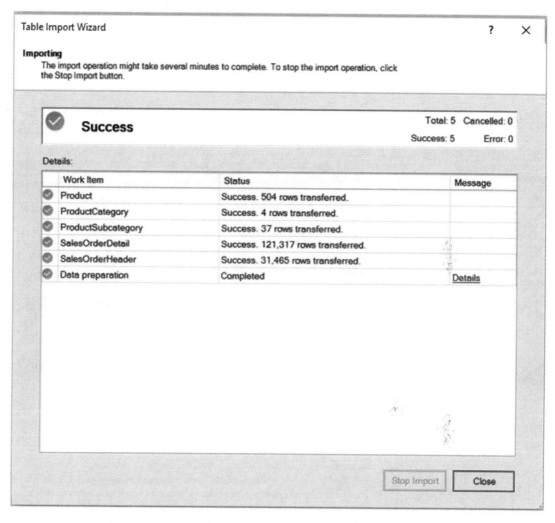

Figure 2-11. *Importing the data into the model*

When the wizard closes, you will see the data in the data view of the Model Designer.

■ **Note**   Remember that Power Pivot is only connected to the data source when it is retrieving the data. Once the data is retrieved, the connection is closed, and the data is part of the model.

If you switch to the diagram view of the Model Designer you will see the tables, and if the table relationships were defined in the database you will see the relationships between the tables. In Figure 2-12 you can see relationships defined between the product tables and one defined between the sales tables, but none defined between the SalesOrderDetail table and the Product table. You can create a relationship in the model even though one was not defined in the data source (more about this later).

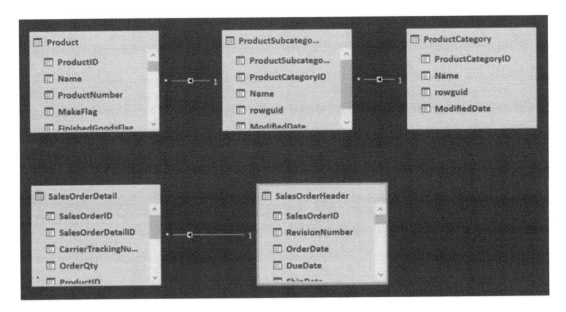

Figure 2-12. *Table relationships defined in the data source*

Although selecting from tables and views is an easy way to get data into the model without needing to explicitly write a query, it is not always possible. At times you may need to write your own queries; for example, you may want to combine data from several different tables and no view is available. Another factor is what is supported by the data source. Some data sources don't allow views and may require you to supply queries to extract the data. In these cases, when you get to the screen that asks how you want to retrieve the data, select the query option (refer to Figure 2-6).

Once you select the query option, you are presented with a screen where you can write in a query (see Figure 2-13). Although you may not write the query from scratch, this is where you would paste in a query written for you or one that you created in another tool such as Microsoft Management Studio or TOAD. Don't forget to name the query. It will become a table in the model with the name of the query.

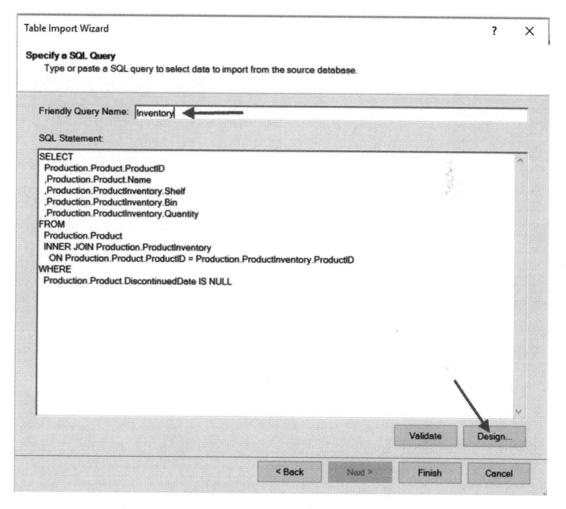

Figure 2-13. Creating your own query

If the data source supports it, you can launch a pretty nice Query Designer by clicking in the lower right corner of the query entry window (see Figure 2-13). This designer (see Figure 2-14) allows you to select the columns you want from the various tables and views. If the table relationships are defined in the database, it will add the table joins for you. You can also apply filters and group and aggregate the data.

■ **Note**   Parameters are not supported in the Power Pivot model, and checking the box will give you an error message when you try to close the Query Designer.

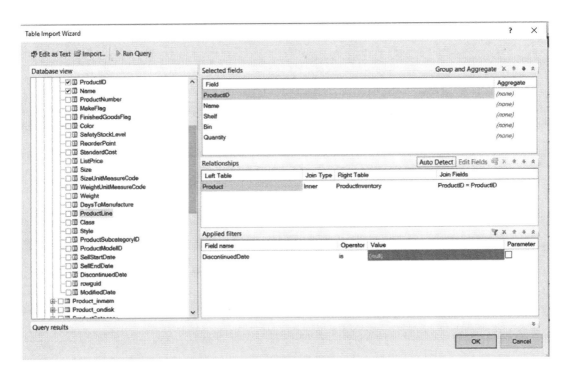

Figure 2-14. *Using the Query Designer*

After you are done designing the query, you should always run it to make sure it works the way you intended (see Figure 2-15).

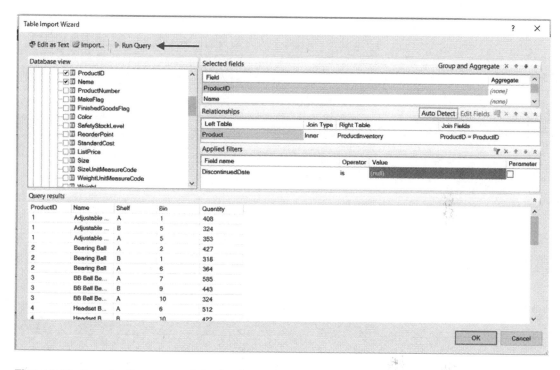

Figure 2-15. *Running the query and viewing the results*

Once you are satisfied with the query, clicking the OK button returns you to the previous screen with the query text entered. You can modify the query in this screen and use the Validate button to ensure that it is still a valid query (see Figure 2-16). Clicking Finish will bring the data and table into the model.

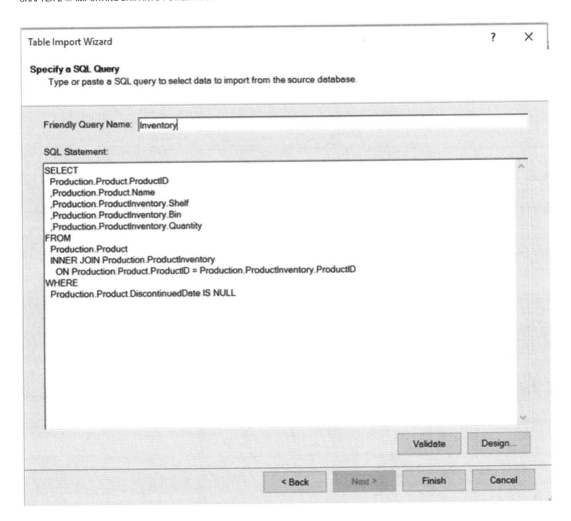

Figure 2-16. *Viewing and validating the query*

Now that you know how to import data from a database, let's see how you can add data to the model from a text file.

Importing Data from Text Files

You may often need to combine data from several different sources. One of the most common sources of data is still the text file. This could be the result of receiving data as an output from another system; for example, you may need information from your company's enterprise resource planning (ERP) system, provided as a text file. You may also get data through third-party services that provide the data in a comma-separated value (CSV) format. For example, you may use a rating service to rate customers, and the results are returned in a CSV file.

Importing data into your model from a text file is similar to importing data from a relational database table. First you select the option to get external data from other sources on the Home menu, which brings up the option to connect to a data source. Scroll down to the bottom of the window, and you can choose to import data from either an Excel file or a text file (see Figure 2-17).

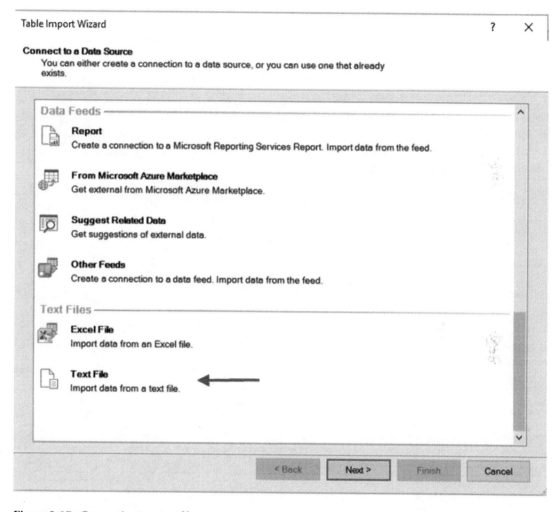

Figure 2-17. Connecting to a text file

Selecting the text file brings up a screen where you enter the path to the file and the file delimiter. Each text file is considered a table, and the friendly connection name will be the name of the table in the model. Once you supply the connection information, the data is loaded for previewing and filtering (see Figure 2-18).

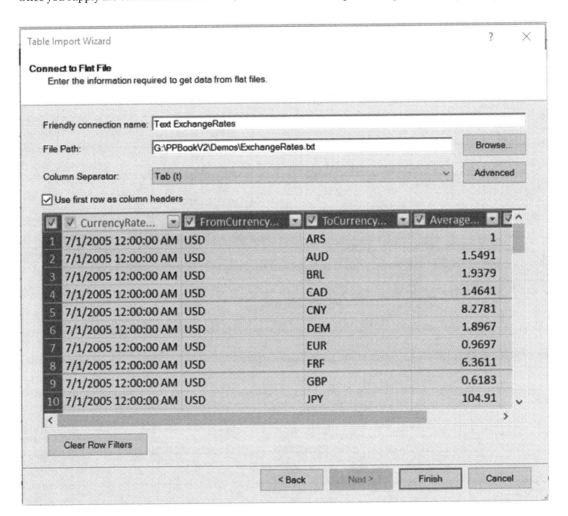

Figure 2-18. Previewing the data

Selecting the drop-down next to the column header brings up the ability to limit the rows brought in based on filter criteria (see Figure 2-19).

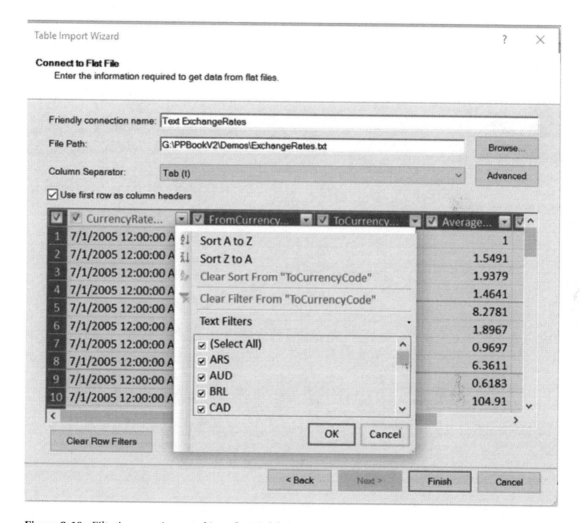

Figure 2-19. *Filtering rows imported into the model*

The main difference between importing data from a text file and importing data from an Excel file is that the Excel file can contain more than one table. By default, each sheet is treated as a table (see Figure 2-20). Once you select the table, you have the option to preview and filter the data just as you did for a text file.

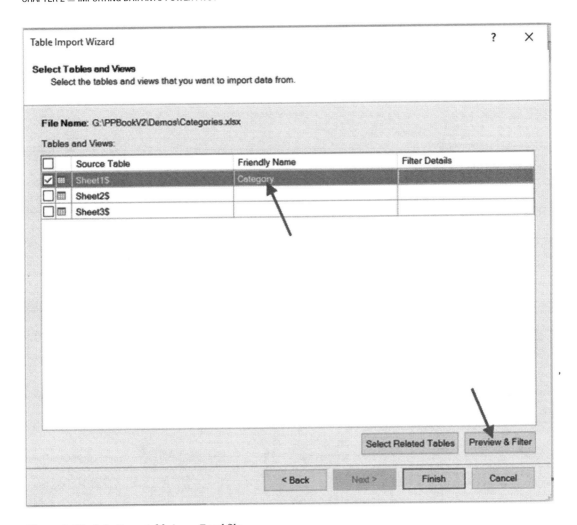

Figure 2-20. Selecting a table in an Excel file

In addition to importing data from a text file, you may need to supplement your data model using data imported from a data feed. This is becoming a very common way to exchange data with business partners, and you will see how to do this next.

Importing Data from a Data Feed

Although text files are one of the most popular ways of exchanging data, data feeds are becoming an increasingly prevalent way of exchanging data. *Data feeds* provide the data through web services, and to connect to the web service, you enter the web address of the web service. In Figure 2-17 you can see the data feed connections available. Most often you will know the address of the data service provided by a partner or data provider. In this case, you choose other feeds that then provide you with a connection information entry window, as shown in Figure 2-21.

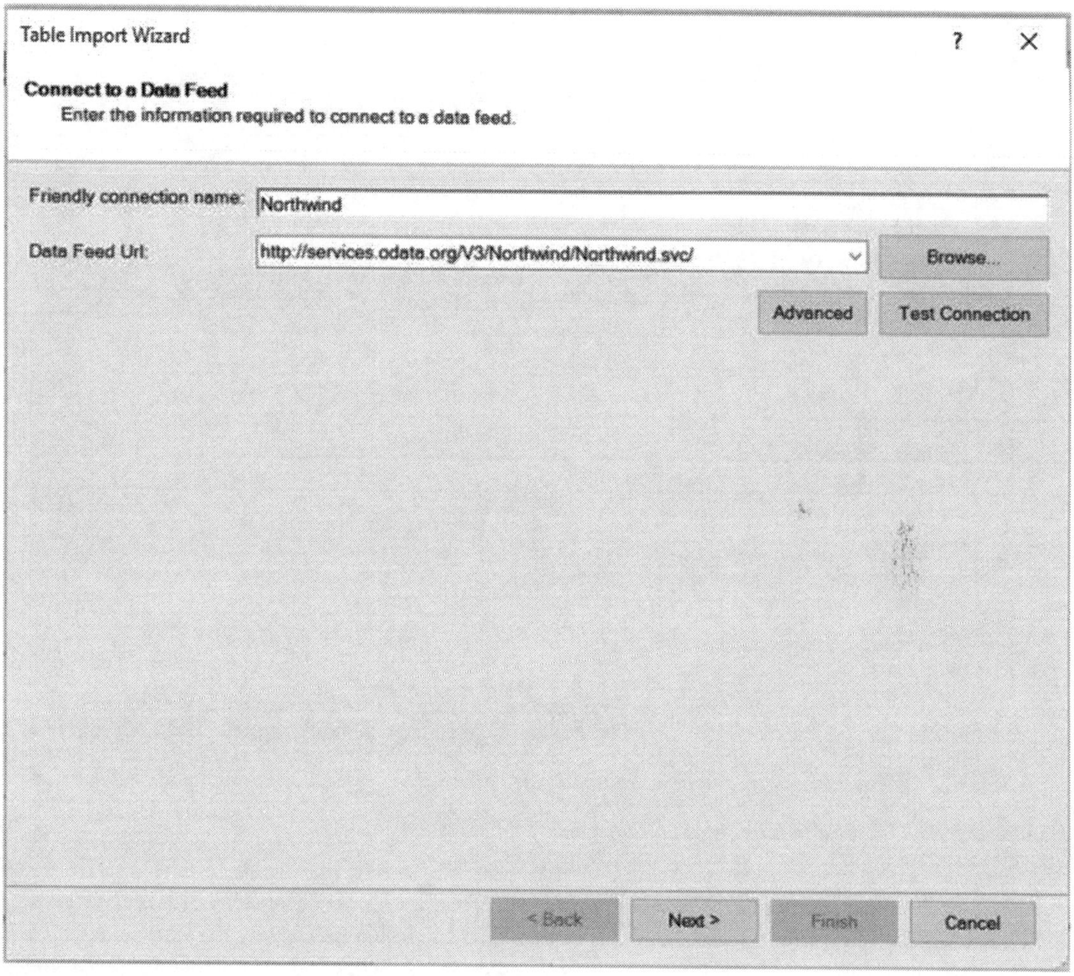

Figure 2-21. Connecting to a data feed

Because the data feed contains not only the data but also the metadata (description of the data), once you make the connection, Power Pivot lets you preview and filter the data, as shown in Figure 2-22.

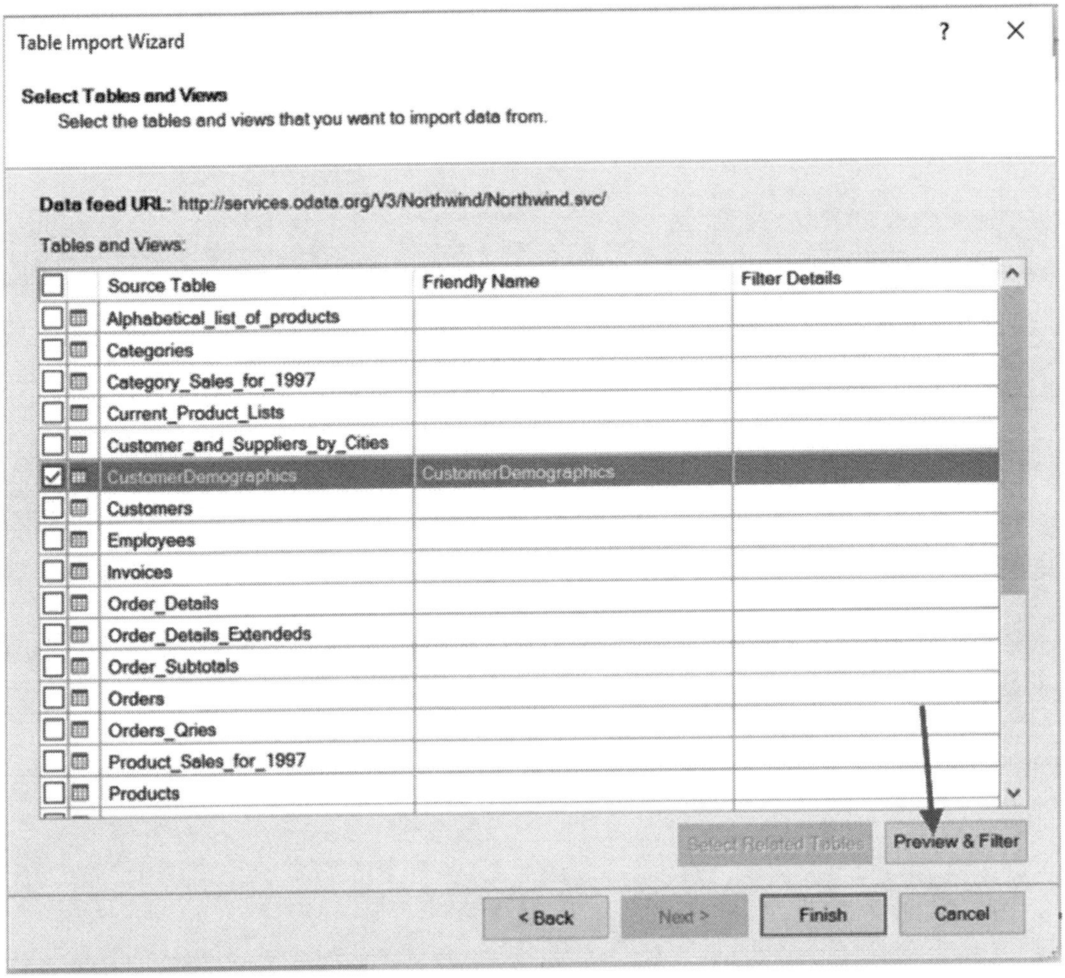

Figure 2-22. Previewing and filtering data from a data feed

A couple of interesting data feeds you can consume are data from Reporting Services reports and SharePoint lists. These applications can easily expose their data as data feeds that you can consume as a data source. In addition, many database vendors such as SAP support the ability to expose their data as data feeds.

Importing Data from an OLAP Cube

Many companies have invested a lot of money and effort into creating an enterprise reporting solution consisting of an enterprise-wide OLAP repository that feeds various dashboards and score cards. Using Power Pivot, you can easily integrate data from these repositories. From the connection choices in the connection window (Figure 2-17), choose the Microsoft SQL Server Analysis Services connection under Multidimensional Services. This launches the connection information window as shown in Figure 2-23. You can either connect to a multidimensional cube or a Power Pivot model published to SharePoint. To connect to a cube, enter the server name and the database name. To connect to a Power Pivot model, enter the URL to the Excel workbook (in a SharePoint library) and the model name.

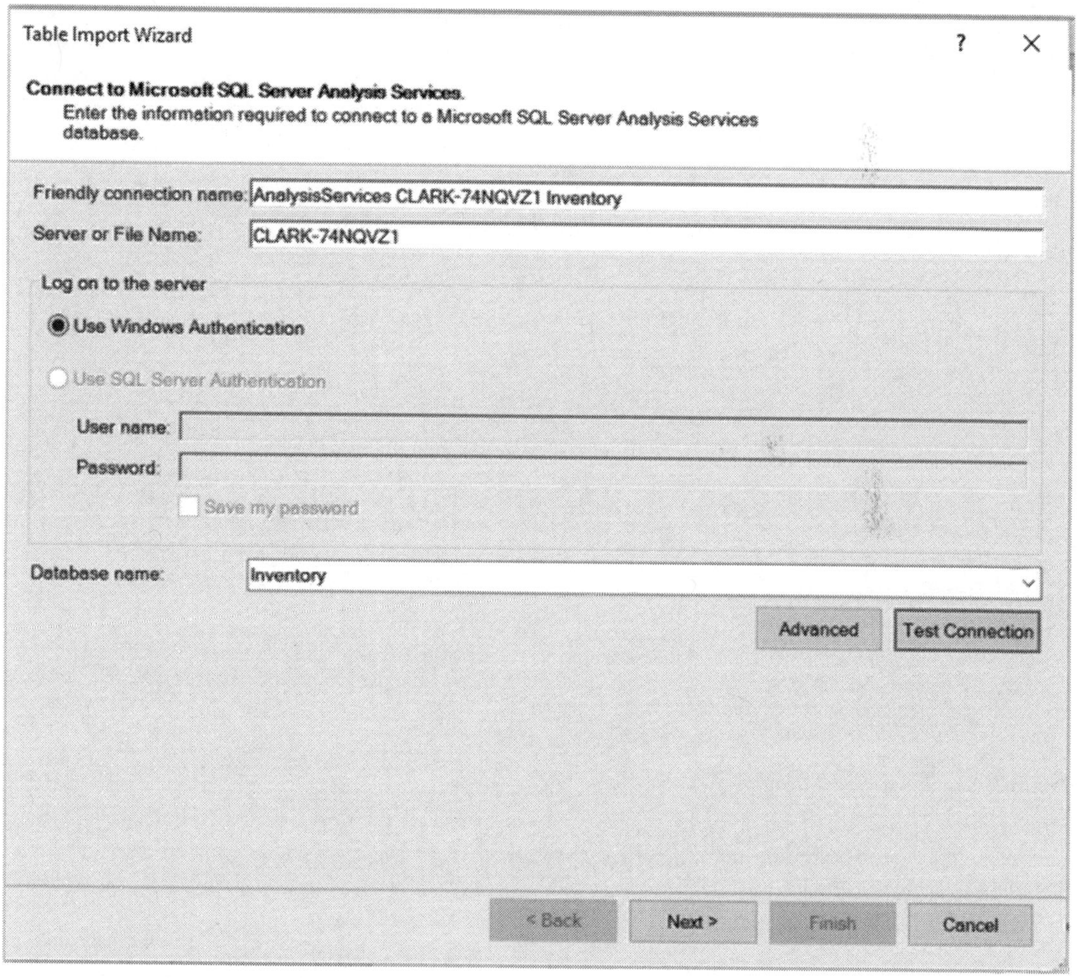

Figure 2-23. Connecting to an Analysis Services cube

Once you are connected to the cube, you can enter an MDX query to retrieve the data (see Figure 2-24). Remember to validate the query to make sure it will run.

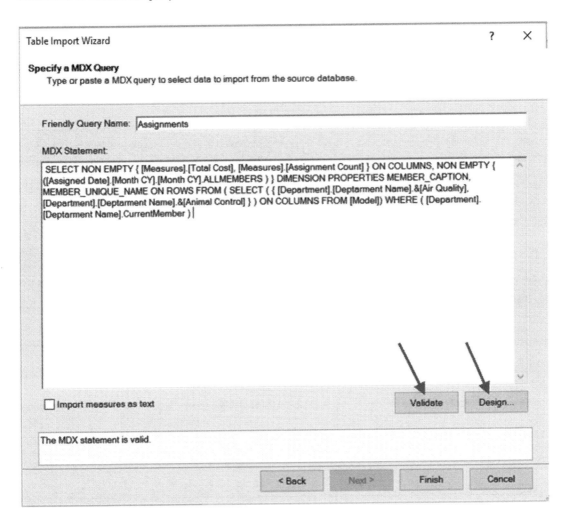

Figure 2-24. *Entering an MDX query*

If you don't know MDX, you can use a visual designer to create it, as shown in Figure 2-25. One of the nice features of the designer is the ability to preview the results.

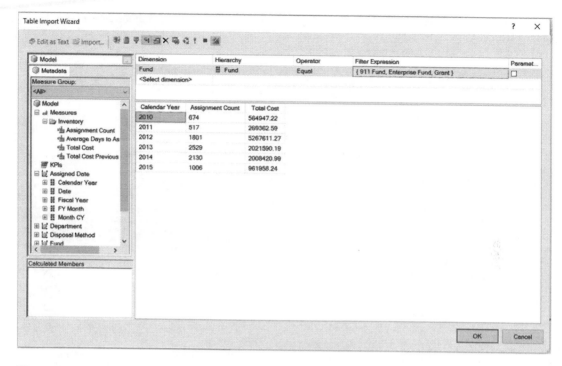

Figure 2-25. *Designing an MDX query*

When you are done designing the query, it is entered in to the MDX statement box, shown in Figure 2-24, where you can finish importing the data.

Reusing Existing Connections to Update the Model

There are two scenarios where you want to reuse an existing connection to a data source. You may need to retrieve additional data from a data source; for example, you need to get data from additional tables or views or issue a new query. In this case, you would choose the Existing Connections button located on the Home tab (see Figure 2-26).

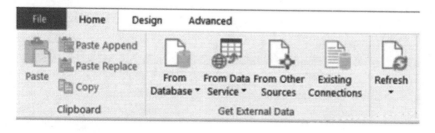

Figure 2-26. *Selecting existing connections*

In the Existing Connections window, select the connection and click the Open button (see Figure 2-27). This will launch the screens (which depend on the connection type) covered previously, where you go through the process of selecting the data you want to import.

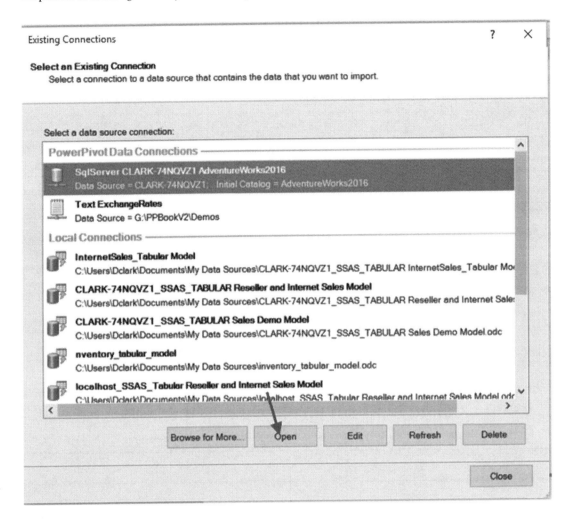

Figure 2-27. *Opening an existing connection*

The other scenario is when you want to change the filtering or add some columns to an existing table in the model. In this case, you need to select the table in the data view mode of the designer, and on the Design tab, select Table Properties (see Figure 2-28).

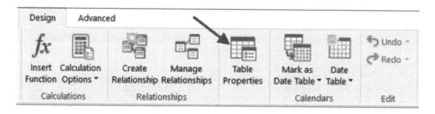

Figure 2-28. *Selecting table properties*

The Edit Table Properties window allows you to update the query used to populate the table with data. You can either update the table in the Table Preview mode (Figure 2-29) or Query Editor mode (Figure 2-30). When in Query Editor mode, you can also launch the Query Designer to update the query.

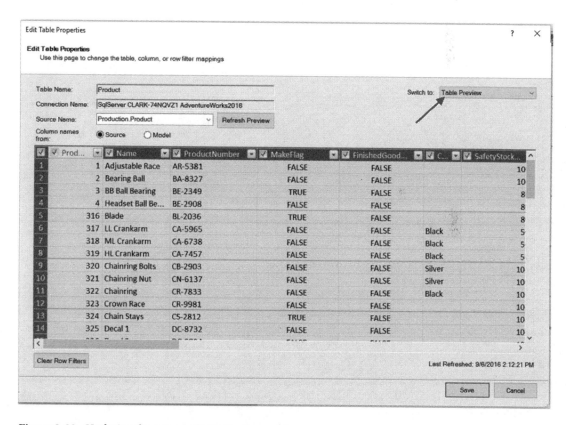

Figure 2-29. *Updating the query in Table Preview mode*

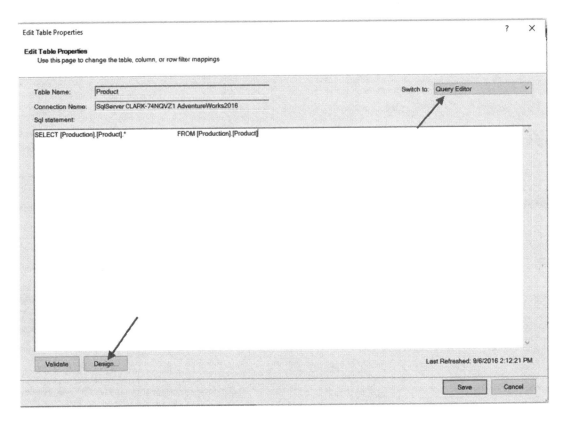

Figure 2-30. *Updating the query in Query Editor mode*

Now that you have seen how to import data from various data sources into the Power Pivot data model, it is time to get some hands-on experience importing the data.

▓ **Note** The following lab uses an Access database. If you are connecting to an Access database for the first time on your computer, you may need to install Access 2013 Runtime.

HANDS-ON LAB: LOADING DATA INTO POWER PIVOT

In the following lab you will

- Import data from an Access database.
- Import data from a text file.

1. Open Excel 2016 and create a new file called Chapter2Lab1.xlsx.

2. On the Power Pivot tab, click the Manage Data Model button (see Figure 2-31). This launches the Power Pivot Model Designer window.

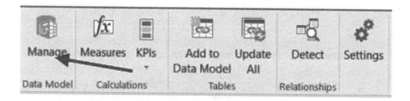

Figure 2-31. *Opening the Model Designer window*

3. On the Home tab in the Get External Data grouping, click the From Database drop-down (see Figure 2-32). In the drop-down, select From Access. This launches the Table Import Wizard.

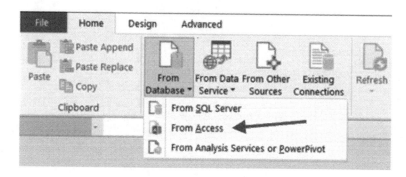

Figure 2-32. *Launching the Table Import Wizard*

4. Browse for the Northwind.acdb database file in the LabStarterFiles\Chapter2Lab1 folder and test the connection. Use the friendly connection name *Access Northwind*. You don't need a user name and password for this database (see Figure 2-33). Test the connection and click Next to advance to the next window.

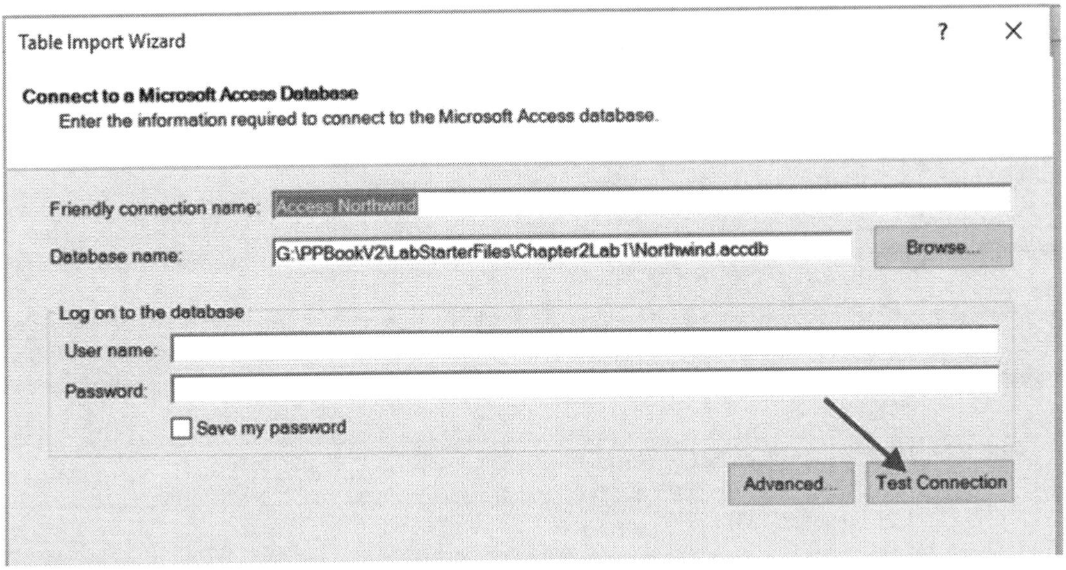

Figure 2-33. *Connecting to an Access database*

5. You have two options for importing the data: you can select from a list of tables and views or chose to write a query to select the data. Select from a list of tables and views.

6. In the Select Tables and Views window, select Customers and click the row to highlight it. At the bottom of the window, select the Preview & Filter button to preview and filter the data (see Figure 2-34).

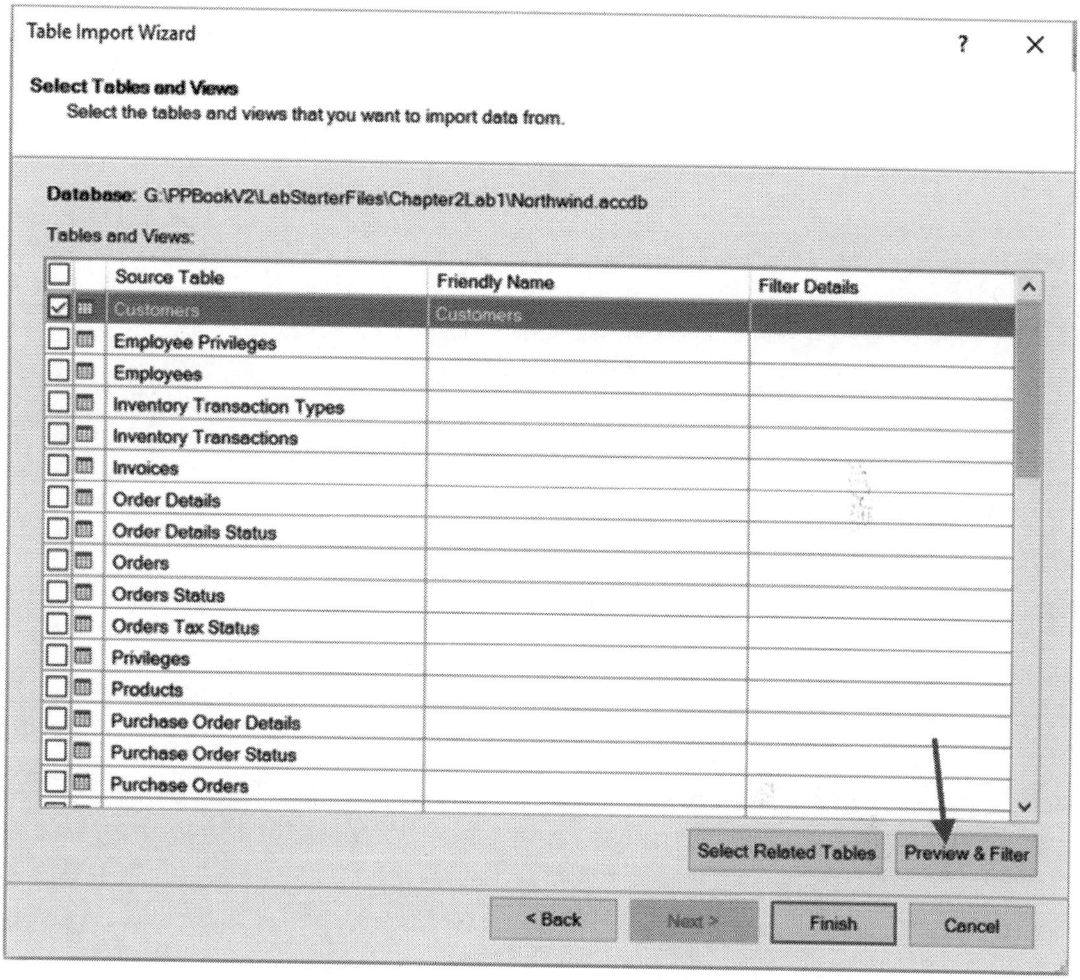

Figure 2-34. *Selecting tables to import*

7. In the Customers table, choose the following fields: ID, Company, Last Name, First Name, City, State/Province, and Country/Region. Uncheck the rest of the fields (see Figure 2-35). Checking the upper left check box will select or deselect all the columns.

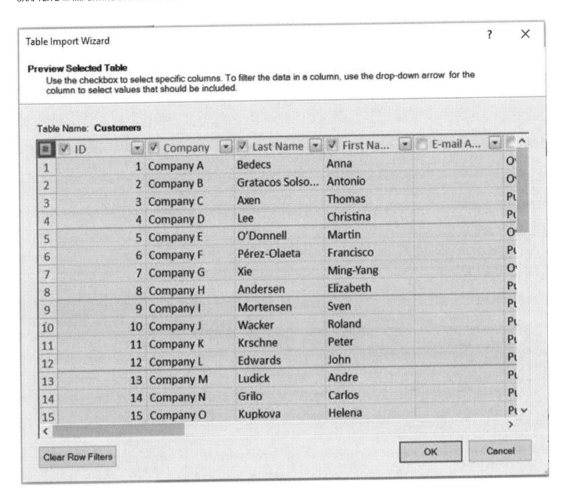

Figure 2-35. *Filtering table columns*

8. From the Employees table, select the following: ID, Last Name, First Name, and Job Title.

9. From the Orders table, select these: Order ID, Employee ID, Customer ID, Order Date, Shipped Date, Shipper ID, Payment Type, and Paid Date. On the Status ID column, click the drop-down to filter the data. Uncheck status 0 and status 2. Status 3 represents a status of closed (see Figure 2-36).

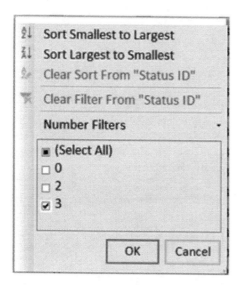

Figure 2-36. *Filtering table rows*

10. When you are done selecting the tables, click the Finish button to import the data. After importing, close the wizard. You should see each table as a tab in the Data View window (see Figure 2-37).

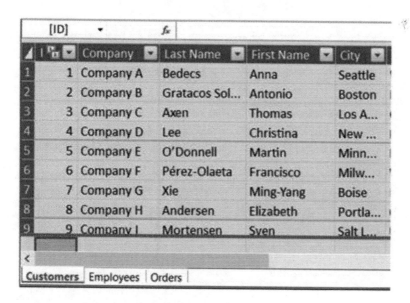

Figure 2-37. *Tables in the Data View window*

11. You are now going to select the order details using a query. In the Power Pivot Model Designer, select the Home tab and click the Existing Connections button. In the connections window, select the Access Northwind connection and click Open.

12. This time, select Write A Query That Will Specify The Data To Import.

13. On the Specify A Query window, name the query OrderDetails and select the Design button to launch the Query Designer. (You could also write the query without the designer.) In the Query Designer, select Import and select OrderDetailQuery. txt in the LabStarterFiles\Chapter2Lab1 folder. Test the query by clicking the red exclamation (!) mark (see Figure 2-38). After testing the query, click the OK button.

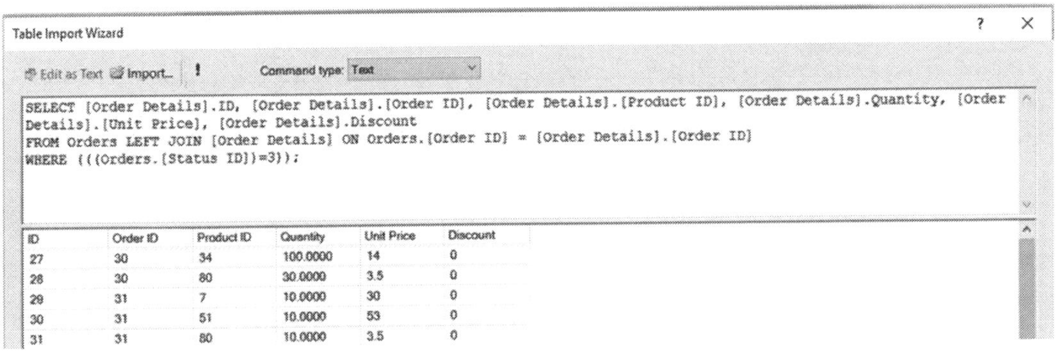

Figure 2-38. *Using a query to get data*

14. In the Table Import Wizard, click the Finish button to import the data. After importing, close the wizard. You should see that an OrderDetail table tab has been added.

15. The final table you are going to import is contained in a tab-delimited text file. On the Home tab in the Get External Data section, click the From Other Sources button. In the data sources list, select Text File and click Next.

16. In the connection information change the connection name to *Product*. In the File Path browse to the ProductList.txt file in the LabStarterFiles\Chapter2Lab1 folder. Select a tab column separator and check the Use First Row As Column Headers box. Click the Finish button to import the data (see Figure 2-39).

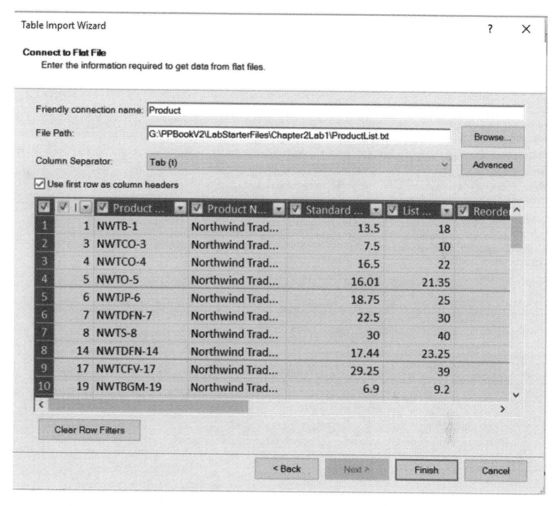

Figure 2-39. Importing data from a text file

17. After importing, close the wizard, and you should see that a Product table tab has been added.

18. When you are finished, save the file and close Excel.

Summary

One of the first steps in creating the Power Pivot model is importing data. In this chapter you learned how to import data from a variety of data sources. One of the nice features of importing data in Power Pivot is that the experience is similar when you import the data from the various data sources. You create a connection, supply a query or select tables, preview and filter the data, and then import it into the model. This works well for importing data that has been cleaned and transformed into a central repository maintained by IT. However, data is coming increasingly from various sources both structured and unstructured. Data from these sources often needs to be scrubbed and transformed before it can be useful and imported into a model. In the next chapter, you will look at a valuable add-in to Excel: Power Query, a powerful tool that provides an easy-to-use interface for discovering, cleaning and transforming data prior to importing it into your Power Pivot models.

CHAPTER 3

▣ ▣ ▣

Data Munging with Power Query

Although Power Pivot provides many types of connections that you can use to query data, there are times when you need to clean and shape it (commonly called *data munging*) before loading it into the model. This is where Power Query really shines and is a very useful part of your BI arsenal. Power Query provides an easy-to-use interface for discovering and transforming data. It contains tools to clean and shape data such as removing duplicates, replacing values, and grouping data. In addition, it supports a vast array of data sources, both structured and unstructured, such as relational databases, web pages, and Hadoop, just to name a few. Once the data is extracted and transformed, you can then easily load it into a Power Pivot model.

After completing this chapter, you will be able to

- Discover and import data from various sources.

- Cleanse data.

- Merge, shape, and filter data.

- Group and aggregate data.

- Insert calculated columns.

Discovering and Importing Data

Traditionally, if you needed to combine and transform data from various disparate data sources, you would rely on the IT department to stage the data for you using a tool such as SQL Server Integration Services (SSIS). This can often be a long, drawn-out effort of data discovery, cleansing, and conforming the data to a relational structure. Although this type of formal effort is needed to load and conform data for the corporate operational data store, there are many times when you just want to add data to your Power Pivot model from a variety of sources in a quick, intuitive, and agile manner. To support this effort, you can use Power Query (also known as Get & Transform) as your self-service BI ETL tool. Prior to Excel 2016, you needed to download and install a free add-in, after which a Power Query tab became available. Starting with Excel 2016, Power Query is natively integrated, and you access it using the Get & Transform section of the Data tab (see Figure 3-1).

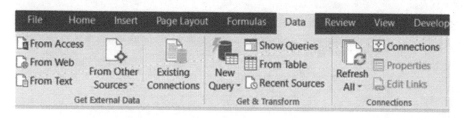

Figure 3-1. *The Get & Transform section of the Data tab*

© Dan Clark 2017
D. Clark, *Beginning Power BI*, DOI 10.1007/978-1-4842-2577-6_3

If you click the New Query drop-down, you can see the variety of data sources available to you. You can get data from the web, files, databases, and a variety of other sources (see Figure 3-2).

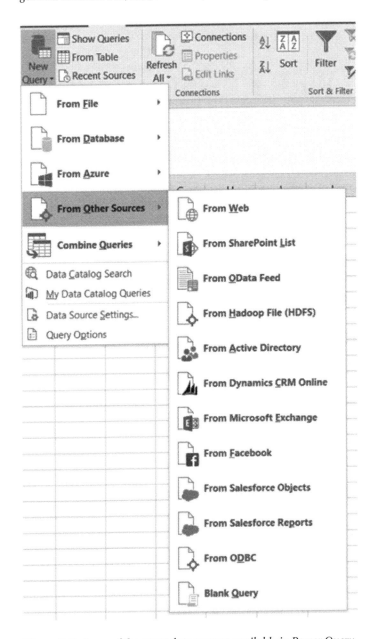

Figure 3-2. Some of the many data sources available in Power Query

The type of connection will dictate what information you need to supply to gain access to the data source. For example, a web source requires a URL whereas a CSV file requires the file path. Once you connect to a data source, the Query Editor window will launch, displaying a sample of the data. For example, Figure 3-3 shows flight delay data contained in a CSV file.

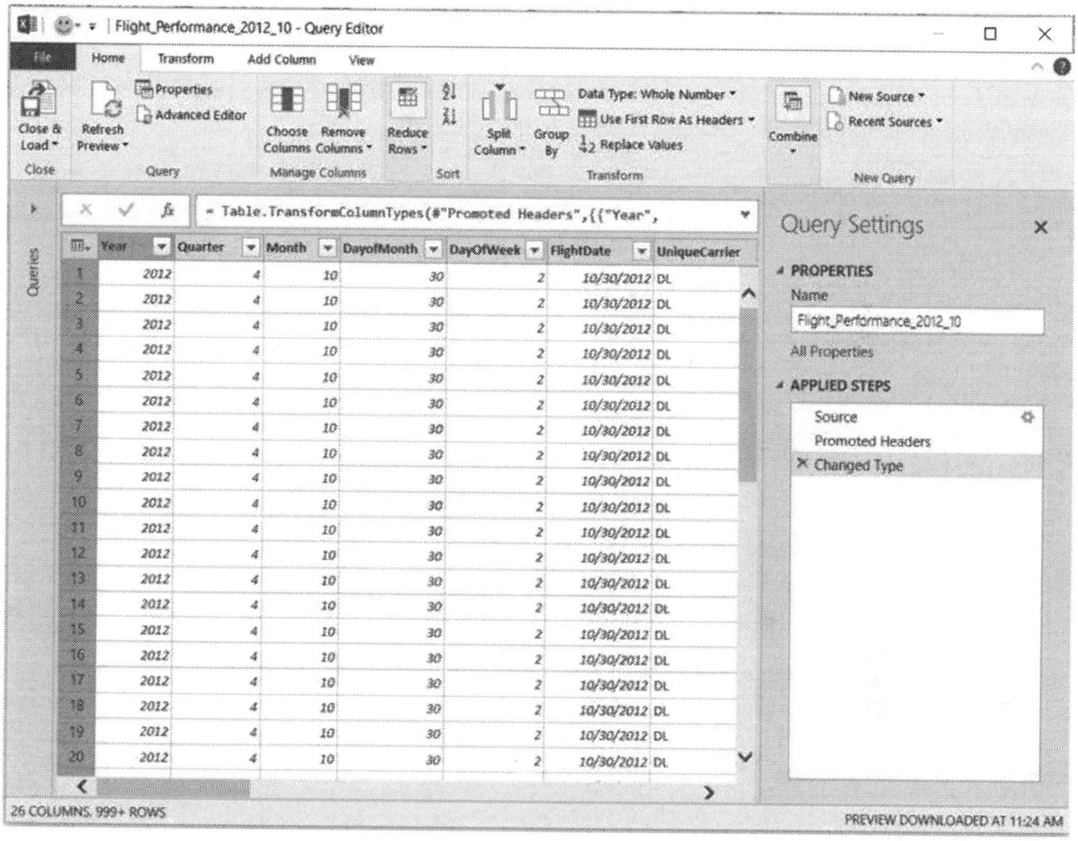

Figure 3-3. *The Query Editor window*

If you select a data source with multiple tables, you will see a Navigator pane displayed in Excel. Figure 3-4 shows the Navigator pane displayed when you connect to an Access source. After you select a table, sample data is displayed, and you can choose to launch the Query Editor or load it directly.

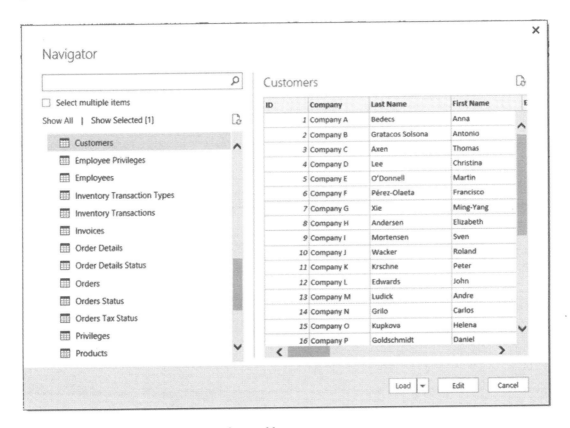

Figure 3-4. Using the Navigator pane to select a table

Once you have connected to the data source, the next step is to transform, cleanse, and filter the data before importing it into the data model.

Transforming, Cleansing, and Filtering Data

After connecting to the data source you are ready to transform and clean the data. This is an important step and will largely determine how well the data will support your analysis effort. Some common transformations that you will perform include removing duplicates, replacing values, removing error values, and changing data types. For example, in Figure 3-5 the FlightDate column is a Text data type in the source CSV file, but you want it to be a Date column in your model.

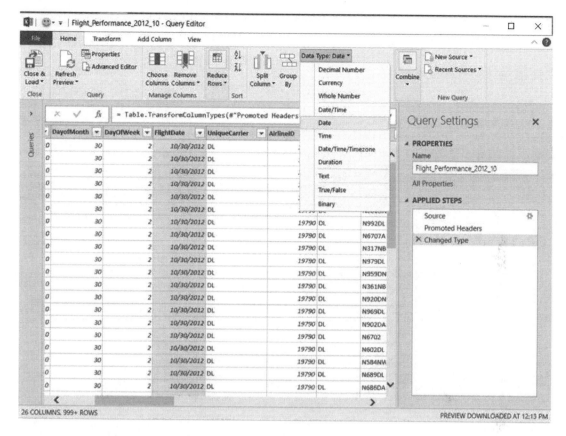

Figure 3-5. *Changing the data type of a column*

Often you need to replace values from a source system so that they sync together in your model. For example, a carrier listed as VX in the CSV file has a value of VG in your existing data. You can easily replace these values as the data is imported by selecting the column and then selecting the Replace Values transformation in the menu. This launches a window in which you can enter the values to find and what to replace them with (see Figure 3-6).

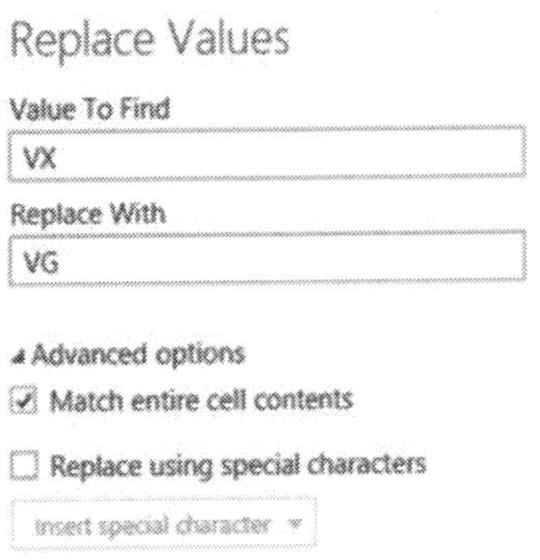

Replace Values

Value To Find

VX

Replace With

VG

◢ Advanced options

☑ Match entire cell contents

☐ Replace using special characters

Insert special character ▼

Figure 3-6. Replacing values in a column

When loading data from a source, another common requirement is filtering out unnecessary columns and rows. To remove columns, simply select the columns and select the Remove Columns button on the Home tab. If you only need a few columns, you can also select the columns you want to keep and then select the Remove Other Columns option. You can filter out rows by selecting the drop-down beside the column name and entering a filter condition (see Figure 3-7).

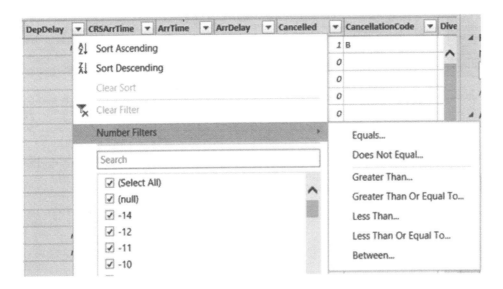

Figure 3-7. Filtering rows

As you apply the data transformations and filtering, the Query Editor lists the steps you have applied. This allows you to organize and track the changes you make to the data. You can rename, rearrange, and remove steps by right-clicking the step in the list (see Figure 3-8).

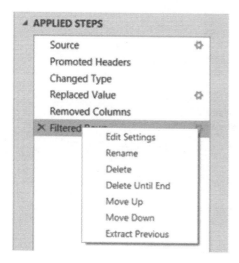

Figure 3-8. *Managing the query steps*

After cleansing and transforming the data, you may need to combine data from several sources into one table in your data model or expand data contained in a column.

Merging and Shaping Data

There are times when you may need to merge data from several tables and/or sources before you load the data into the model—for example, if you have codes in a table that link to another look-up table that contains the full value for the field. One way to deal with this is to import both tables into your model and create a link between the tables in the Power Pivot model. Another option is to merge the tables together before importing the data. For example, in the flight data you saw earlier, there is a UniqueCarrier column that contains carrier codes. You can merge these with another CSV file that contains the carrier codes and the carrier name. First create and save a query for each set of data with the Query Editor. For the look-up table, you can uncheck the Load to Worksheet and Load to Data Model check boxes, which you don't need because the data will be loaded after the merge. Next open the main query and click the Merge button on the Home tab. This will launch the Merge window (see Figure 3-9), where you select the look-up query and the columns that link the data together.

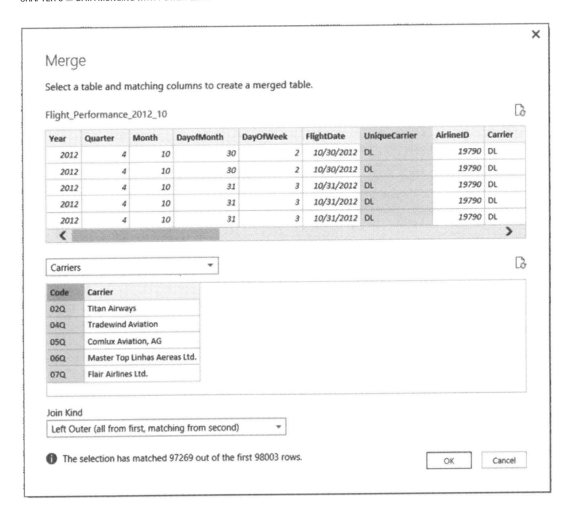

Figure 3-9. Merging data from two queries

Once you merge the queries, you can choose which columns to merge (see Figure 3-10). Once the columns are merged you will probably want to rename the columns in the main query.

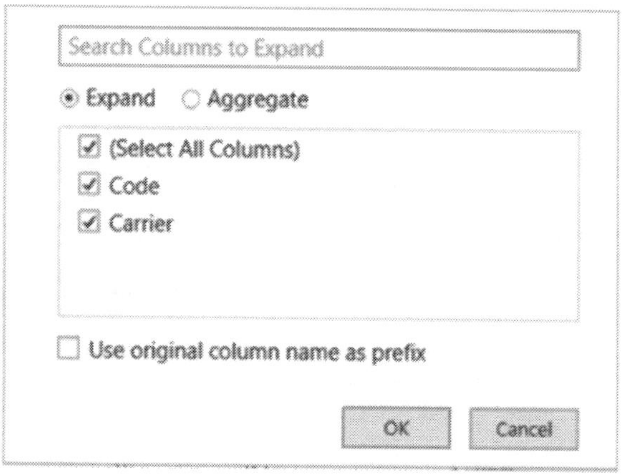

Figure 3-10. *Choosing columns to merge*

Along with merging data from look-up tables, you may also need to append data from two different sources. For example, say you have flight data for each year separated into different source files or tables and want to combine multiple years into the same table. In this case, you would create two similar queries, each using a different source. First open one of the queries in the Query Editor and select the Append Queries button on the Home tab. You can then select the other query as the table to append (see Figure 3-11).

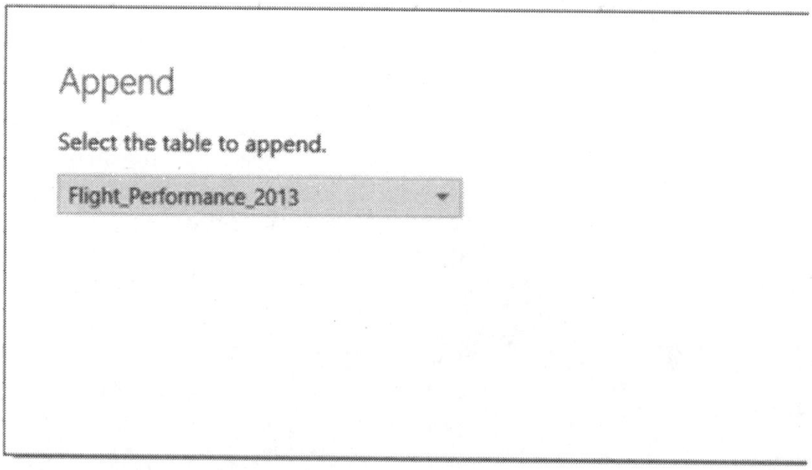

Figure 3-11. *Appending two queries*

Sometimes a source may provide you with data in a column that needs to be split up among several columns. For example, you may need to split the city and state, or the first name and last name. To do that, select the column in the Query Editor and on the Home tab choose Split Column. You can either split the column by a delimiter or by the number of characters (see Figure 3-12).

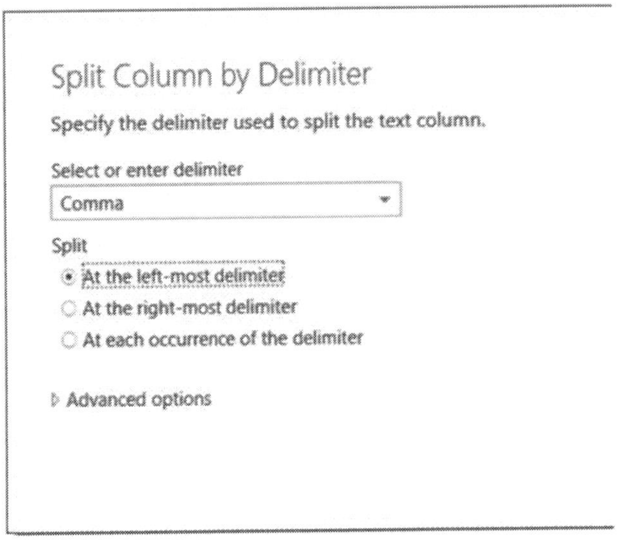

Split Column by Delimiter

Specify the delimiter used to split the text column.

Select or enter delimiter

Comma ▾

Split

◉ At the left-most delimiter
○ At the right-most delimiter
○ At each occurrence of the delimiter

▷ Advanced options

Figure 3-12. Spliting a column using a delimiter

Another scenario you may run into is when the data source contains data that is not in tabular form, but rather in a matrix, as in Figure 3-13.

Carrier	10/1/2012	10/2/2012	10/3/2012	10/4/2012	10/5/2012
AA	27579	18675	19041	21242	21115
DL	18763	11226	15112	16914	12681
UA	13784	11043	20777	20327	16497
US	3242	4083	7362	7567	4443

Figure 3-13. Using a matrix as a data source

In order to import this data into the data model, you will need to unpivot the data to get it in a tabular form. In the Query Editor, select the columns that need to be unpivoted (see Figure 3-14).

▦▾	Carrier	▾	10/1/2012	▾	10/2/2012	▾	10/3/2012	▾	10/4/2012	▾	10/5/2012	▾
1	AA		27579		18675		19041		21242		21115	
2	DL		18763		11226		15112		16914		12681	
3	UA		13784		11043		20777		20327		16497	
4	US		3242		4083		7362		7567		4443	

Figure 3-14. Selecting columns to unpivot

On the Transform tab, select the Unpivot transform. Once the data is unpivoted, you will get an Attribute column from the original column headers and a Value column (see Figure 3-15). You should rename these columns before importing the data.

⊞▾	Carrier ▾	Attribute ▾	Value ▾
1	AA	10/1/2012	27579
2	AA	10/2/2012	18675
3	AA	10/3/2012	19041
4	AA	10/4/2012	21242
5	AA	10/5/2012	21115
6	AA	10/6/2012	12749
7	AA	10/7/2012	20850
8	AA	10/8/2012	25678
9	AA	10/9/2012	20299
10	AA	10/10/2012	18974
11	AA	10/11/2012	21275
12	AA	10/12/2012	15887
13	AA	10/13/2012	11643
14	AA	10/14/2012	26060
15	AA	10/15/2012	15929
16	AA	10/16/2012	12281

Figure 3-15. *Resulting rows from the unpivot transformation*

As you bring data into the model, you often don't need the detail level data; instead, you need an aggregate value at a higher level—for example, product level sales or monthly sales. Using Power Query, you can easily group and aggregate the data before importing it.

Grouping and Aggregating Data

The need to group and aggregate data is a common scenario you may run into when importing raw data. For example, you may need to roll the data up by month or sales territory, depending on the analysis you want. To aggregate and group the data in the Query Editor, select the column you want to group by and select the Group By transform in the Home tab. You are presented with a Group By window (see Figure 3-16).

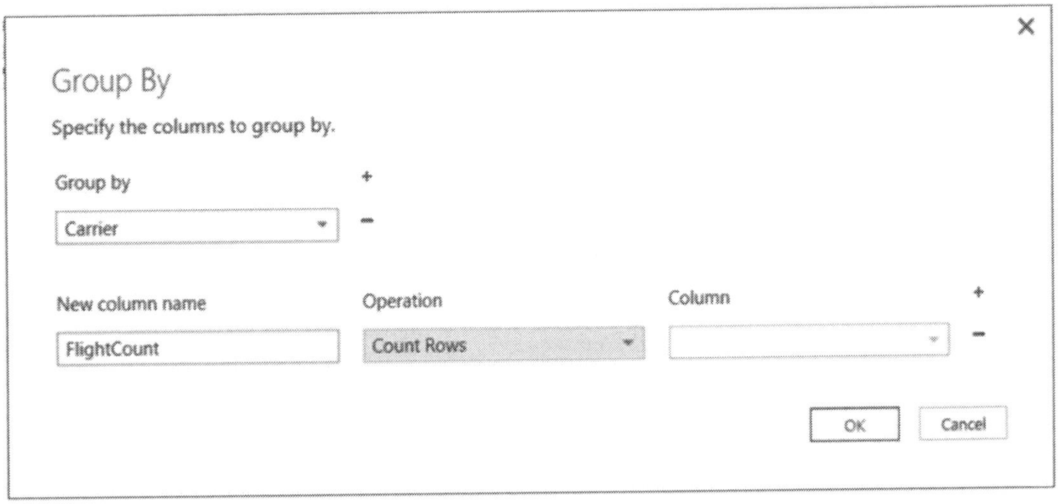

Figure 3-16. *Grouping data in Power Query*

You can group by multiple columns and aggregate multiple columns using the standard aggregate functions. Figure 3-17 shows some of the results from grouping by origin and carrier and aggregating the average and maximum departure delays.

	Origin	Carrier	FlightCount	MaxDelay	AveDelay
1	MSP	Delta Air Lines	610	336	45.45737705
2	ATL	Delta Air Lines	3278	820	34.08084198
3	JFK	Delta Air Lines	196	345	47.19387755
4	SFO	Delta Air Lines	119	307	54.84033613
5	LAS	Delta Air Lines	102	493	49.69607843
6	PBI	Delta Air Lines	78	247	40.98717949
7	MKE	Delta Air Lines	41	162	40.82926829
8	SLC	Delta Air Lines	282	479	43.4751773
9	SDF	Delta Air Lines	39	566	61.56410256
10	CVG	Delta Air Lines	77	327	44.05194805
11	LAX	Delta Air Lines	303	447	35.3630363
12	ELP	Delta Air Lines	10	83	35
13	JAX	Delta Air Lines	63	155	39.47619048
14	DTW	Delta Air Lines	568	433	45.57042254

Figure 3-17. *Grouping and aggregating flight data*

The final requirement you may run into as you import data using Power Query is inserting a calculated column. This is a little more advanced because you need to write code, as you will see in the next section.

Inserting Calculated Columns

Until now you have been building and executing queries using the visual interfaces provided by Power Query. Behind the scenes, however, the Power Query Editor was creating scripts used to execute the queries. A Power Query script is written in a new language called M. As you have seen, you can get a lot of functionality out of Power Query without ever having to know about M or learn how it works. Nevertheless, at the very least, you should know it is there and that it is what gets executed when you run the query. If you navigate to the View tab in the Query Editor, you will see an option to open the Advanced Editor, which will display the M code used to build the query (see Figure 3-18).

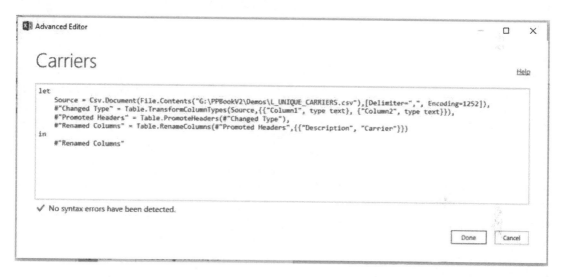

Figure 3-18. *Building a query with M*

You can use the Advanced Editor to write the query directly with M, thereby exposing some advanced data processing not exposed in the visual interface tools.

If you want to insert a calculated column into the query, you need to use the M functions. On the Add Column tab of the Query Editor you can duplicate columns, insert an index column, merge columns, and insert a custom column. When you select the Add Custom Column option, you are presented with an Add Custom Column editor where you insert the M function used to create the column (see Figure 3-19).

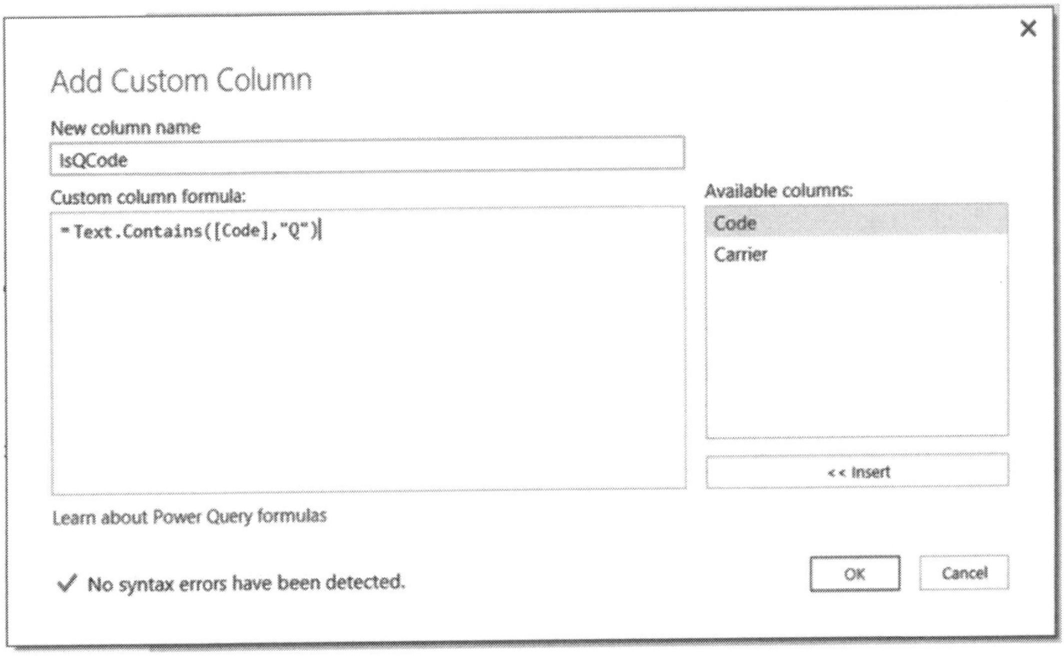

Figure 3-19. *Creating columns using M formulas*

Figure 3-20 shows the results of the query with the custom column added.

⊞⌄	Code ⌄	Carrier ⌄	IsQCode ⌄
1	02Q	Titan Airways	TRUE
2	04Q	Tradewind Aviation	TRUE
3	05Q	Comlux Aviation, AG	TRUE
4	06Q	Master Top Linhas Aereas Ltd.	TRUE
5	07Q	Flair Airlines Ltd.	TRUE
6	09Q	Swift Air, LLC	TRUE
7	0BQ	DCA	TRUE
8	0CQ	ACM AIR CHARTER GmbH	TRUE
9	0GQ	Inter Island Airways, d/b/a Inter Island Air	TRUE
10	0HQ	Polar Airlines de Mexico d/b/a Nova Air	TRUE
11	0J	JetClub AG	FALSE
12	0JQ	Vision Airlines	TRUE
13	0KQ	Mokulele Flight Services, Inc.	TRUE

Figure 3-20. *Displaying the results of the query*

So, if you need to create columns using Power Query before inserting the data into the Power Pivot model, you use M formulas. If you create the columns after importing the data into the Power Pivot model, you use DAX formulas (covered in later chapters).

Now that you have seen how Power Query works, it is time to get some hands-on experience using it to import, cleanse, and shape data.

HANDS-ON LAB: IMPORTING AND SHAPING DATA WITH POWER QUERY

In the following lab you will

- Create a query to import data.

- Filter and transform data.

- Append and shape data.

- Group and aggregate data.

1. In the LabStarterFiles\Chapter3Lab1 folder, open the Chapter3Lab1.xlsx file. This file contains a basic Power Pivot model that you will add to using Power Query.

2. Select the Data tab in Excel. Under the Get & Transform section, select the New Query drop-down and under From File choose the From CSV option. Navigate to the FlightPerformance_2012_10.csv file in the LabStarterFiles\Chapter3Lab1 folder. You should see the Query Editor window with airline delay data, as shown in Figure 3-21.

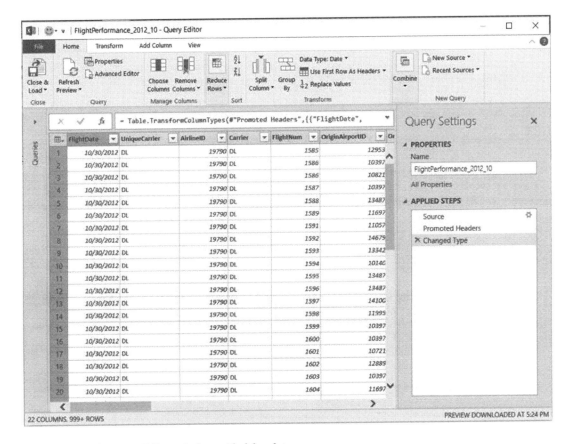

Figure 3-21. The Query Editor window with delay data

3. In the Query Settings pane, rename the query to FlightDelays.

4. In the Applied Steps list, if the Query Editor did not automatically add the transform to set the first row as headers, add it now.

5. Check the types of each column to see whether the Query Editor updated the FlightDate to a Date data type and the number type columns to a Number data type. If it did not, change them now.

6. On the Home tab select Choose Columns. Select the Carrier, Origin, OriginCityName, and DepDelay columns.

7. Filter the data so that it only pulls rows that have a flight departure delay of greater than 15 minutes.

8. On the Home tab, select the Close & Load drop-down and then choose Close & Load To. In the Load To window, uncheck the Add this data to the Data Model option (see Figure 3-22).

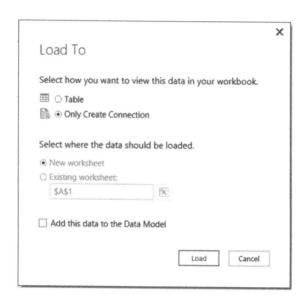

Figure 3-22. *Saving and Loading a query*

9. Complete steps 2–8 for the FlightPerformance_2012_11.csv file, except this time, name the query FlightDelays2.

10. You should now have two workbook queries, as shown in Figure 3-23.

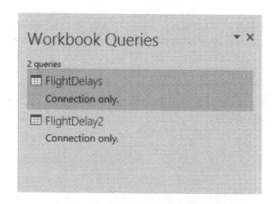

Figure 3-23. *Current workbook queries*

11. Double-click the FlightDelays query to open it back up in the Query Editor.

12. Select the Append Queries option in the Combine section of the Home tab. Append the FlightDelays2 query to the FlightDelays query.

13. Select the OriginCityName column and split it into two columns, named OriginCity and OriginState, using the comma. Do the same for the DestCityName column.

14. Replace West Palm Beach/Palm Beach in the OriginCity column with just Palm Beach.

15. On the Home tab, select Close & Load.

16. In the Workbook Queries pane, hover over the FlightDelays query and click the ellipses at the bottom of the preview window. In the menu that displays, select Load To (see Figure 3-24).

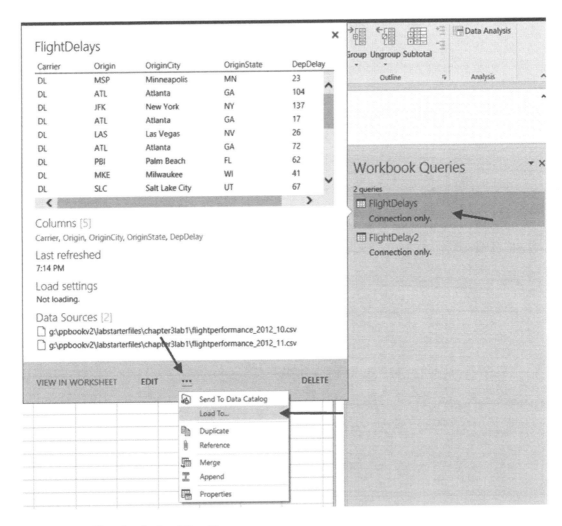

Figure 3-24. *Changing the Load To setting*

17. In the Load To window, check Add this data to the Data Model and click Load.

18. Once the query finishes loading, open the Power Pivot model and verify that the table was loaded.

19. Close the Model Explorer and on the Data tab in Excel select the New Query drop-down. Select From File and choose the From CSV option. Navigate to FlightPerformance_2012_12.csv in the LabStarterFiles\Chapter3Lab1 folder.

20. In the Query Settings pane, rename the query to DelaySummary.

21. Keep the Carrier, Origin, and DepDelay columns and remove the rest.

22. Filter out delays that are less than 15 minutes.

23. Find the average delay and max delay grouping by the origin and carrier (see Figure 3-25).

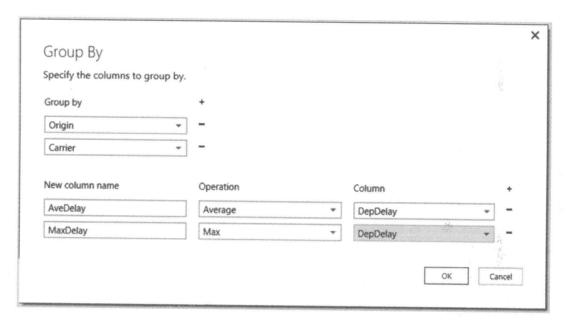

Figure 3-25. Grouping by origin and carrier.

24. On the Home tab, select the Close & Load drop-down and then choose Close & Load To. In the Load To window, uncheck the Add this data to the Data Model option.

25. Add a query called Carriers that gets the code and description from the Carriers. csv file.

26. Open the DelaySummary query and select the Merge Queries option on the Home tab. Using the Carriers query, merge the Description column matching the Carrier column in the DelaySummary query with the Code column in the Carriers query (see Figure 3-26).

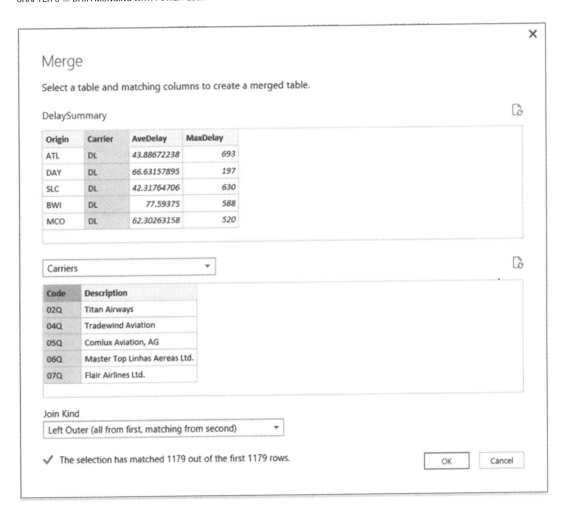

Figure 3-26. *Merging data from two queries*

27. Rename the Carrier column to *CarrierCode* and the Description column to *Carrier*.

28. When you are done, repeat step 16 to load the query into the data model.

29. Open the Power Pivot model and verify that the table was added to the model.

Summary

Power Query is a very useful tool you can use to get data from many different types of sources. In this chapter, you learned how to use Power Query to do some data munging—shaping, cleansing, and transforming data using intuitive interfaces without having to use code. Power Query builds the code for you but doesn't hide it from you. If you need to alter or enhance the code, you can use the Advanced Editor view. Although this chapter only touched on the M query language, we will return to this topic in Chapter 12, where we will dive deeper into it.

Now that you know how to get, clean, and shape data, the next step is to understand what makes a good model. This is very important when dealing with data in Power Pivot. A good model will make Power Pivot perform incredibly fast and allow you to analyze the data in new and interesting ways. A bad model will cause Power Pivot to perform very slowly and at worst give distorted results when performing the data analysis. The next chapter guides you through the process of creating solid models on which to build your analytical reports and dashboards.

CHAPTER 4

▓ ▓ ▓

Creating the Data Model

Now that you know how to get data into the Power Pivot model, the next step is to understand what makes a good model. This is very important when dealing with data in Power Pivot. A good model will make Power Pivot perform amazingly fast and allow you to analyze the data in new and interesting ways. A bad model will cause Power Pivot to perform very slowly and at worst give misleading results when performing the data analysis. Traditional Excel pivot tables are based on a single table contained in an Excel sheet. Power Pivot tables are based off of multiple tables contained in the data model. This chapter guides you through the process of creating a solid model that will become the foundation for your data analysis. In addition, you will look at how to present a user-friendly model to client tools. This includes renaming tables and fields, presenting appropriate data types, and hiding extraneous fields.

After completing this chapter, you will be able to

- Explain what a data model is.

- Create relationships between tables in the model.

- Create and use a star schema.

- Understand when and how to denormalize the data.

- Create and use linked tables.

- Create and use hierarchies.

- Make a user-friendly model.

What Is a Data Model?

Fundamentally a *data model* is made up of tables, columns, data types, and table relations. Typically, data tables are constructed to hold data for a business entity; for example, customer data is contained in a customer table and employee data is contained in an employee table. Tables consist of columns that define the attributes of the entity. For example, you may want to hold information about customers such as name, address, birth date, household size, and so on. Each of these attributes has a data type that depends on what information the attribute holds—the name would be a string data type, the household size would be an integer, and the birth date would be a date. Each row in the table should be unique. Take a customer table, for example; if you had the same customer in multiple rows with different attributes, say birth date, you would not know which was correct.

In the previous example, you would know that one of the rows was incorrect because the same person could not have two different birthdays. There are many times, however, when you want to track changes in attribute values for an entity. For example, a product's list price will probably change over time. To track the change, you need to add a time stamp to make the row unique. Then each row can be identified by the product number and time stamp, as shown in Figure 4-1.

© Dan Clark 2017
D. Clark, *Beginning Power BI*, DOI 10.1007/978-1-4842-2577-6_4

	ProductNumber	StandardCost	ListPrice	ProductLine	DealerPrice	ModelName	StartDate
1	FR-R38B-58	176.1997	297.6346	R	178.5808	LL Road Frame	2005-07-01 00:00:00.000
2	FR-R38B-58	170.1428	306.5636	R	183.9382	LL Road Frame	2006-07-01 00:00:00.000
3	FR-R38B-58	204.6251	337.22	R	202.332	LL Road Frame	2007-07-01 00:00:00.000

Figure 4-1. Using a time stamp to track changes

Once you have the tables of the model identified, it is important that you recognize whether the tables are set up to perform efficiently. This process is called *normalizing* the model. Normalization is the process of organizing the data to make data querying easier and more efficient. For example, you should not mix attributes of unrelated entities together in the same table—you would not want product data and employee data in the same table. Another example of proper normalization is to not hold more than one attribute in a column. For example, instead of having one customer address column, you would break it up into street, city, state, and zip code. This would allow you to easily analyze the data by state or by city. The spread sheet shown in Figure 4-2 shows a typical non-normalized table. If you find that the data supplied to you is not sufficiently normalized, you can use Power Query to break the data up into multiple tables that you can then relate together in your model.

Customer Name	Address
Tom Smith	128 Elm St. Littleton, PA 12555
Jannet Jones	1399 Firestone Drive, San Francisco, CA 94109
Jon Yang	9539 Glenside Dr, Phoenix AZ 85004
Tom Smith	9707 Coldwater Drive, Orlando, FL 32804

Order Date	Item 1	Item 1 Description	Item 1 Price	Item 2	Item 2 Description	Item 2 Price
7/23/2013	FR-R38B-58	LL Road Frame	183	HB-R504	LL Road Handlebars	26.75
7/23/2013	FW-R623	Road Front Wheel	85.5			
8/1/2013	RB-9231	Rear Brakes	21.98			
8/1/2013	FW-R623	LL Road Front Wheel	85.5	RB-9231	Breaks	21.98

Figure 4-2. A non-normalized table

Once you are satisfied the tables in your model are adequately normalized, the next step is to determine how the tables are related. For example, you need to relate the customer table, sales table, and product table in order to analyze how various products are selling by age group. The way you relate the different tables is through the use of *keys*. Each row in a table needs a column or a combination of columns that uniquely identifies the row. This is called the *primary key*. The key may be easily identified, such as a sales order number or a customer number that has been assigned by the business when the data was entered. Sometimes you will need to do some analysis of a table to find the primary key, especially if you get the data from an outside source. For example, you may get data that contains potential customers. The fields are name, city, state, zip, birth date, and so on. You cannot just use the name as the key because it is very likely that you have more than one customer with the same name. If you use the combination of name and city, you have less of a chance of having more than one customer identified by the same key. As you use more columns, such as zip and birth date, your odds get even better.

When you go to relate tables in the model, the primary key from one table becomes a *foreign* key in the related table. For example, to relate a customer to their sales, the customer key needs to be contained in the sales table where it is considered a foreign key. When extracting the data, the keys are used to get the related data. By far, the best type of key to use for performance reasons is a single column integer. For this reason, a lot of database tables are designed with a surrogate key. This key is an integer that gets assigned to the record when it is loaded. Instead of using the natural key, the surrogate is used to connect the tables. Figure 4-3 shows a typical database table containing both the surrogate key (CustomerKey) and the natural key (CustomerAlternateKey).

CustomerKey	GeographyKey	CustomerAlternateKey	Title	FirstName	MiddleName	LastName	NameStyle	BirthDate
11000	26	AW00011000	NULL	Jon	V	Yang	0	1966-04-08
11001	37	AW00011001	NULL	Eugene	L	Huang	0	1965-05-14
11002	31	AW00011002	NULL	Ruben	NULL	Torres	0	1965-08-12
11003	11	AW00011003	NULL	Christy	NULL	Zhu	0	1968-02-15
11004	19	AW00011004	NULL	Elizabeth	NULL	Johnson	0	1968-08-08
11005	22	AW00011005	NULL	Julio	NULL	Ruiz	0	1965-08-05
11006	8	AW00011006	NULL	Janet	G	Alvarez	0	1965-12-06
11007	40	AW00011007	NULL	Marco	NULL	Mehta	0	1964-05-09
11008	32	AW00011008	NULL	Rob	NULL	Verhoff	0	1964-07-07
11009	25	AW00011009	NULL	Shannon	C	Carlson	0	1964-04-01

Figure 4-3. *A table containing both a surrogate key and a natural key*

It is important that you are aware of the keys used in your sources of data. If you can retrieve the keys from the source, you are much better off. This is usually not a problem when you are retrieving data from a relational database, but if you are combining data from different sources, make sure you have the appropriate keys.

Once you have the keys between the tables identified, you are ready to create the relationships in the Power Pivot model.

Creating Table Relations

There are a few rules to remember when establishing table relationships in a Power Pivot model. First, you can't use composite keys in the model. If your table uses a composite key, you will need to create a new column by concatenating the composite columns together and using this column as the key. Second, you can only have one active relationship path between two tables, but you can have multiple inactive relationships. Third, relationships are one-to-many; in other words, creating a relationship between the customer table (one side) and the sales table (many sides) is okay. Creating a direct relationship between the customer table and the products table is not allowed, however, because the customer can buy many products, and the same product can be bought by many customers. In these cases, you create a junction table to connect the tables together.

To create a relationship between two tables in the Power Pivot model, you open up the Data Model Manager and switch to the diagram view. Right-click the table that represents the *many* side of the relationship and select Create Relationship. This launches the Create Relationship window. Select the related table and the key column in each table. Figure 4-4 shows creating a relationship between the Sales table and the Store table. By default, the first relationship created between the tables is marked as the active relationship.

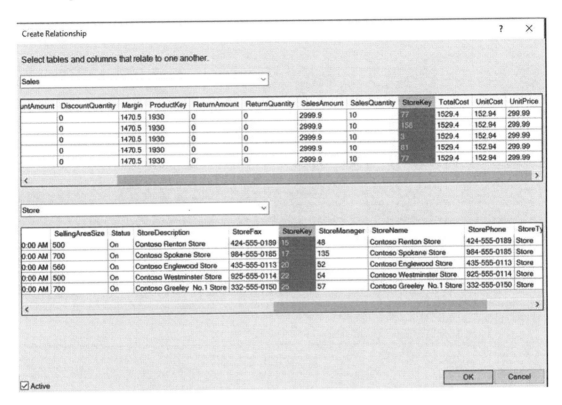

Figure 4-4. Creating a table relationship

Figure 4-5 shows the resulting relationship in the diagram view. If you click the relationship arrow, the two key columns of the relationship are highlighted. The * indicates the *many* side of the relationship. For each row in the Store table, there can be many related rows in the Sales table.

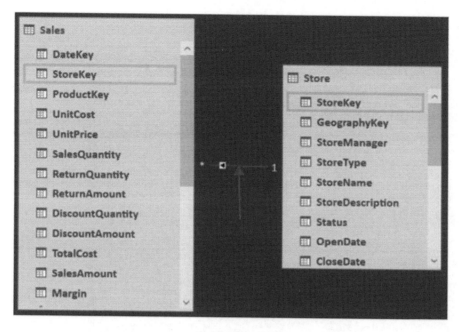

Figure 4-5. *Viewing a relationship in the diagram view*

You can create more than one relationship between two tables, but remember, only one can be the active relationship. If you try to make two active relationships, you'll get an error like the one shown in Figure 4-6.

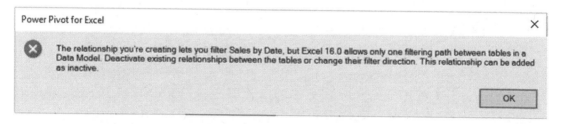

Figure 4-6. *Trying to create a second active relationship between two tables*

Sometimes the active relationship is not so obvious. Figure 4-7 shows an active relationship between the Sales table and the Date table and another one between the Sales table and the Store table. There is also an inactive relationship between the Store table and the Date table. If you try to make this one active, you get the same error message shown in Figure 4-6. This is because you can trace an active path from the Date table to the Sales table to the Store table.

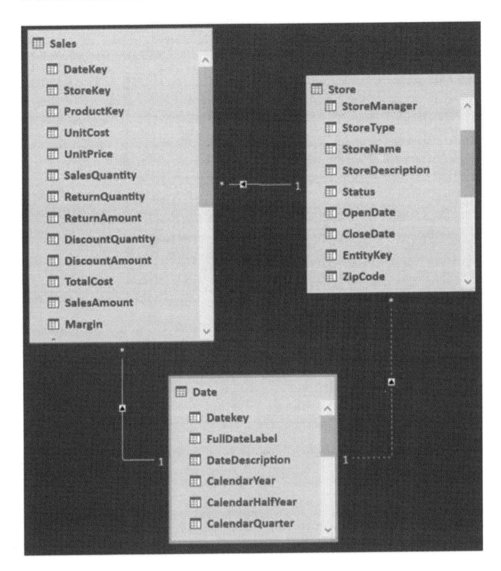

Figure 4-7. *An indirect active relationship*

Another common error you may run into is when you try to create a relationship between two tables and the key is not unique in at least one of the tables. Figure 4-8 shows a Product table and a Sales table that both contain duplicate ProductNumbers.

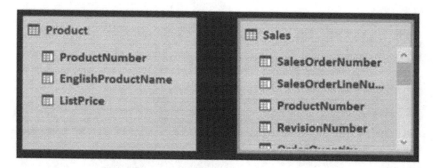

Figure 4-8. *The Product and Sales tables*

When you try to create a relationship between the tables you get the error shown in Figure 4-9.

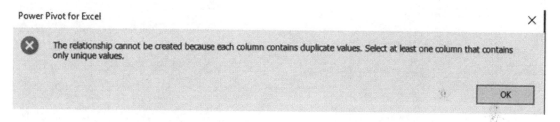

Figure 4-9. *Getting a duplicate value error*

In this example the ProductNumber is supposed to be unique in the Product table, but it turns out there are duplicates. In order to fix this, you would have to change the query for the Product table data to ensure that you are not getting duplicates.

Now that you know how to create table relationships in the model, you are ready to look at the benefits of using a star schema.

Creating a Star Schema

When creating a data model, it is important to understand what the model is being used for. The two major uses of databases are for capturing data and for reporting/analyzing the data. The problem is that when you create a model for efficient data capture, you decrease its efficiency to analyze the data. To combat this problem, many companies split off the data-capturing database from their reporting/analysis database. Fortunately, when creating the data model in Power Pivot, we only need to tune it for reporting.

One of the best models to use when analyzing large sets of data is the star schema. The *star schema* consists of a central fact table surrounded by dimension tables, as shown in Figure 4-10.

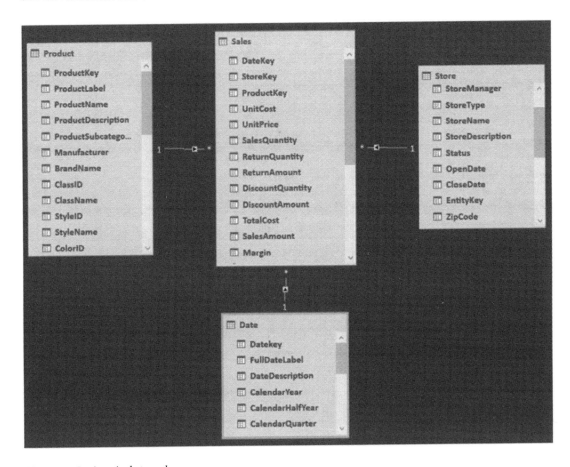

Figure 4-10. *A typical star schema*

The fact table contains quantitative data related to the business or process. For example, the Sales table in Figure 4-10 contains measurable aspects of a sale, such as total costs, sales amount, and quantity. Fact tables usually contain many rows and have a date or time component that records the time point at which the event occurred. The dimension tables contain attributes about the event. For example, the Date table can tell you when the sale occurred and allows you to roll up the data to the month, quarter, or year level. The Product table contains attributes about the product sold, and you can look at sales by product line, color, and brand. The Store table contains attributes about the store involved in the sale. Dimension tables usually don't contain as many rows as fact tables but can contain quite a few columns. When you ask a question like "Which bikes are selling the best in the various age groups?" the measures (sales dollar values) come from the fact table, whereas the categorizations (age and bike model) come from the dimension tables.

The main advantage of the star schema is that it provides fast query performance and aggregation processing. The disadvantage is that it usually requires a lot of preprocessing to move the data from a highly normalized transactional system to a more denormalized reporting system. The good news is that your business may have a reporting system feeding a traditional online analytical processing (OLAP) database such as Microsoft's Analysis Server or IBM's Cognos. If you can gain access to these systems, they are probably the best source for your core business data.

In order to create a star schema from your source data systems, you may have to perform some data denormalization, which is covered in the following section.

Understanding When to Denormalize the Data

Although transactional database systems tend to be highly normalized, reporting systems are denormalized into the star schema. If you don't have access to a reporting system where the denormalization is done for you, you will have to denormalize the data into a star schema to load your Power Pivot model. As an example, Figure 4-11 shows the tables that contain customer data in the Adventureworks transactional sales database.

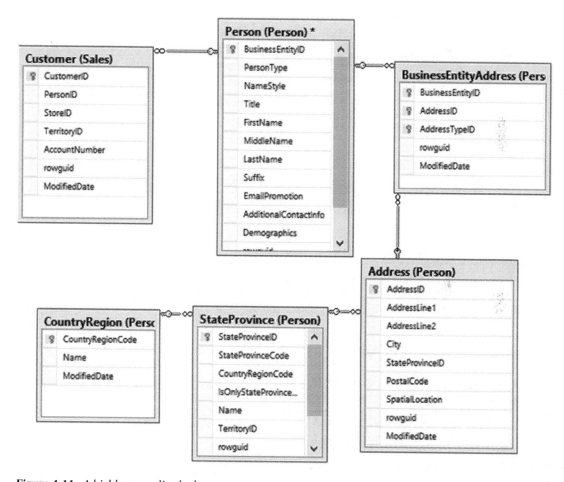

Figure 4-11. *A highly normalized schema*

In order to denormalize the customer data into your model, you need to create a query that combines the data into a single customer dimension table. If you are not familiar with creating complex queries, the easiest way to do this is to have the database developers create a view you can pull from that combines the tables for you. If the query isn't too complex, you can create it yourself using Power Query. For example, Figure 4-12 shows a Customer table and a Geography table.

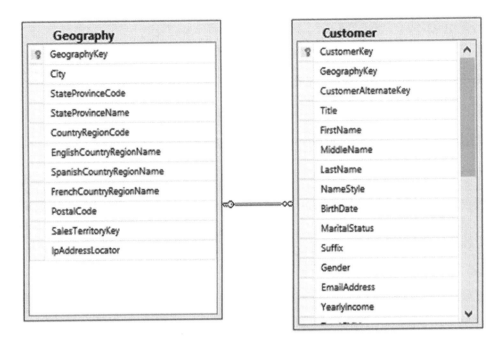

Figure 4-12. *Combining customer and customer location data*

You can combine these into one customer dimension table using the merge function in Power Query. Although you do not have to be a query expert to get data into your Power Pivot model, it is very beneficial to know the basics of querying the data sources, even if it just helps to ask the right questions when you talk to the database developers.

Creating Linked Tables

One thing to remember about the data contained in the Power Pivot model is that it is read only. For the most part, this is a good thing. You want to make sure that the data only gets changed in the source system. At times, however, as part of the data analysis, you will want to make adjustments on the fly and see how it affects the results. One example that happens fairly often is *bucket analysis*. For example, say you want to look a continuous measure such as age in discrete buckets (ranges) and you need to adjust the ranges during analysis. This is where *linked* tables shine.

To create the linked table, you first set up the table on an Excel sheet. After entering the data, you highlight it and click the quick analysis menu (see Figure 4-13). Under the Tables tab, click the Table button.

Age Group	Min Age	Max Age
Infant	0	2
Child	3	12
Teenager	13	18
Young Adult	19	25
Adult	25	59
Older Adult	60	120

Formatting   Charts   Totals   **Tables**   Sparklines

Table   Blank PivotTable

Tables help you sort, filter, and summarize data.

Figure 4-13. *Creating an Excel table*

Once the table is created, it is a good idea to name it before importing it into the Power Pivot data model. You can do this by selecting the table and then entering the table name under the Tables tab in the Table Tools Design tab (see Figure 4-14).

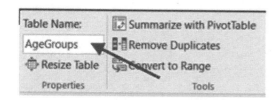

Table Name:	
AgeGroups	
⊕ Resize Table	
Properties	Tools

Summarize with PivotTable
Remove Duplicates
Convert to Range

Figure 4-14. *Renaming an Excel table*

Once you have the table named, select it, and on the Power Pivot tab, select Add To Data Model (see Figure 4-15).

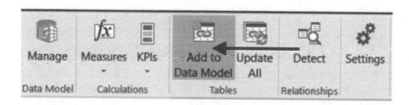

Manage	Measures	KPIs	Add to Data Model	Update All	Detect	Settings
Data Model	Calculations		Tables		Relationships	

Figure 4-15. *Adding the table to the model*

After the table is imported into the model, if you change some of the table values in the Excel sheet and select Update All on the PowerPivot tab (see Figure 4-15), the linked table in the model will update with the new values.

Creating Hierarchies

When analyzing data, it is often helpful to use hierarchies to define various levels of aggregations. For example, it is common to have a calendar-based hierarchy based on year, quarter, and month levels. An aggregate like sales amount is then rolled up from month to quarter to year. Another common hierarchy might be from department to building to region. You could then roll cost up through the different levels. Creating hierarchies in a Power Pivot model is very easy. In the diagram view of the Model Designer, select the table that has the attributes (columns) you want in the hierarchy. You will then see a Create Hierarchy button in the upper right corner of the table (see Figure 4-16). Click the button to add the hierarchy and rename it. You can then drag and drop the fields onto the hierarchy to create the different levels. Make sure you arrange the fields so that they go from a higher level down to a lower level.

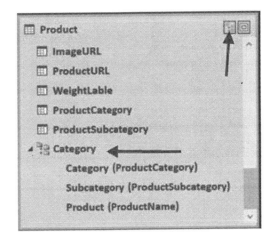

Figure 4-16. *Creating a hierarchy*

Creating hierarchies is one way to increase the usability of your model and help users instinctively gain more value in their data analysis. In the next section you will see some other things you can do to the model to increase its usability.

Making a User-Friendly Model

As you are creating your model, one thing to keep in mind is making the model easy and intuitive to use. Chances are that the model may get used by others for analysis. There are properties and settings you can use that will make your models more user friendly.

One of the most effective adjustments you can make is to rename the tables and columns. Use names that make sense for business users instead of a cryptic naming convention that only makes sense to the database developers. Another good practice is to make sure the data types and formats of the columns are set correctly. A field from a text file may come in typed as a string when in reality it is numeric data. In addition, you can hide fields that are of no use to the user, such as the surrogate keys used for linking the tables.

A common requirement is to change the sort order of a column from its natural sorting. The most common example is the months of the year. Because they are text by default, they are sorted alphabetically. In reality, you want them sorted by month number. To fix this, you can sort one column by any other column in the table (see Figure 4-17). This is a nice feature and allows you to create your own business-related custom sorting.

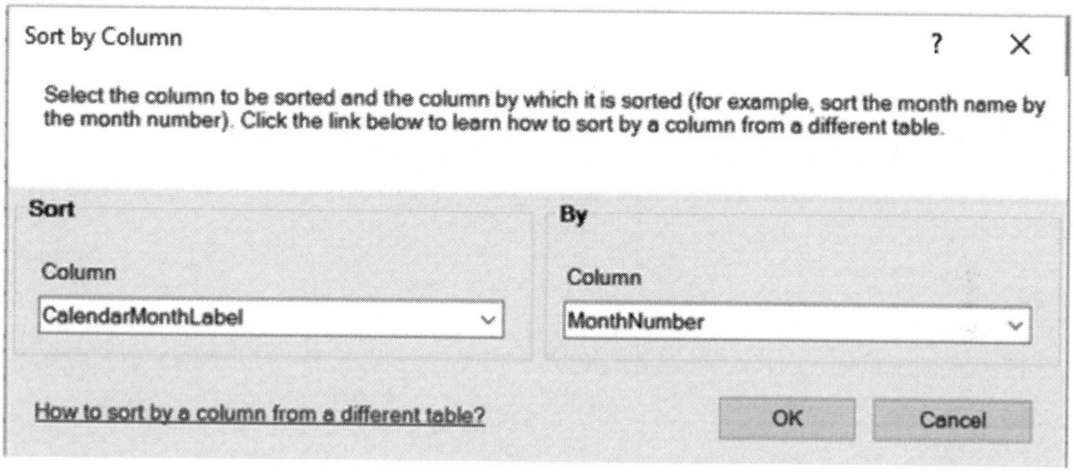

Figure 4-17. *Sorting one column by another column*

You can use some other settings to create good models for the various client tools. We will revisit this topic in more detail in Chapter 11.

The following hands-on lab will help you solidify the topics covered in this chapter.

HANDS-ON LAB: CREATING A DATA MODEL IN POWER PIVOT

In the following lab you will

- Create table relations.

- Denormalize data.

- Create a linked table.

- Set up a hierarchy.

- Make a user-friendly model.

1. Open Excel 2016 and create a new file called Chapter4Lab1.xlsx.

2. Open the Power Pivot Model Designer by clicking the Manage button on the Power Pivot tab. Connect to the Adventureworks.accdb file in the LabStarterFiles\Chapter4Lab1 folder.

3. Select the tables and fields listed and import the data.

Source Table Name	Friendly Name	Fields
DimDate	Date	DateKey FullDateAlternateKey EnglishMonthName MonthNumberOfYear CalendarQuarter CalendarYear
DimCustomer	Customer	CustomerKey BirthDate MaritalStatus Gender YearlyIncome TotalChildren HouseOwner NumberOfCars
FactInternetSales	Internet Sales	ProductKey OrderDateKey ShipDateKey CustomerKey SalesTerritoryKey SalesOrderNumber SalesOrderLineNumber OrderQuantity' UnitPrice TotalProductCost SalesAmount

4. In the data view mode of the Power Pivot Model Designer, rename and hide the columns indicated in the table. To rename or hide a column, right-click it and choose Rename or Hide From Client Tools in the context menu.

Table	Column	Friendly Name	Hide
Date	DateKey		X
	FullDateAlternateKey	Date	
	EnglishMonthName	Month	
	MonthNumberOfYear	Month No	X
	CalendarQuarter	Quarter	
	CalendarYear	Year	
Customer	CustomerKey		X
	BirthDate	Birth Date	
	MaritalStatus	Marital Status	
	Gender	Gender	
	YearlyIncome	Income	
	TotalChildren	Children	
	HouseOwner	Home Owner	
	NumberOfCars	Cars	
Internet Sales	ProductKey		X
	OrderDateKey		X
	ShipDateKey		X
	CustomerKey		X
	SalesTerritoryKey		X
	SalesOrderNumber	Order Number	
	SalesOrderLineNumber	Order Line Number	
	OrderQuantity	Quantity	
	UnitPrice	Unit Price	
	TotalProductCost	Product Cost	
	SalesAmount	Sales Amount	

5. Switch the Power Pivot window to diagram view. You should see the Date, Customer, and Internet Sales. The Customer table and the Internet Sales table have a relationship defined between them. This was discovered by the Table Import Wizard.

6. Drag the DateKey from the Date table and drop it on the OrderDateKey in the Internet Sales table. Similarly, create a relationship between the DateKey and the ShipDateKey. Double-click this relationship to launch the Edit Relationship window (see Figure 4-18). Try to make it an active relationship. You should get an error because you can only have one active relationship between two tables in the model.

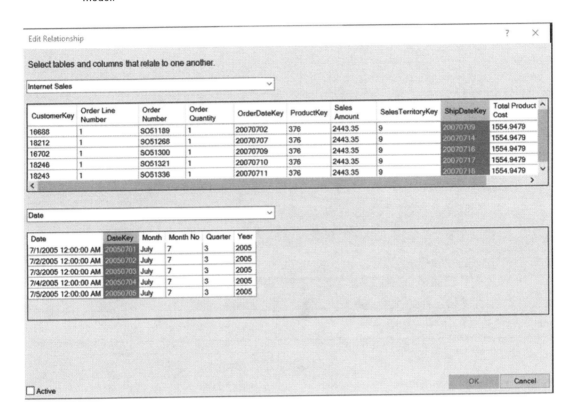

Figure 4-18. *Creating the table relationship*

7. Close the Model Designer. Select the Data tab in Excel and under the New Query drop-down select From Database and then From Microsoft Access Database (see figure 4-19).

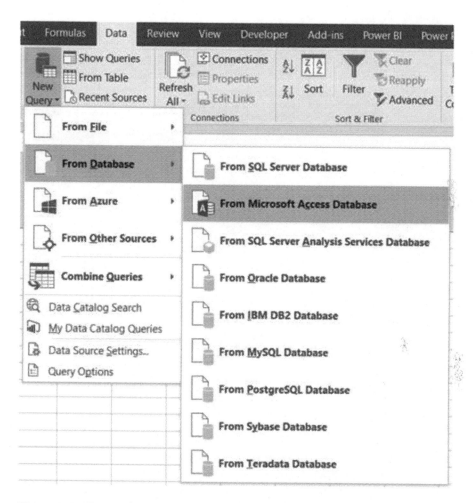

Figure 4-19. Connecting to Access using Power Query

8. Connect to the Adventureworks.accdb file in the LabStarterFiles\Chapter4Lab1 folder. In the Navigator window check the Select multiple items box. Select the DimProduct, DimProductCategory, and the DimProductSubcategory tables and click the Edit button (see Figure 4-20).

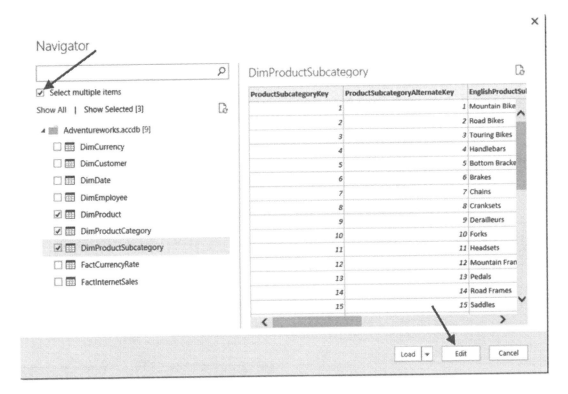

Figure 4-20. *Selecting tables in Power Query*

9. Using the Power Query designer, select the ProductKey, ProductAlternateKey, WeightUnitMeasureCode, SizeUnitMeasureCode, EnglishProductName, ListPrice, Size, SizeRange, Weight, and Color columns from the DimProduct query. Change the Name of the query to `Product`.

10. Merge the DimProductSubcategory to the `Product` query using a Left Outer join (see Figure 4-21).

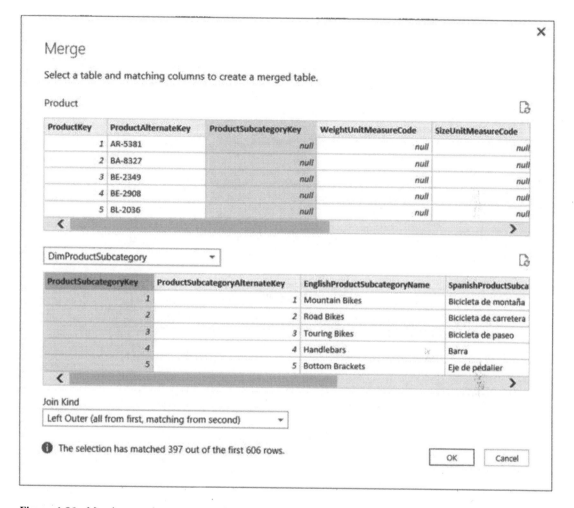

Figure 4-21. Merging queries

11. Expand the resulting column and select the EnglishProductSubcategoryName and the ProductCategoryKey columns. Uncheck the Use original column name as prefix check box (see Figure 4-22).

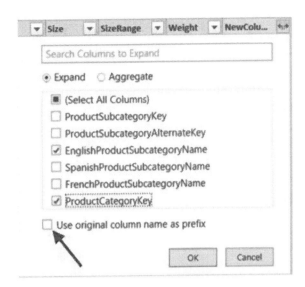

Figure 4-22. *Selecting merged columns*

12. Repeat the previous steps to merge the EnglishProductCategoryName from the DimProductCategory query into the `Product` query.

13. Now that the queries have been merged, you can remove the ProductSubcategoryKey and the ProductCategoryKey columns from the `Product` Query.

14. Rename the columns as follows:

Table	Column	Friendly Name
Product	ProductKey	
	ProductAlternateKey	Product Code
	WeightUnitMeasureCode	Weight UofM Code
	SizeUnitMeasureCode	Size UofM Code
	EnglishProductName	Product Name
	ListPrice	List Price
	Size	
	SizeRange	Size Range
	Weight	
	Color	
	EnglishProductCategoryName	Category
	EnglishProductSubcategoryName	Subcategory

15. Select the DimProductCategoryQuery. On the Home tab, select the Close & Load drop-down and then choose Close & Load To. In the Load To window, uncheck the Add this data to the Data Model option (see Figure 4-23).

Figure 4-23. *Loading the queries.*

16.   Repeat step 14 for the DimProductSubcategory. For the `Product` query, make sure you check the option to load it in the Data Model.

17.   After loading the product data, open the Model Designer and hide the ProductKey from client tools.

18.   Create a relationship between the Internet Sales and the Product tables using the ProductKey. Your final diagram should look like Figure 4-24.

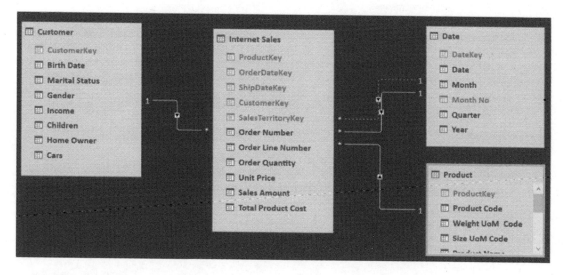

Figure 4-24. *Viewing the data model relationships*

19. To create a linked table, enter the data shown in Figure 4-25 into an empty spreadsheet tab in Excel.

	A	B	C	D
1	SalesTerritoryKey	Region	Country	Group
2	1	Northwest	United States	North America
3	2	Northeast	United States	North America
4	3	Central	United States	North America
5	4	Southwest	United States	North America
6	5	Southeast	United States	North America
7	6	Canada	Canada	North America
8	7	France	France	Europe
9	8	Germany	Germany	Europe
10	9	Australia	Australia	Pacific
11	10	United Kingdom	United Kingdom	Europe
12	11	NA	NA	NA

Figure 4-25. *The linked table data*

20. Select the cells and right-click. In the Quick Analysis context menu, select the Tables tab and click the Table button (see Figure 4-26). In the Table Tools Design tab, rename the table SalesTerritory.

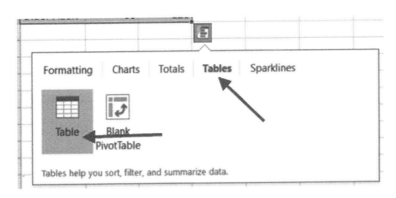

Figure 4-26. *The Quick Analysis Tables tab*

21. On the Power Pivot tab, click the Add To Data Model button. Once the table is in the model, change the name to Sales Territory, hide the SalesTerritoryKey, and create a relationship to the Internet Sales table.

22. To create a hierarchy, select the Sales Territory table in the Power Pivot window's diagram view and click the Create Hierarchy button. Drag and drop the Sales Territory Group, Country, and Region on the hierarchy. Rename the hierarchy *Sales Territory* (see Figure 4-27).

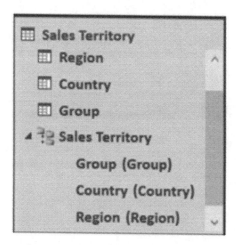

Figure 4-27. *The Sales Territory hierarchy*

23. Create a Calendar hierarchy named *Calendar* in the Date table using Year, Quarter, and Month.

24. Switch to the data view in the designer and select the Date Table tab. Select the Month column and set its Sort By Column to the Month No. column.

25. When done, save and close Excel.

Summary

When working in Power Pivot, it is very important to understand what makes a good model. A good model will make Power Pivot perform incredibly fast and allow you to easily analyze large amounts of data. Unlike traditional Excel pivot tables, which are based on a single table contained in an Excel sheet, Power Pivot pivot tables are based off of multiple tables contained in the data model. This chapter guided you through the process of creating a solid model that will become the foundation for your data analysis. In addition, you saw how to present a user-friendly model to client tools.

Now that you have a solid foundation for your model, you are ready to extend the model with custom calculations. The next chapter introduces the Data Analysis Expressions (DAX) language and explains how to create calculated columns in the data model. It includes plenty of examples to help you create common calculations in the model.

CHAPTER 5

■ ■ ■

Creating Calculations with DAX

Now that you know how to create a robust data model to base your analysis on, the next step is to add to the model any calculations required to aid your exploration of the data. For example, you may have to translate code values into meaningful descriptions or parse out a string to obtain key information. This is where Data Analysis Expressions (DAX) comes into play. This chapter introduces you to DAX and shows you how to use DAX to create calculated columns to add to the functionality of your model.

After completing this chapter, you will be able to

- Use DAX to add calculated columns to a table.

- Implement DAX operators.

- Work with text functions in DAX.

- Use DAX date and time functions.

- Use conditional and logical functions.

- Get data from a related table.

- Use math, trig, and statistical functions.

What Is DAX?

DAX is a formula language used to create calculated columns and measures in the Power Pivot model. It is a language developed specifically for the tabular data model Power Pivot is based on. If you are familiar with Excel's formula syntax, you will find that the DAX syntax is very familiar. In fact, some of the DAX formulas have the same syntax and functionality as their Excel counterparts. The major difference—and one that you need to wrap your head around—is that Excel formulas are cell based whereas DAX is column based. For example, if you want to concatenate two values in Excel, you would use a formula like the following:

```
=A1 & " " & B1
```

© Dan Clark 2017
D. Clark, *Beginning Power BI*, DOI 10.1007/978-1-4842-2577-6_5

where A1 is the cell in the first row and first column, and B1 is the cell in the second column of the first row (see Figure 5-1).

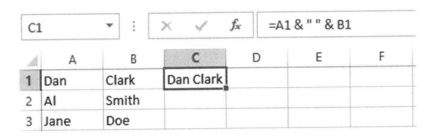

Figure 5-1. *Entering a formula in Excel*

This is very similar to the DAX formula:

```
=[First Name] & " " & [Last Name]
```

where First Name and Last Name are columns in a table in the model (see Figure 5-2).

[Full Name]	*fx* =[FirstName] & " " & [LastName]			
FirstName	LastName	Middle...	Full Name	
1 Guy	Gilbert	R	Guy Gilbert	
2 Barry	Johnson	K	Barry Johnson	
3 Sidney	Higa	M	Sidney Higa	
4 Jeffrey	Ford	L	Jeffrey Ford	
5 Steven	Selikoff	T	Steven Selikoff	
6 Stuart	Munson	V	Stuart Munson	
7 Greg	Alderson	F	Greg Alderson	
8 David	Johnson	N	David Johnson	

Figure 5-2. *Entering a formula in Power Pivot*

The difference is that the DAX formula is applied to all rows in the table, whereas the Excel formula only works on the specific cells. In Excel you need to re-create the formula in each row.

What this means is that, although you can do something like this in Excel

```
=A1 & " " & B2
```

where you are taking a cell from the first row and concatenating a cell from the second row (see Figure 5-3), you can't do that in DAX.

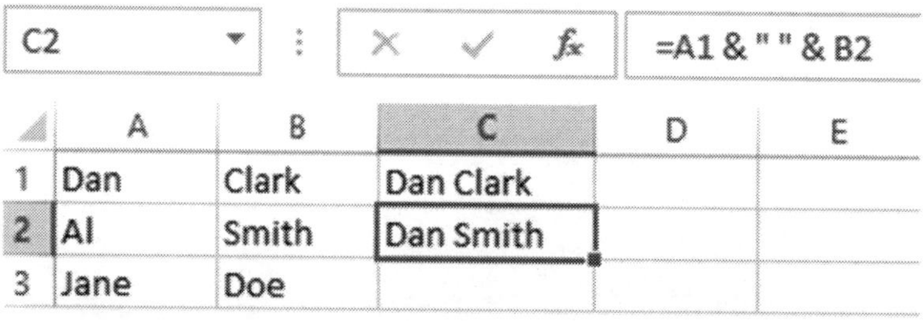

Figure 5-3. *Using cells in different rows*

When creating DAX formulas, it is important to consider the data types and any conversions that may take place during the calculations. If you don't take these into account, you may experience errors in the formula or unexpected results. The supported data types in the model are whole number, decimal number, currency, Boolean, text, and date. DAX also has a table data type that is used in many functions that take a table as an input value and return a table.

When you try to add a numeric data type with a text data type, you get an implicit conversion. If DAX can convert the text to a numeric value it will add them as numbers; if it can't, you will get an error. On the other hand, if you try to concatenate a numeric data type with a text data type, DAX will implicitly convert the numeric data type to text. Although most of the time implicit conversions give you the results you are looking for, they come at a performance cost and should be avoided if possible. For example, if you import data from a text file, and the column is set to a text data type but you know it is in fact numeric, you should change the data type in the model.

When creating calculations in DAX you will need to reference tables and columns. If the table name doesn't contain spaces, you can just refer to it by name. If the table name contains spaces, you need to enclose it in single quotes. Columns and measures are enclosed in brackets. If you just list the column name in the formula, it is assumed that the column exists in the same table. If you are referring to a column in another table, you need to use the fully qualified name, which is the table name followed by the column name. The following code demonstrates the syntax:

```
=[SalesAmount] - [TotalCost]
=Sales[SalesAmount] - Sales[TotalCost]
='Internet Sales'[SalesAmount] - 'Internet Sales'[TotalCost]
```

Here are some other points to keep in mind when working with DAX:

- DAX formulas and expressions can't modify or insert individual values in tables.

- You can't create calculated rows using DAX. You can create only calculated columns and measures.

- When defining calculated columns, you can nest functions to any level.

The first thing to understand when creating a calculation is which operators are supported and what the syntax to use them is. In the next section you will investigate the various DAX operators.

Implementing DAX Operators

DAX contains a robust set of operators, including arithmetic, comparison, logic, and text concatenation. Most of these should be familiar to you and are listed in Table 5-1.

Table 5-1. *DAX Operators*

Category	Symbol	Use
Arithmetic operators		
	+	Addition
	-	Subtraction
	*	Multiplication
	/	Division
	^	Exponentiation
Comparison operators		
	=	Equal to
	>	Greater than
	<	Less than
	>=	Greater than or equal to
	<=	Less than or equal to
	<>	Not equal to
Text concatenation operator		
	&	Concatenation
Logic operators		
	&&	And
	||	Or

As an example of the arithmetic operator, the following code is used to divide the Margin column by the Total Cost column to create a new column, the Margin Percentage.

```
=[Margin]/[TotalCost]
```

It is very common to have several arithmetic operations in the same calculation. In this case, you have to be aware of the order of operations. Exponents are evaluated first, followed by multiplication/division, and then addition/subtraction. You can control order of operations by using parentheses to group calculations; for example, the following formula will perform the subtraction before the division:

```
=([Sales Amount]-[Total Cost])/[Total Cost]
```

The comparison operators are primarily for IF statements. For example, the following calculation checks to see whether a store's selling area size is greater than 1000. If it is, it is classified as a large store; if not, it is classified as small:

```
=IF([Selling Area Size]>1000,"Large","Small")
```

The logical operators are used to create multiple comparison logic. The following code checks to see whether the store size area is greater than 1000 or if it has more than 35 employees to classify it as large:

```
=IF([Selling Area Size]> 1000 || [Employee Count] > 35,"Large","Small")
```

When you start stringing together a series of logical conditions, it is a good idea to use parentheses to control the order of operations. The following code checks to see whether the store size area is greater than 1000 and if it has more than 35 employees to classify it as large. It will also classify it as large if it has annual sales of more than $1,000,000 regardless of its size area or number of employees:

```
=IF((([Selling Area Size]> 1000 && [Employee Count] > 35) || [Annual Sales] >
1000000,"Large","Small")
```

When working with DAX calculations, you may need to nest one formula inside another. For example, the following code nests an IF statement inside the false part of another IF statement. If the employee count is not greater than 35, it jumps to the next IF statement to check whether it is greater than 20:

```
=IF(Store[EmployeeCount]>35,"Large",IF(Store[EmployeeCount]>20,"Medium","Small"))
```

DAX contains many useful functions for creating calculations and measures. These functions include text functions, date and time functions, statistical functions, math functions, and informational functions. The next few sections look at using the various function types in your calculations.

Working with Text Functions

A lot of calculations involve some kind of text manipulation. You may need to truncate, parse, search, or format the text values that you load from the source systems. DAX contains many useful functions for working with text. The functions are listed in Table 5-2 along with a description of what they are used for.

Table 5-2. *DAX Text Functions*

Function	Description
BLANK	Returns a blank.
CONCATENATE	Joins two text strings into one text string.
EXACT	Compares two text strings and returns TRUE if they are exactly the same, and FALSE otherwise.
FIND	Returns the starting position of one text string within another text string.
FIXED	Rounds a number to the specified number of decimals and returns the result as text.
FORMAT	Converts a value to text according to the specified format.
LEFT	Returns the specified number of characters from the start of a text string.
LEN	Returns the number of characters in a text string.
LOWER	Converts all letters in a text string to lowercase.
MID	Returns a string of characters from a text string, given a starting position and length.
REPLACE	Replaces part of a text string with a different text string.
REPT	Repeats text a given number of times. Use REPT to fill a cell with a number of instances of a text string.
RIGHT	Returns the last character or characters in a text string, based on the number of characters you specify.
SEARCH	Returns the number of the character at which a specific character or text string is first found, reading left to right.
SUBSTITUTE	Replaces existing text with new text in a text string
TRIM	Removes all spaces from text except for single spaces between words.
UPPER	Converts a text string to all uppercase letters.
VALUE	Converts a text string that represents a number to a number.

As an example of using a text function in a calculation, let's say you have a product code column in a products table where the first two characters represent the product family. To create the product family column, you would use the Left function as follows:

```
=Left([Product Code],2)
```

You can use the FIND function to search a text for a subtext. You can use a (?) to match any single character and a (*) to match any sequence of characters. You have the option of indicating the starting position for the search. The FIND function returns the starting position of the substring found. If it doesn't find the substring, it can return a 0, –1, or a blank value. The following code searches the product description column for the word *mountain*:

```
=FIND("mountain",[Description],1,-1)
```

The FORMAT function converts a value to text based on the format provided. For example, you may need to convert a date to a specific format. The following code converts a date data type to a string with a format like "Mon - Dec 02, 2013":

```
=FORMAT([StartDate],"ddd - MMM dd, yyyy")
```

Along with the ability to create your own format, there are also predefined formats you can use. The following code demonstrates using the Long Date format "Monday, December 2, 2013":

```
=FORMAT([StartDate],"Long Date")
```

Now that you have seen how to use some of the text functions, the next types of functions to look at are the built-in date and time functions.

Using DAX Date and Time Functions

Most likely you will find that your data analysis has a date component associated with it. You may need to look at sales or energy consumption and need to know the day of the week the event occurred. You may have to calculate age or maturity dates. DAX has quite a few date and time functions to help create these types of calculations. Table 5-3 summarizes the various date and time functions available.

Table 5-3. DAX Date and Time Functions

Function	Description
DATE	Returns the specified date in datetime format
DATEVALUE	Converts a date in the form of text to a date in datetime format
DAY	Returns the day of the month
EDATE	Returns the date that is the indicated number of months before or after the start date
EOMONTH	Returns the date in datetime format of the last day of the month, before or after a specified number of months
HOUR	Returns the hour as a number from 0 (12:00 a.m.) to 23 (11:00 p.m.)
MINUTE	Returns the minute as a number from 0 to 59
MONTH	Returns the month as a number from 1 (January) to 12 (December)
NOW	Returns the current date and time in datetime format
SECOND	Returns the seconds of a time value, as a number from 0 to 59
TIME	Converts hours, minutes, and seconds given as numbers to a time in datetime format
TIMEVALUE	Converts a time in text format to a time in datetime format
TODAY	Returns the current date
WEEKDAY	Returns a number from 1 to 7 identifying the day of the week of a date
WEEKNUM	Returns the week number for the given date
YEAR	Returns the year of a date as a four-digit integer
YEARFRAC	Calculates the fraction of the year represented by the number of whole days between two dates

As an example of using the date functions, say you need to calculate years of service for employees. The first thing to do is find the difference between the current year and the year they were hired. The following code gets the year from today's date:

```
=YEAR(Today())
```

Now you can subtract the year of their hire date. Notice we are nesting one function inside another. Nesting functions is a common requirement for many calculations:

```
=YEAR(TODAY()) - YEAR([HireDate])
```

Astute readers will realize that this calculation is only correct if the current month is greater than or equal to the month they were hired. You can adjust for this using a conditional If statement as follows:

```
= If (MONTH(TODAY())>=MONTH([HireDate]) ,YEAR(TODAY()) - YEAR([HireDate]),YEAR(TODAY()) -
YEAR([HireDate])-1)
```

As you can see, calculations can get quite complicated pretty quickly. The challenge is making sure that the open and closing parentheses of each function line up correctly. One way to organize the code is to use multiple lines and indenting. To get a new line in the formula editor bar, you need to hold down the Shift key while you press Enter. I find the following easier to understand:

```
= If (MONTH(TODAY())>=MONTH([HireDate]),
        YEAR(TODAY()) - YEAR([HireDate]),
        YEAR(TODAY()) - YEAR([HireDate])-1
     )
```

There is often more than one way to create a calculation. You may find an easier way to make the calculation or one that performs better. The following calculates the years of service using the YEARFRAC function and the TRUNC function (one of the math functions) to drop the decimal part of the number:

```
=TRUNC(YEARFRAC([HireDate],TODAY()))
```

The next group of functions you are going to investigate are the informational and logical functions. These functions are important when you want to determine whether a condition exists such as a blank value, or whether an error is occurring due to a calculation. These functions allow you to trap for conditions and respond to them in an appropriate way.

Using Informational and Logical Functions

As you start building more complex calculations, you often need to use informational and logical functions to check for conditions and respond to various conditions. One common example is the need to check for blank values. The ISBLANK function returns TRUE if the value is blank and FALSE if it is not. The following code uses a different calculation depending on whether the middle name is blank:

```
=IF(ISBLANK([MiddleName]),
[FirstName] & " " & [LastName],
[FirstName] & " " & [MiddleName] & " " & [LastName]
)
```

The ISERROR function is used to check whether a calculation or function returns an error. The following calculation checks to see if a divide by zero error occurs during a division:

```
=IF(ISERROR([TotalProductCost]/[SalesAmount]),
    BLANK(),
    [TotalProductCost]/[SalesAmount]
   )
```

Another way to create this calculation is to use the IFERROR function, which returns the value if no error occurs and an alternate value if an error occurs:

```
=IFERROR([TotalProductCost]/[SalesAmount],BLANK())
```

Tables 5-4 and 5-5 list the logical and informational functions available in DAX.

Table 5-4. The DAX Logical Functions

Function	Description
AND	Checks whether both arguments are TRUE.
FALSE	Returns the logical value FALSE.
IF	Checks whether a condition provided as the first argument is met. Returns one value if the condition is TRUE, and another value if the condition is FALSE.
IFERROR	Evaluates an expression and returns a specified value if the expression returns an error; otherwise, returns the value of the expression itself.
NOT	Changes FALSE to TRUE, or TRUE to FALSE.
OR	Checks whether one of the arguments is TRUE to return TRUE.
SWITCH	Evaluates an expression against a list of values and returns one of multiple possible result expressions.
TRUE	Returns the logical value TRUE.

Table 5-5. The DAX Informational Functions

Function	Description
CONTAINS	Returns TRUE if values for all referred columns exist, or are contained, in those columns
ISBLANK	Checks whether a value is blank
ISERROR	Checks whether a value is an error
ISLOGICAL	Checks whether a value is a Boolean value
ISNONTEXT	Checks whether a value is not text (blank cells are not text)
ISNUMBER	Checks whether a value is a number
ISTEXT	Checks whether a value is text
LOOKUPVALUE	Returns the value in the column for the row that meets all criteria specified by a search

When you are analyzing data, you often need to look up corresponding data from a related table. You may need to obtain descriptions from a related code or summarize data and import it into a table, such as lifetime sales. The following section looks at how you go about looking up related data using DAX.

Getting Data from Related Tables

There are times when you need to look up values in other tables to complete a calculation. If a relationship is established between the tables, you can use the RELATED function. This allows you to denormalize the tables and make it easier for users to navigate. For example, you may have a Customer table related to a Geography table (see Figure 5-4).

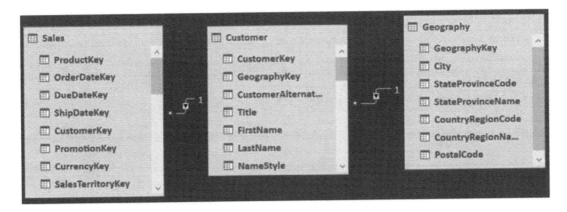

Figure 5-4. *Using the* RELATED *function*

If you need to look at sales by customer's country, you can use the RELATED function to create a Country column in the Customers table:

```
=RELATED(Geography[CountryRegionName])
```

You can then hide the Geography table from client tools to keep the model cleaner and less confusing to users.

Although the related table returns a single value, there are times when you want to look at a set of related data and aggregate it before displaying the value in the column. For example, you may want to add a column to the Customers table that lists their lifetime sales amount. In this case, you would use the RELATEDTABLE function to get the related sales and then sum them up for each customer:

```
=SUMX(RELATEDTABLE(Sales),[SalesAmount])
```

___

■ **Note**   The previous code uses the SUMX function, which is used instead of the SUM function because you are applying a filter. Chapter 6 discusses this in more detail.

___

The final set of functions to look at are the math, trig, and statistical functions. These functions allow you to perform common analysis such as logs, standard deviation, rounding, and truncation.

Using Math, Trig, and Statistical Functions

Along with the functions discussed thus far, DAX also includes quite a few math, trig, and statistical functions. The math functions (see Table 5-6) are used for rounding, truncating, and summing up the data. They also contain functions you may use in scientific, engineering, and financial calculations; for example, you may need to calculate the volume of a sphere given the radius. This is calculated in DAX as follows:

```
=4*PI()*POWER([Radius],3)/3
```

As another example, say you want to calculate compounding interest on an investment. The following DAX calculation determines the compounding rate of return for an investment:

```
=[Principal]*POWER(1+([IntRate]/[CompoundRate]),[CompoundRate]*[Years])
```

Table 5-6. *Some of the Math and Trig Functions Available in DAX*

Function	Description
ABS	Returns the absolute value of a number
CEILING	Rounds a number up to the nearest integer or to the nearest multiple of significance
EXP	Returns *e* raised to the power of a given number
FACT	Returns the factorial of a number
FLOOR	Rounds a number down, toward zero, to the nearest multiple of significance
LOG	Returns the logarithm of a number to the base you specify
PI	Returns the value of pi, 3.14159265358979, accurate to 15 digits
POWER	Returns the result of a number raised to a power
ROUND	Rounds a number to the specified number of digits
SQRT	Returns the square root of a number
SUM	Adds all the numbers in a column
TRUNC	Truncates a number to an integer by removing the decimal, or fractional, part of the number

When you are analyzing data, you often want to look at not only the relationship between the data but also the quality of the data and how well you can trust your predictions. This is where the statistical analysis of the data comes in to play. With statistics, you can do things like determine and account for outliers in the data, examine the volatility of the data, and detect fraud. As an example, you can use DAX to determine and filter out the outliers in your data using the standard deviation. The following DAX function calculates the standard deviation of the sales amount:

=STDEVX.P(RELATEDTABLE(Sales),Sales[SalesAmount])

Table 5-7 lists some of the statistical functions available in DAX.

Table 5-7. *Some Statistical Functions Available in DAX*

Function	Description
AVERAGE	Returns the average of all the numbers in a column
COUNT	Counts the number of cells in a column that contain numbers
COUNTA	Counts the number of cells in a column that are not empty
COUNTBLANK	Counts the number of blank cells in a column
COUNTROWS	Counts the number of rows in the specified table
DISTINCTCOUNT	Counts the number of different cells in a column of numbers
MAX	Returns the largest numeric value in a column
MIN	Returns the smallest numeric value in a column
RANK.EQ	Returns the ranking of a number in a list of numbers
RANKX	Returns the ranking of a number in a list of numbers for each row in the table argument
STDEV.S	Returns the standard deviation of a sample population
TOPN	Returns the top *N* rows of the specified table
VAR.S	Returns the variance of a sample population

Now that you have seen what functions you have available in Power Pivot and DAX. I want to review some tips on creating functions in general.

Tips for Creating Calculations in Power Pivot

Before turning you loose on a hands-on lab, I want to give you a few pointers on creating these calculations in Power Pivot. When entering a formula for a calculated column, right-click a column in the table in the Data View window of the model builder. In the context menu, select Insert Column (see Figure 5-5).

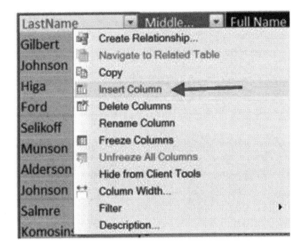

Figure 5-5. *Adding a calculated column*

Rename the column and then enter the formula in the formula editor bar. Formulas start with an equal sign (=) and table names are contained in single quotes (' '), which is optional if the table name does not contain spaces. Table columns are contained in square brackets ([ ]). The formula editor bar supplies an autocomplete feature that you should take advantage of (see Figure 5-6). Select the function, table, or column from the drop-down list and press the Tab key to insert it into the formula. If you don't see the autocomplete drop-down, chances are there is an error in your formula.

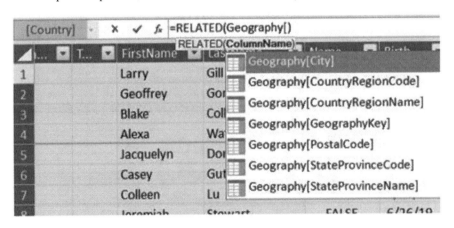

Figure 5-6. *Using autocomplete when creating calculations*

There are three buttons next to the formula editor bar: The X is used to cancel the changes you made; the check mark is used to commit the changes; and the function symbol is used to launch an Insert Function window (see Figure 5-7). You can peruse the various functions and gain information on the parameters expected by the functions.

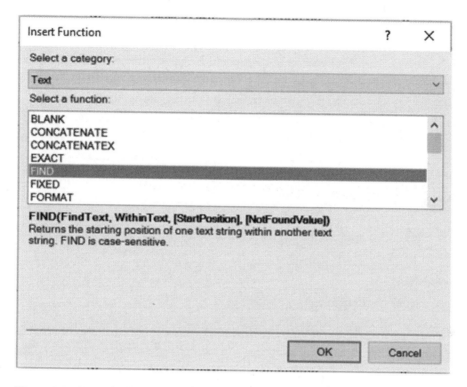

Figure 5-7. *Using the function helper*

When you create a calculation incorrectly, you may get an error indicator. You should click the error drop-down and select Show Error (see Figure 5-8). This will display an error message (see Figure 5-9) that will give you useful information that can help you fix the error.

Country	Lifeti... ◇	CalculatedCol...
Germany	#ERROR	◇ (Ctrl) ▾
United Kingdom	#ERROR	Show Error...
United Kingdom	#ERROR	
Germany	#ERROR	

Figure 5-8. *Showing error information*

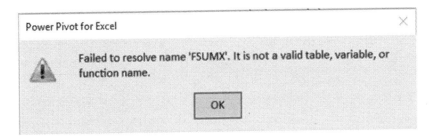

Figure 5-9. *Viewing the error message*

Now that you have seen how to create calculations with DAX and are familiar with the DAX functions available to you, it is time to gain some hands-on experience.

HANDS-ON LAB: CREATING CALCULATED COLUMNS IN POWER PIVOT

In the following lab you will

- Create calculated columns.

- Use DAX text functions.

- Use date functions in a DAX expression.

- Use data from a related table in an expression.

- Implement conditional logic in an expression.

1. In the LabStarterFiles\Chapter5Lab1 folder, open the Chapter5Lab1.xlsx file. This file contains a data model consisting of sales data, product data, and store data.

2. View the model in the Power Pivot Model Designer using the diagram view (see Figure 5-10).

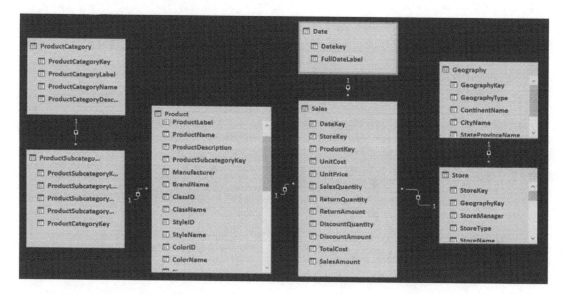

Figure 5-10. *The data model for store sales*

3. Switch to data view in the Power Pivot Window and select the Sales table.

4. After the SalesAmount column, click the Add Column. In the formula bar above the table, enter the following to calculate margin:

   ```
   =[SalesAmount] - [TotalCost]
   ```

5. Right-click the new column and rename it *Margin*.

6. Repeat this procedure to create a Margin Percent column with the following formula:

   ```
   =[Margin]/[SalesAmount]
   ```

7. In the Data View window, select the Date table.

8. Use the Date functions to create a Year, Month Number, and Weekday Number column. Use the Format function to get the Month and Weekday (names) column. Your Date table should look similar to figure 5-11.

	Datekey	FullDate...	Year	Month Nu...	Month	Weekday Numb...	Weekday
1	1/1/2005 12:00:00 ...	2005-01-01	2005	1	January	7	Sat
2	1/2/2005 12:00:00 ...	2005-01-02	2005	1	January	1	Sun
3	1/3/2005 12:00:00 ...	2005-01-03	2005	1	January	2	Mon
4	1/4/2005 12:00:00 ...	2005-01-04	2005	1	January	3	Tue
5	1/5/2005 12:00:00 ...	2005-01-05	2005	1	January	4	Wed
6	1/6/2005 12:00:00 ...	2005-01-06	2005	1	January	5	Thu
7	1/7/2005 12:00:00 ...	2005-01-07	2005	1	January	6	Fri
8	1/8/2005 12:00:00 ...	2005-01-08	2005	1	January	7	Sat

[Weekday] *fx* =Format([Datekey],"ddd")

Figure 5-11. Adding calculated columns to the date table

9. Using the Year and Month columns, create a Calendar hierarchy in the Date table.

10. In the Data View window, select the Product table.

11. Insert a Weight Label column with the following formula:

    ```
    =if(ISBLANK([Weight]),BLANK(), [Weight] & " " & [WeightUnitMeasureID])
    ```

12. Next to ProductSubcategoryKey, create a Product Category column using the RELATED function:

    ```
    =RELATED('ProductCategory'[ProductCategoryName])
    ```

13. Using the RELATED function, create a ProductSubcategory column.

14. Hide the ProductCategory and ProductSubcategory tables from the client tools.

15. Switch to the Store table and create a Years Open column with the following formula:

    ```
    =TRUNC(YEARFRAC([OpenDate],
            If(ISBLANK([CloseDate]),TODAY(),[CloseDate]))
              ,0)
    ```

16. Create a LifetimeSales column using the following formula:

    ```
    =SUMX(RELATEDTABLE(Sales),Sales[SalesAmount])
    ```

17. Save and close the Excel file.

Summary

This chapter introduced you to the DAX language and the built-in functions that you can use to create calculations. At this point, you should be comfortable with creating calculated columns and using the DAX functions. I strongly recommend that you become familiar with the various functions available and how to use them in your analysis.

In the next chapter you will continue working with DAX to create measures. *Measures* are one of the most important parts of building your model in Power Pivot—the measures are the reason you are looking at your data. You want to answer questions such as how sales are doing or what influences energy consumption. Along with creating measures, you will also see how filter context effects measures. Filter context is one of the most important concepts you need to master in order to get the most out of Power Pivot.

CHAPTER 6

■ ■ ■

Creating Measures with DAX

Creating measures in DAX is the most important skill necessary to create solid data models. This chapter covers the common functions used to create measures in the data model. It also covers the important topic of data context and how to alter or override the context when creating measures.

After completing this chapter, you will be able to

- Understand the difference between measures and attributes.

- Understand how context affects measurements.

- Create common aggregates.

- Know how and when to alter the filter context.

- Create KPIs.

Measures vs. Attributes

If you look at a typical star model for a data warehouse, you have a fact table surrounded by dimension tables. For example, Figure 6-1 shows a financial fact table surrounded by several dimension tables.

© Dan Clark 2017
D. Clark, *Beginning Power BI*, DOI 10.1007/978-1-4842-2577-6_6

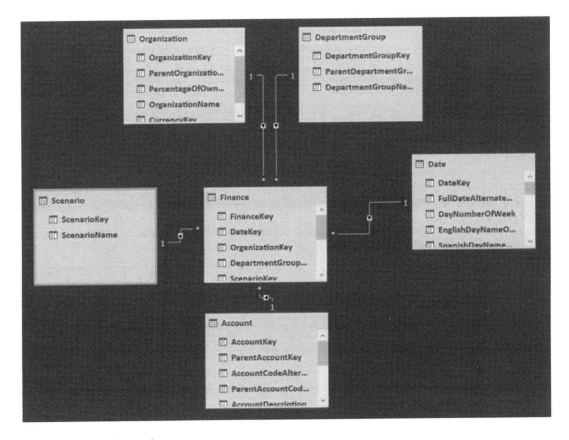

Figure 6-1. *Typical star schema*

Remember, the fact table contains numbers that you need to aggregate; for example, in the finance table, you have the amount, which is a monetary value that needs to be aggregated. In a sales fact table, you may have a sales amount and item counts. In a human resources system, you might have hours worked. The dimension tables contain the attributes that you are using to categorize and roll up the measures. For example, the financial measures are classified as profit, loss, and forecasted. You want to roll the values up to the department and organization level and you want to compare values between months and years.

When you start slicing and dicing the data in a pivot table, the attributes become the row and column headers, whereas the measures are the values in the cells. Attributes are also commonly used as filters either in a filter drop-down or in a slicer. Figure 6-2 shows a pivot table containing research and development spending, actual and budgeted, for the months in the fiscal year 2006.

DepartmentGroupName	Research and Development			OrganizationName	
FiscalYear	2006				
				Canadian Division	
SumAmount	Column Labels			Central Division	
Row Labels	Actual	Budget	Grand Total	Northeast Division	
1	$1,993,567.08	$1,915,370.00	$3,908,937.08	Northwest Division	
July	$392,972.36	$359,390.00	$752,362.36		
August	$961,235.94	$938,490.00	$1,899,725.94	Southeast Division	
September	$639,358.78	$617,490.00	$1,256,848.78	Southwest Division	
2	$2,706,643.34	$2,794,280.00	$5,500,923.34	AdventureWorks C...	
October	$709,493.00	$732,960.00	$1,442,453.00	Australia	
November	$1,177,389.73	$1,248,960.00	$2,426,349.73		
December	$819,760.61	$812,360.00	$1,632,120.61		
3	$2,424,910.23	$2,384,100.00	$4,809,010.23		
January	$518,208.94	$441,300.00	$959,508.94		
February	$916,732.01	$899,900.00	$1,816,632.01		
March	$989,969.28	$1,042,900.00	$2,032,869.28		
4	$2,805,397.73	$2,766,330.00	$5,571,727.73		
April	$697,205.89	$640,910.00	$1,338,115.89		
May	$1,154,369.01	$1,157,810.00	$2,312,179.01		
June	$953,822.83	$967,610.00	$1,921,432.83		
Grand Total	$9,930,518.38	$9,860,080.00	$19,790,598.38		

Figure 6-2. Analyzing data in a pivot table

If you look at the filtering for each cell, you should realize they are all filtered a little differently. The two measures indicated by the green (horizontal) arrows differ by month, whereas the measures indicated by the red (diagonal) arrows differ by actual versus budgeted amount. As you change the fiscal year, department, or organization, the values for the measures must be recalculated because the query context has changed.

In the following section you will see how you can create some common aggregation measures in your Power Pivot model.

Creating Common Aggregates

It is very easy to create common aggregates such as sum, count, or average in Power Pivot. First you need to determine which table you want to associate the measure with. If you follow the star schema model, this will most likely be the fact table, but it doesn't have to be. In the data view mode of the Power Pivot Model Designer, select the tab of the table that is associated with the measure. The area below the data grid is where you place the measure formulas (see Figure 6-3). If you don't see a measures grid, you may need to unhide it by selecting the Calculation Area button on the Home tab (see Figure 6-4).

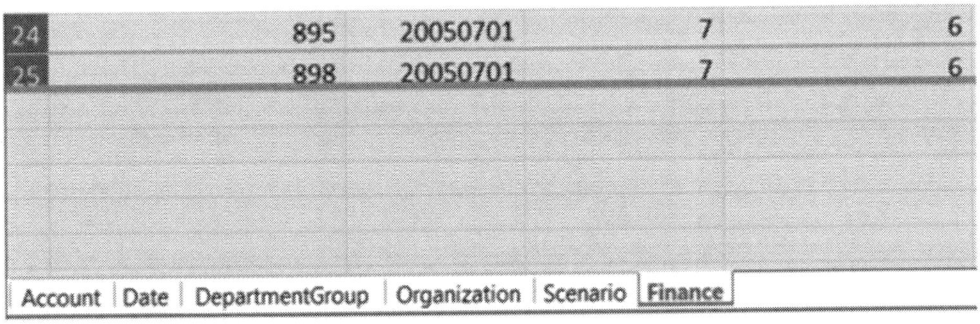

24
895
20050701
7
6
25
898
20050701
7
6
Account
Date
DepartmentGroup
Organization
Scenario
Finance

Figure 6-3. *The measure grid for the Finance table*

Data View
Diagram View
Show Hidden
Calculation Area
View

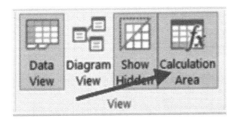

Figure 6-4. *Showing or hiding the measure grid*

The easiest way to create an aggregate is to select the column you want to aggregate, select the AutoSum drop-down, and choose the aggregate you need (see Figure 6-5).

AutoSum
Sum
Average
Count
Distinct Count
Max
Min
Find
Find
Diagram View

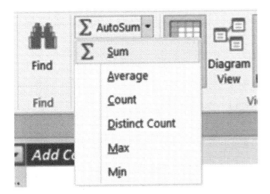

Figure 6-5. *Using the AutoSum for common aggregates*

The aggregate is placed in the measure grid below the column (see Figure 6-6). If you select the cell, you will see the formula in the formula bar (see Figure 6-7). The name of the measure is placed before the formula followed by a colon and equal sign (:=). Once you add the measure, you can rename it by editing it in the formula editor.

1	83	143	7/1/2005 12:...
1	84	119	7/1/2005 12:...
	Sum of Amount: 1358640412.7		

Figure 6-6. *The resulting measure below the column*

[Amount] ▾	*fx* Sum of Amount:=SUM([Amount])
▲ FinanceKey ▾	DateK... 🔒▾	Organiz... 🔒▾
1	850	20050701	7

Figure 6-7. *Editing the measure formula*

The other way to create an aggregate measure is to select any cell in the measures grid and enter the formula in the formula bar. Although you can define a measure in any cell in the measures grid, it is a good idea to organize the measures in some fashion. I generally try to organize the measures along the left side of the grid so they are not spread out all over the grid (see Figure 6-8). You can easily move a definition from one cell to another using cut and paste.

23		894	20050701	7
24		895	20050701	7
Sum Amount: $1,358,640,412.70				
Ave Amount: $34,475.38				
Max Amount: $4,820,988.00				

| Account | Date | DepartmentGroup | Organization | Scenario | Finance |

Figure 6-8. *Organizing your measures*

You may have noticed that the aggregate functions such as SUM, AVE, MIN, and MAX have corresponding SUMX, AVEX, MINX, and MAXX functions. The X functions are used when you are evaluating an expression for each row in the table and not just a single column. As an example, the SUMX function is defined as follows:

SUMX(<table>, <expression>)

where the table is the table containing the rows to be evaluated, and the expression is what will be evaluated for each row.

As an example, say you have a sales table that contains a Cost and a Gross column. To figure out the total net sales amount, you can take the gross amount minus the cost and sum the result for each row, as in the following formula:

```
SumNet:=SUMX(Sales,[Gross]-[Cost])
```

Another way to get the same result is to create a net calculated column first and then use the SUM function on the net column. The difference is that calculated columns are pre-calculated and stored in the model. Measures are calculated when filters are applied to them in the pivot table and have to be recalculated every time the data context changes. So, the more calculated columns you have, the greater the size of your Power Pivot file. The more measures you have, and the greater their complexity increases, the more memory is necessary when you are working with the file. In most cases, you are better off doing as much calculation in memory rather than creating lots of calculated columns.

Understanding how data context changes the measurement value is very important when creating measures and is explored in the next section.

Mastering Data Context

Context plays an important role when creating measures in the Power Pivot model. Unlike static reports, Power Pivot models are designed for dynamic analysis by the client. When the user changes filters, drills down, and changes column and row headers in a pivot table, the context changes, and the values are recalculated. Knowing how the context changes and how it affects the results is very essential to being able to build and troubleshoot formulas.

There are three types of context you need to consider: row, query, and filter. The row context comes into play when you are creating a calculated column. It includes the values from all the other columns of the current row as well as the values of any table related to the row. If you create a calculated column, say margin,

```
=[Gross] - [Cost]
```

DAX uses the row context to look up the values from the same row to complete the calculation. If you create a calculated column, such as lifetime sales

```
=SUMX(RELATEDTABLE(Sales),[SalesAmount])
```

DAX automatically looks up the related values using the row context of the current row. The row context is set once the model is loaded and will not change until new data is loaded. This is why calculated columns are pre-calculated and only need to be recalculated when data is refreshed.

Query context is the filtering applied to a cell in the pivot table. When you drop a measure into a pivot table, the DAX query engine examines the row and column headers and any filters applied. Each cell has a different query context applied to it (see Figure 6-9) and returns the value associated with the context. Because you can change the query context on the fly by changing row or column headers and filter values, the cell values are calculated dynamically, and the values are not held in the Power Pivot model.

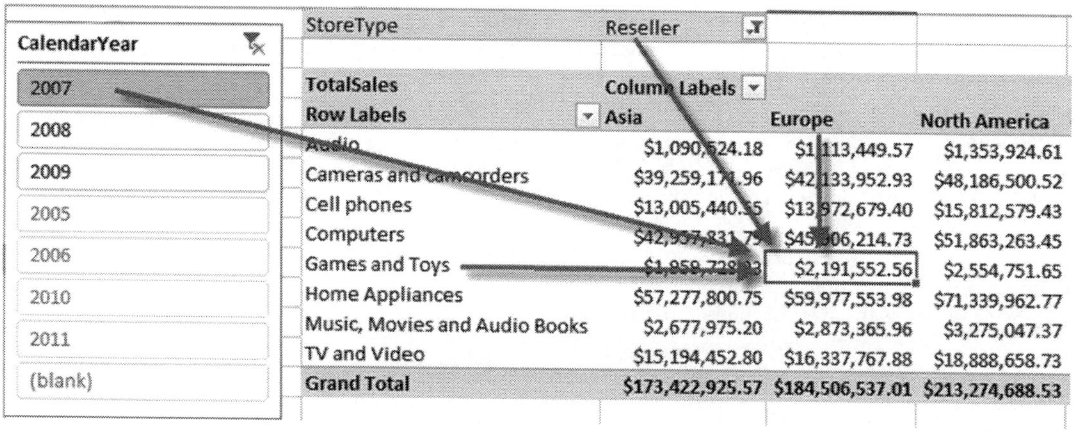

Figure 6-9. The query context of a measure

Filter context is added to the measure using filter constraints as part of the formula. The filter context is applied in addition to the row and query contexts. You can alter the context by adding to it, replacing it, or selectively changing it using filter expressions. For example, if you used the following formula to calculate sales,

```
AllStoreSales:=CALCULATE(SUM(Sales[SalesAmount]),ALL(Store[StoreType]))
```

the filter context would clear any StoreType filter implemented by the query context.

In the next section you will see why knowing when and how to alter the query context is an important aspect of creating measures.

Altering the Query Context

When creating calculations, you often need to alter the filter context being applied to the measure. For example, say you want to calculate the sales of a product category compared to the sales of all products (see Figure 6-10).

Row Labels	ProductSales	ProductSalesRatio
Audio	$28,327,054.16	1.17 %
Cameras and camcorders	$497,254,487.87	20.50 %
Cell phones	$171,965,337.05	7.09 %
Computers	$635,370,758.16	26.19 %
Games and Toys	$31,323,167.21	1.29 %
Home Appliances	$771,257,471.64	31.79 %
Music, Movies and Audio Books	$32,047,454.50	1.32 %
TV and Video	$258,602,375.72	10.66 %
Grand Total	$2,426,148,106.30	100.00 %

Figure 6-10. Viewing the product sales ratio

To calculate the sales ratio, you need to take the sales filtered by the query context (in this case, categories) and divide it by the sales of all products regardless of the product query context. To calculate sales, you just use the SUM function. To calculate the sum of all product sales, you need to override any product filtering applied to the cell. To do that, you use the CALCULATE function, which evaluates an expression in a context that is modified by the specified filters and has the following syntax:

```
CALCULATE(<expression>,<filter1>,<filter2>...)
```

where expression is essentially a measure to be evaluated, and the filters are Boolean expressions or a table expression that defines the filters.

So, to override any product filters, you use the following code:

```
AllProductSales:=CALCULATE(SUM([SalesAmount]), ALL(Product))
```

This uses the ALL function, which returns all the rows in a table or all the values in a column, ignoring any filters that might have been applied. On this case, it clears all filters placed on the Product table. Figure 6-11 shows the measures in a pivot table.

Row Labels	ProductSales	AllProductSales	ProductSalesRatio
Audio	$28,327,054.16	$2,426,148,106.30	1.17 %
Cameras and camcorders	$497,254,487.87	$2,426,148,106.30	20.50 %
Cell phones	$171,965,337.05	$2,426,148,106.30	7.09 %
Computers	$635,370,758.16	$2,426,148,106.30	26.19 %
Games and Toys	$31,323,167.21	$2,426,148,106.30	1.29 %
Home Appliances	$771,257,471.64	$2,426,148,106.30	31.79 %
Music, Movies and Audio Books	$32,047,454.50	$2,426,148,106.30	1.32 %
TV and Video	$258,602,375.72	$2,426,148,106.30	10.66 %
Grand Total	$2,426,148,106.30	$2,426,148,106.30	100.00 %

Figure 6-11. Verifying the AllProductSales measure

Notice the ProductSales measure is affected by the product filter (category), whereas the AllProductSales is not. The final step to calculate the ProductSalesRatio measure is to divide the ProductSales by the AllProductSales. You can use a measure inside another measure as long as you don't have a circular reference. So, the ProductSalesRatio is calculated as follows:

```
ProductSalesRatio:=[ProductSales]/[AllProductSales]
```

You can hide the AllProductSales measure from the client tools because, in this case, it is used as an intermediate measure and is not useful on its own.

In this section you saw how to use the CALCULATE function and a filter function to alter the filters applied to a measure. There are many filter functions available in DAX, and it is important that you understand when to use them. The next section looks at several more important filter functions you can use.

Using Filter Functions

The filter functions in DAX allow you to create complex calculations that require you to interrogate and manipulate the data context of a row or cell in a pivot table. Table 6-1 lists and describes some of the filter functions available in DAX.

Table 6-1. *Some DAX Filter Functions*

Function	Description
ALL	Returns all the rows in a table, or all the values in a column, ignoring any filters that might have been applied.
ALLEXCEPT	Removes all context filters in the table except filters that have been applied to the specified columns.
ALLNONBLANKROW	Returns all rows but the blank row and disregards any context filters that might exist.
ALLSELECTED	Removes context filters from columns and rows, while retaining all other context filters or explicit filters.
CALCULATE	Evaluates an expression in a context that is modified by the specified filters.
CALCULATETABLE	Evaluates a table expression in a context modified by the given filters.
DISTINCT	Returns a one-column table that contains the distinct values from the specified column.
FILTER	Returns a table that represents a subset of another table or expression.
FILTERS	Returns the values that are directly applied as filters.
HASONEVALUE	Returns TRUE when the context has been filtered down to one distinct value.
ISFILTERED	Returns TRUE when a direct filter is being applied.
ISCROSSFILTERED	Returns TRUE when the column or another column in the same or related table is being filtered.
KEEPFILTERS	Modifies how filters are applied while evaluating a CALCULATE or CALCULATETABLE function. Keeps applied filters and adds additional filters.
RELATED	Returns a related value from another table.
USERELATIONSHIP	Specifies the relationship to be used in a specific calculation.
VALUES	Returns a one-column table that contains the distinct values from the specified column.

You have already seen how you can use the CALCULATE function in combination with the ALL function to calculate the total product sales, ignoring any product filtering applied. Let's take a look at a few more examples.

Figure 6-12 shows a Power Pivot model for reseller sales. In the model, there is an inactive relationship between the Employee and the SalesTerritory tables. You can use this relationship to calculate the number of salespeople in each country.

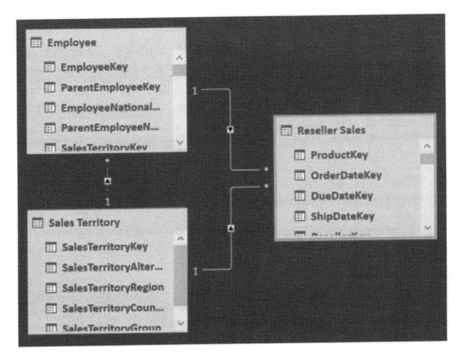

Figure 6-12. *An inactive relationship in the Power Pivot model*

You calculate the number of sales reps in each country using the following code:

```
Sales Rep Cnt:=CALCULATE(
DISTINCTCOUNT(Employee[EmployeeNationalIDAlternateKey]),
USERELATIONSHIP(Employee[SalesTerritoryKey],
'Sales Territory'[SalesTerritoryKey]))
```

In this case, you need to use the CALCULATE function so that you can apply the filter function USERELATIONSHIP to tell the DAX query engine which relationship to use. Figure 6-13 shows the resulting pivot table. It also shows the result you would get if you just used the DISTINCTCOUNT function without the USERELATIONSHIP filter.

Row Labels	Sales Rep Cnt	Sales Rep Cnt2
Australia	1	17
Canada	2	17
France	1	17
Germany	1	17
NA	3	17
United Kingdom	1	17
United States	8	17
Grand Total	17	17

Figure 6-13. *Count of sales reps in each country*

The next example looks at the difference between the ALL and the ALLSELECTED filter functions. You can create three sales amount measures as follows:

```
Reseller Sales:=SUM([SalesAmount])
Reseller Grand Total:=calculate(sum([SalesAmount]), ALL('Reseller Sales'))
Reseller Visual Total:=calculate(sum([SalesAmount]), ALLSELECTED())
```

Reseller Sales keeps all the data contexts applied to the measure. Reseller Grand Total removes all context associated with the ResellerSales table and any related table. Reseller Visual Total removes the column and row context from the measure. Figure 6-14 shows the resulting measures in a pivot table.

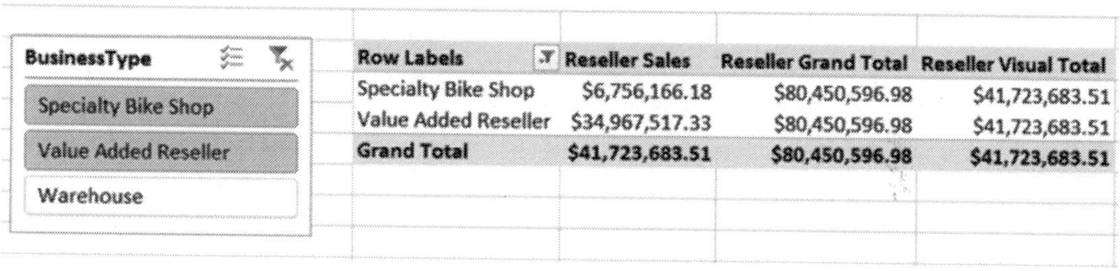

BusinessType				Row Labels	Reseller Sales	Reseller Grand Total	Reseller Visual Total
Specialty Bike Shop				Specialty Bike Shop	$6,756,166.18	$80,450,596.98	$41,723,683.51
Value Added Reseller				Value Added Reseller	$34,967,517.33	$80,450,596.98	$41,723,683.51
Warehouse				Grand Total	$41,723,683.51	$80,450,596.98	$41,723,683.51

Figure 6-14. Results of using different filters

Now let's look at a more complex example. In this example, you want to determine the best single-order customers in a particular time period. The final pivot table is shown in Figure 6-15.

Row Labels	Large Sales	Top Sale	Date of Top Sale
Brooks	$36,965.25	$3,028.02	12/1/2007
Bryant	$43,876.23	$3,036.95	11/10/2007
Butler	$36,828.66	$2,457.95	12/9/2007
Coleman	$37,424.27	$2,492.32	9/22/2007
Cox	$34,169.36	$2,428.05	9/28/2007
Diaz	$38,220.87	$4,677.24	12/15/2007
Flores	$31,637.93	$2,438.06	11/26/2007
Gonzales	$40,326.89	$2,479.94	8/1/2007
Griffin	$32,743.94	$2,443.55	12/8/2007
Hernandez	$40,074.48	$3,086.31	12/3/2007
Kelly	$32,683.80	$2,447.05	7/30/2007
Powell	$33,407.10	$2,478.34	8/21/2007
Reed	$31,468.15	$2,453.04	11/15/2007
Rodriguez	$35,110.80	$2,543.44	9/30/2007
Ross	$44,472.36	$3,182.00	1/22/2007
Russell	$33,569.17	$2,554.20	11/9/2007
Sanchez	$32,111.48	$4,950.93	7/31/2007
Washington	$38,801.68	$3,316.26	10/22/2007

CalendarYear
- 2005
- 2006
- 2007
- 2008
- 2009

CountryRegionNa...
- Australia
- Canada
- France
- Germany
- United Kingdom
- United States

Figure 6-15. Finding best single-order customers

The first step is to find the customers who spent a lot of money during the time period. To calculate customer sales, you use the following measure:

```
Sum Sales:=SUM([SalesAmount])
```

Next you want to only look at large spenders (over $30,000 spent during the period) so you can filter out smaller values:

```
Large Sales:=IF([Sum Sales]>=30000,[Sum Sales],Blank())
```

The next step is to find the order amounts for the customer and take the maximum value:

```
Top Sale:=MAXX(VALUES(Date[DateKey]),[Sum Sales])
```

Because you only want to list the top sales for top customers, you can add an IF statement to make sure the customer has large sales:

```
Top Sale:=
IF(ISBLANK([Large Sales]),Blank(),MAXX(VALUES(Date[DateKey]),[Sum Sales]))
```

As a final example, say you are working with the HR department and you want to create a pivot table that will allow them to list employee counts for the departments at a particular date. There is an EmployeeDepartmentHistory table that lists employee, department, start date, and end date. There is also a Dates table that has a row for every date spanning the department histories. Figure 6-16 shows the pivot table containing employee counts for each department.

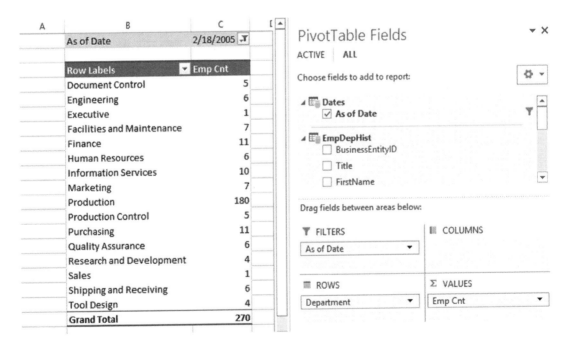

Figure 6-16. *Employee counts as of the selected date*

As of Date is used as a filter, and Emp Cnt is the measure. When the As of Date is changed the Emp Cnt, it is recalculated to show the employee counts on that date. Figure 6-17 shows new counts after the date is changed.

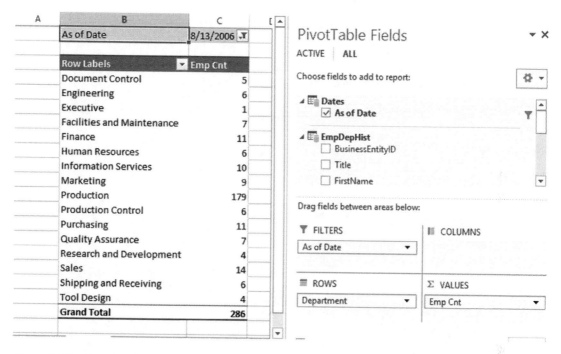

Figure 6-17. *Changing the As of Date*

The first step to creating the Emp Cnt is to use the COUNT function because you want to count the EmployeeID in the table:

```
Emp Cnt:=COUNT(EmpDepHist[BusinessEntityID])
```

Because you need to filter the table to only active employees at the date chosen, you need to change this to the COUNTX function:

```
Emp Cnt:=COUNTX(EmpDepHist, EmpDepHist[BusinessEntityID])
```

To filter the EmpDepHist table, you use the FILTER function:

```
FILTER(<table>,<filter>)
```

The FILTER function is a Boolean expression that evaluates to TRUE. In this case, you need to have the date that the employee started in the department less than or equal to the As of Date:

```
EmpDepHist[StartDate]<=Dates[As of Date]
```

Now, because the pivot table user can select more than one date, and you want to make sure you only compare it to a single date, you can use the MAX function:

```
EmpDepHist[StartDate]<=MAX(Dates[As of Date])
```

You also want to make sure the date the employee left the department is greater than the As of Date:

```
EmpDepHist[EndDate] > Max(Dates[As of Date]
```

If the employee is currently in the department, the EndDate will be blank:

```
ISBLANK(EmpDepHist[EndDate])
```

When you combine these filter conditions, you get the following filter condition:

```
EmpDepHist[StartDate]<=MAX(Dates[As of Date])
&& (ISBLANK(EmpDepHist[EndDate]) || EmpDepHist[EndDate] > Max(Dates[As of Date]))
```

The final FILTER function then becomes the following:

```
FILTER(EmpDepHist,
EmpDepHist[StartDate]<=MAX(Dates[As of Date])
&& (ISBLANK(EmpDepHist[EndDate]) || EmpDepHist[EndDate] > Max(Dates[As of Date])))
```

And the final employee count measure becomes the following:

```
Emp Cnt:=COUNTX(FILTER(EmpDepHist,
EmpDepHist[StartDate]<=MAX(Dates[As of Date])
&& (ISBLANK(EmpDepHist[EndDate]) || EmpDepHist[EndDate] > Max(Dates[As of Date]))),
EmpDepHist[BusinessEntityID])
```

As you can see, creating a measure can be quite complex, but if you break it up into steps, it becomes very manageable. Rest assured—the more you work with DAX and creating measures, the more intuitive and easier it becomes.

One type of measure commonly used in performance dashboards is the *Key Performance Indicator (KPI)*. A KPI is used to show performance and trends in a visual format. In the next section, you will investigate creating KPIs in the Power Pivot model.

Creating KPIs

KPIs are a staple of many dashboards and provide a great way to quickly see trends and spot areas that need further analysis. The base value of a KPI is based on a measure; for example, you can create a KPI for current sales. The base value is then compared to a target value. The target value can be another measure; for example, last year's sales or an absolute numeric value like a target sales quota. The status thresholds establish what range is considered good, neutral, and bad. These thresholds are then used to determine the visual component of the KPI (that is, green, yellow, red). Figure 6-18 shows KPIs for current sales compared to the previous sales.

Row Labels ▼	PrevQuarterSales	CurrentQuarterSales	SalesPerformance
⊟2005		$1,812,850.77	
3		$1,453,522.89	
4	$1,453,522.89	$1,812,850.77	●
⊟2006	$1,812,850.77	$1,327,799.32	●
1	$1,812,850.77	$1,791,698.45	○
2	$1,791,698.45	$2,014,012.13	●
3	$2,014,012.13	$1,396,833.62	●
4	$1,396,833.62	$1,327,799.32	◐
⊟2007	$1,327,799.32	$4,009,218.46	●
1	$1,327,799.32	$1,413,530.30	●
2	$1,413,530.30	$1,623,971.06	●
3	$1,623,971.06	$2,744,340.48	●
4	$2,744,340.48	$4,009,218.46	●
⊟2008	$4,009,218.46	$50,840.63	●
1	$4,009,218.46	$4,283,629.96	●
2	$4,283,629.96	$5,436,429.15	●
3	$5,436,429.15	$50,840.63	●

Figure 6-18. *Sales KPI comparing current to previous sales*

To create a KPI, first create the base measure it will be based on. For example, production keeps track of scrapped parts, so you can base a KPI on the sum of the number of scrapped parts:

```
SumScrappedQty:=SUM([ScrappedQty])
```

You can compare this to the number of parts processed:

```
SumOrderQuantity:=SUM([OrderQty])
```

After creating the measures, right-click the base measure in the Power Pivot model designer. In the context menu, select Create KPI, which launches the KPI design window (see Figure 6-19).

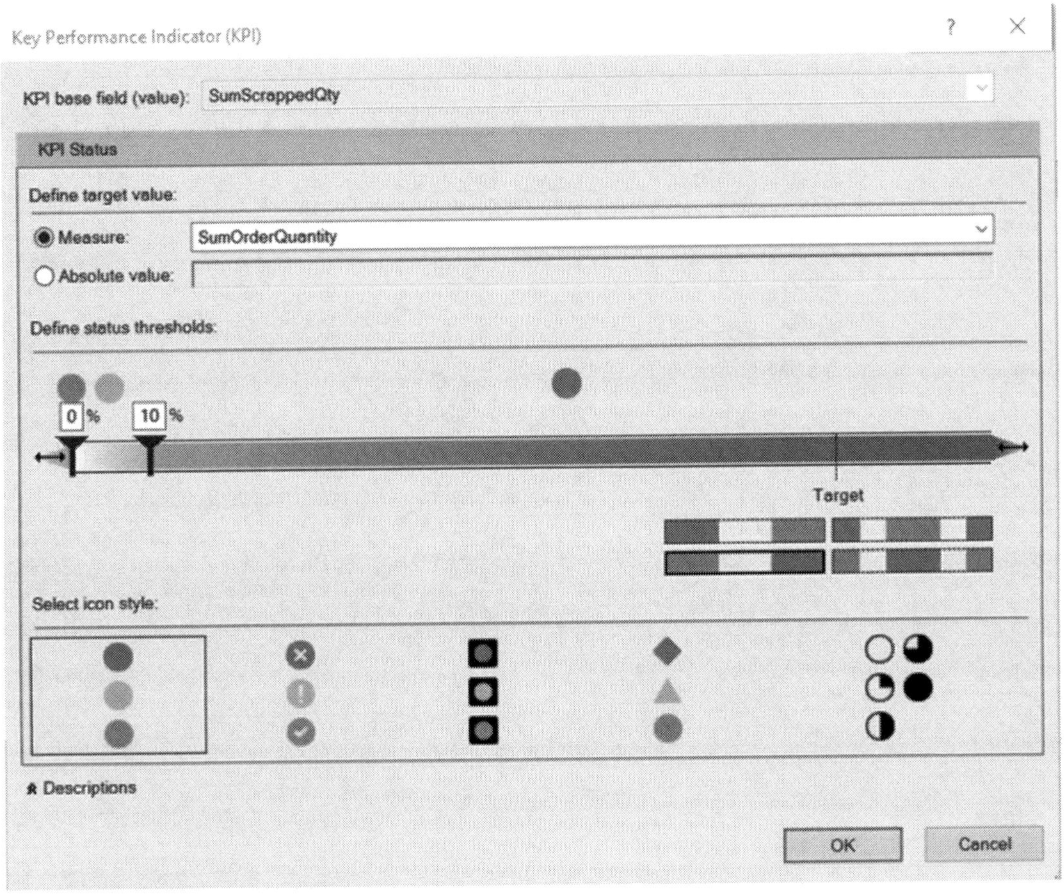

Figure 6-19. The KPI design window

You then set the target to the SumOrderQuantity measure and define the status thresholds. The style icons are used to show the status of the KPIs. When you are done creating the KPI, you can use it in a pivot table in Excel (see Figure 6-20).

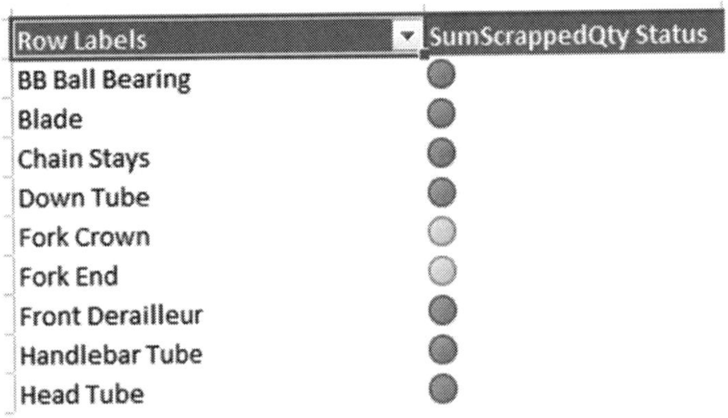

Figure 6-20. Viewing a KPI in a pivot table

Now that you have seen how to create measures and alter the data context using DAX, it is time to get your hands dirty and create some measures in the following lab.

HANDS-ON LAB: CREATING MEASURES IN POWER PIVOT

In the following lab you will

- Create aggregate measures.

- Alter the data context in a measure.

- Use a non-active relationship in a measure.

- Create a complex measure.

- Create a KPI.

1. In the LabStarterFiles\Chapter6Lab1 folder, open the Chapter6Lab1.xlsx file. This file contains a data model consisting of sales data, product data, and store data.

2. View the model in the Power Pivot Model Designer using the diagram view (Figure 6-21).

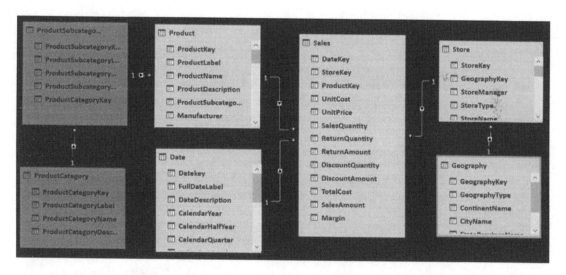

Figure 6-21. *The Power Pivot model*

3. Switch to data view in the Power Pivot window and select the Sales table.

4. Select the SalesAmount column. In the AutoSum drop-down, select Sum (see Figure 6-22). You should see a measure added below the column. Rename the measure to Sum Sales.

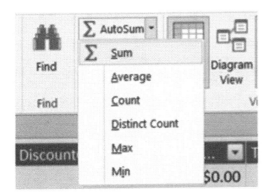

Figure 6-22. *Selecting the AutoSum drop-down*

5. Using the same technique as in step 4, create a Max Sales Quantity, a Min Sales Quantity, and an Ave Sales Quantity measure.

6. To test how the measures are recalculated as the filter context changes, click the PivotTable in the Home tab and insert the PivotTable in Sheet1 cell B2 (see Figure 6-23).

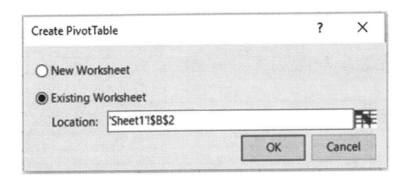

Figure 6-23. *Creating a pivot table*

7. If you don't see the field list, click the pivot table to show it.

8. From the Sales node, check the Sum Sales and Max Sales Quantity. This will add the measures to the Values drop area. Under the Product node, check the ProductCategory attribute. This will add the attribute to the Row Labels drop area.

9. On the Insert tab, click the Slicer button. In the Insert Slicers window, select the All tab and select the ContinentName under the Geography node (see Figure 6-24).

Figure 6-24. *Creating a slicer*

10. The pivot table should look like the one shown in Figure 6-25. Test the measures by clicking the different continents. This changes the query context. Notice how the measure values are recalculated as the query context changes.

Row Labels	▾	Sum Sales	Max Sales Quantity
Audio		$28,327,054.16	100
Cameras and camcorders		$497,254,487.87	100
Cell phones		$171,965,337.05	2880
Computers		$635,370,758.16	180
Games and Toys		$31,323,167.21	400
Home Appliances		$771,257,471.64	96
Music, Movies and Audio Books		$32,047,454.50	72
TV and Video		$258,602,375.72	100
Grand Total		$2,426,148,106.30	2880

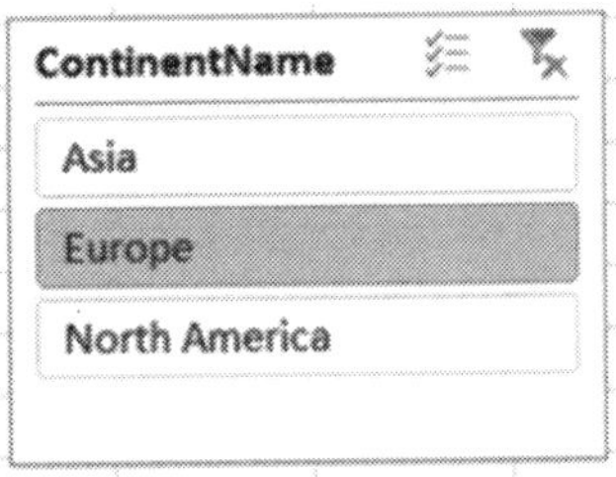

ContinentName
Asia
Europe
North America

Figure 6-25. Testing the query context

11. Now suppose we want a sales ratio comparing the sales to the total sales for all products. Open the Power Pivot Model Designer in data view mode. Select the Sales table. Add the following measure to the Sales table:

```
All Product Sales:=CALCULATE([Sum Sales],ALL('Product'))
```

12. The All Product Sales measure uses the CALCULATE function to override any product filter applied to the query context. Format the measure as currency.

13. Switch to the pivot table. Replace the Max Sales Quantity measure with the All Product Sales measure.

14. Test the pivot table by clicking different continents and notice that the All Product Sales measure is equal to the total product sales for each continent (see Figure 6-26).

Row Labels	▾	Sum Sales	All Product Sales
Audio		$86,552,608.02	$7,287,305,516.43
Cameras and camcorders		$1,520,696,696.88	$7,287,305,516.43
Cell phones		$525,926,798.18	$7,287,305,516.43
Computers		$1,904,003,431.02	$7,287,305,516.43
Games and Toys		$76,256,100.91	$7,287,305,516.43
Home Appliances		$2,278,755,400.00	$7,287,305,516.43
Music, Movies and Audio Books		$99,362,624.96	$7,287,305,516.43
TV and Video		$795,751,856.47	$7,287,305,516.43
Grand Total		$7,287,305,516.43	$7,287,305,516.43

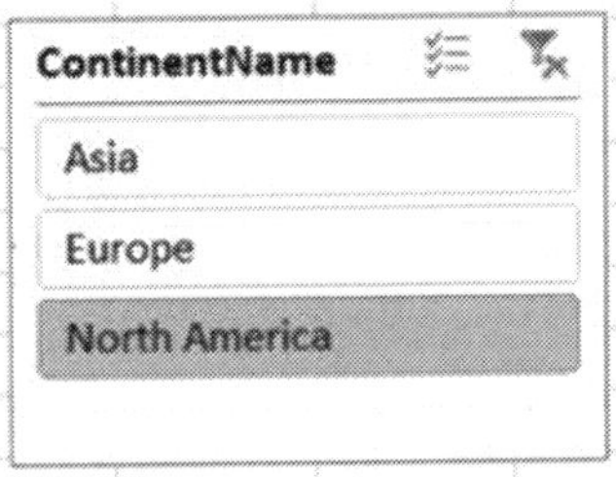

ContinentName
Asia
Europe
North America

Figure 6-26. Testing the measure

15. Switch back to the Power Pivot window and add the following measure to the Sales table (format the measure as percentage):

```
Product Sales Ratio:=[Sum Sales]/[All Product Sales]
```

16. Open the Power Pivot window in diagram view mode. To create a relationship between the Date table and the Store table, drag the OpenDate field from the Store table and drop it on top of the DateKey in the Date table (see Figure 6-27). Notice that this is not the active relationship between the Store and the Date tables as indicated by the dashed line. This is because the active relationship goes from the Store table, through the Sales table, and then to the Date table.

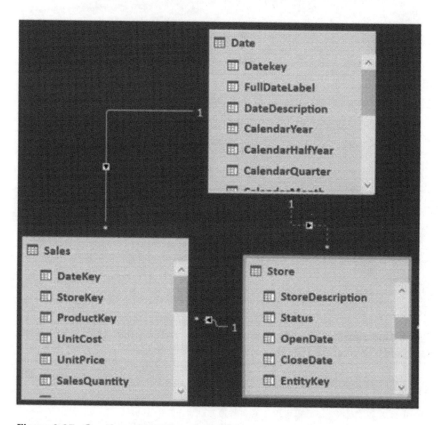

Figure 6-27. *Creating an inactive relationship*

17. Switch to the data view mode and add the following measure to the Store table. Because you are using a non-active relationship, you need to use the USERELATIONSHIP function:

```
Store Count:=CALCULATE(DISTINCTCOUNT([StoreKey]),
USERELATIONSHIP(Store[OpenDate],'Date'[Datekey]))
```

18. To test the store count measure, create a pivot table on Sheet2. Use the ContinentName as the column labels and the CalendarMonth as the row labels. Insert a slicer using CalendarYear. Your pivot table should look like Figure 6-28.

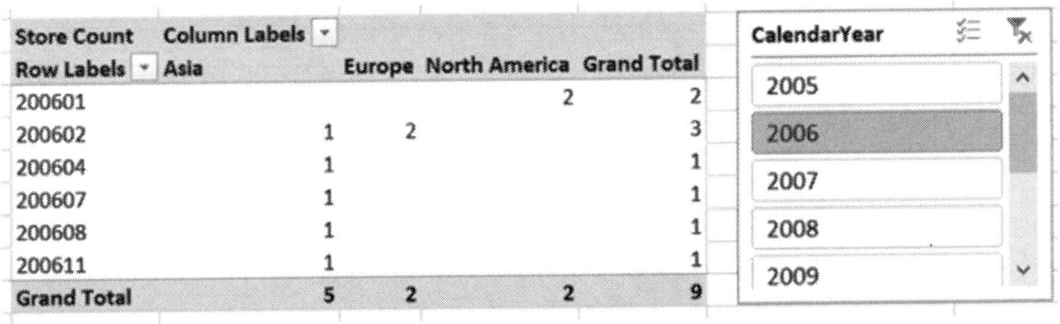

Store Count	Column Labels				CalendarYear
Row Labels	Asia	Europe	North America	Grand Total	
200601			2	2	2005
200602	1	2		3	2006
200604	1			1	2007
200607	1			1	
200608	1			1	2008
200611	1			1	2009
Grand Total	5	2	2	9	

Figure 6-28. *Testing the store count measure*

19. The pivot table represents the number of stores opened during a month. Click the various years and observe the changes in the data.

20. To find out the best sales day for a product category, create a Sale Quantity measure in the Sales table:

```
Sale Quantity:=SUM([SalesQuantity])
```

21. Use the Sale Quantity measure to create a Top Sale Day Quantity measure. The MAXX function is used to break any ties and returns the most recent DateKey:

```
Top Sale Day Quantity:=MAXX(values('Date'[Datekey]),[Sale Quantity])
```

22. To figure out the date of the top sales day, you first create a filter function that returns the dates when the Sale Quantity equals the Top Sale Day Quantity for the period:

```
Filter(VALUES('Date'[Datekey]),
[Sale Quantity]=CALCULATE([Top Sale Day Quantity],
VALUES('Date'[Datekey])))
```

23. This filter is then inserted into a CALCULATE function that returns the most recent date. Format the measure as a short date (select More Formats in the Format dropdown):

```
Top Sale Day:=CALCULATE(MAX('Date'[Datekey]),
    Filter(VALUES('Date'[Datekey]),[Sale Quantity]=
    CALCULATE([Top Sale Day Quantity],VALUES('Date'[Datekey])))))
```

24. Create a pivot table like the one in 6-29 to test your measures.

Row Labels	Top Sale Day Quantity	Top Sale Day
⊟ Audio	2477	11/26/2009
Bluetooth Headphones	1329	11/26/2009
MP4&MP3	1037	11/7/2009
Recording Pen	518	7/16/2009
⊟ Cameras and camcorders	9251	11/2/2007
Camcorders	3241	11/30/2007
Cameras & Camcorders Accessories	2055	12/21/2009
Digital Cameras	2966	12/20/2007
Digital SLR Cameras	2897	11/22/2007
⊞ Cell phones	27438	8/20/2009
⊞ Computers	12898	12/20/2009
⊞ Games and Toys	9674	7/15/2009
⊞ Home Appliances	12096	11/15/2009
⊞ Music, Movies and Audio Books	2344	2/15/2007
⊞ TV and Video	4334	12/18/2007
Grand Total	69757	12/27/2009

Figure 6-29. *Testing the Top Sale Day measure*

25. Create the following measures in the Sales table and format them as currency:

```
Ave Sales:=AVERAGE([SalesAmount])
Total Ave Sales:=If(ISBLANK([Ave Sales]),BLANK(),
                CALCULATE([Ave Sales],ALLSELECTED()))
```

26. Select the Ave Sales measure in the measure grid. Right-click it and select Create KPI in the context menu. In the KPI dialog, notice that the base measure is Ave Sales. Set the target value to Total Ave Sales. Set the low threshold to 90% and the high threshold to 110% (see Figure 6-30).

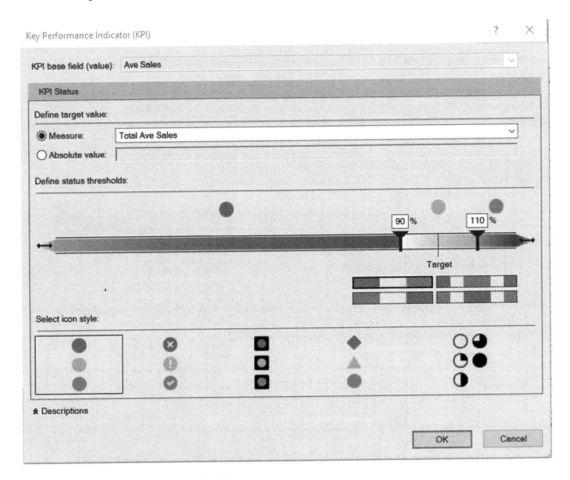

Figure 6-30. *Creating the average sales KPI*

27. Close the dialog and notice that the Ave Sales measure has an icon indicating it has a KPI associated with it.

28. Create a pivot table like the one in Figure 6-31 to test the KPI. You can compare the average sales of a store with the total average sales of all the stores showing.

Row Labels	Ave Sales	Total Ave Sales	Ave Sales Status
Contoso Albany Store	$3,155.12	$3,644.55	●
Contoso Alexandria Store	$3,182.60	$3,644.55	●
Contoso Amsterdam Store	$2,842.46	$3,644.55	●
Contoso Anchorage Store	$3,196.82	$3,644.55	●
Contoso Annapolis Store	$3,273.27	$3,644.55	●
Contoso Appleton Store	$3,235.19	$3,644.55	●
Contoso Arlington Store	$3,199.75	$3,644.55	●
Contoso Ashgabat No.2 Store	$3,353.28	$3,644.55	○
Contoso Ashgabat No.1 Store	$3,367.00	$3,644.55	○
Contoso Asia Online Store	$4,580.45	$3,644.55	●
Contoso Asia Reseller	$4,322.91	$3,644.55	●

Figure 6-31. Viewing the KPI

Summary

This was a long and meaty chapter. You now have a firm grasp of how to create measures in your Power Pivot model. You should also understand data context and how it affects the measurements. This can be a very confusing concept when you start to develop more complex measures. Don't worry—the more you work with it the clearer it becomes.

The next chapter extends the concepts of this chapter. One of the most common types of data analysis is comparing values over time. Chapter 7 shows you how to correctly implement time-based analysis in Power Pivot. It includes setting up a date table and using the various built-in functions for analyzing values to date, comparing values from different periods, and performing semi-additive aggregations.

CHAPTER 7

■ ■ ■

Incorporating Time Intelligence

One of the most common types of data analysis is comparing values over time. This chapter shows you how to correctly implement time-based analysis in Power Pivot. It includes setting up a date table and using the various built-in functions for analyzing values to date, comparing values from different periods, and performing semi-additive aggregations.

After completing this chapter, you will be able to

- Create a date table.

- Use DAX for time period-based evaluations.

- Shift the date context using filter functions.

- Create semi-additive measures.

Date-Based Analysis

A large percentage of data analysis involves some sort of datetime-based aggregation and comparison. For example, you may need to look at usage or sales for the month-to-date (MTD) or year-to-date (YTD), as shown in Figure 7-1.

Row Labels	Sum of Sales	MTD Sales	YTD Sales
⊟ 2007	$571,204,151.10	$55,148,659.27	$571,204,151.10
January	$33,937,209.25	$33,937,209.25	$33,937,209.25
February	$39,627,318.77	$39,627,318.77	$73,564,528.02
March	$43,055,837.85	$43,055,837.85	$116,620,365.87
April	$45,152,238.05	$45,152,238.05	$161,772,603.92
May	$49,678,655.61	$49,678,655.61	$211,451,259.53
June	$49,431,542.53	$49,431,542.53	$260,882,802.06
July	$53,458,586.99	$53,458,586.99	$314,341,389.05
August	$50,771,841.27	$50,771,841.27	$365,113,230.32
September	$49,242,024.87	$49,242,024.87	$414,355,255.19
October	$47,437,924.07	$47,437,924.07	$461,793,179.26
November	$54,262,312.57	$54,262,312.57	$516,055,491.83
December	$55,148,659.27	$55,148,659.27	$571,204,151.10
⊞ 2008	$600,175,898.67	$56,659,783.37	$600,175,898.67
⊞ 2009	$543,817,781.67	$46,788,451.58	$543,817,781.67

ChannelName

- Catalog
- Online
- Reseller
- Store

Figure 7-1. Calculating month-to-date and year-to-date sales

Another common example is looking at performance from one time period to the next. For example, you may want to compare previous months' sales with current sales (see Figure 7-2) or sales for the current month to the same month a year before.

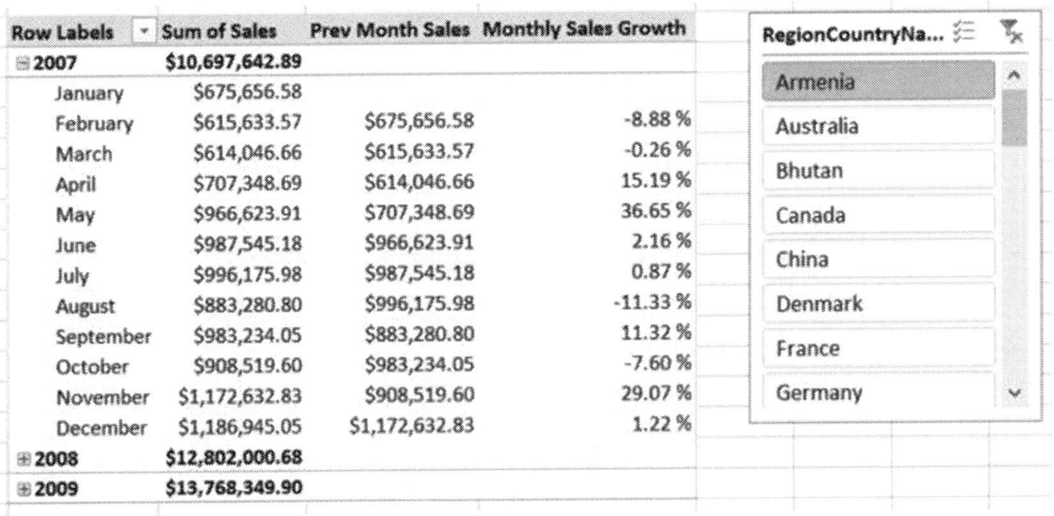

Row Labels	Sum of Sales	Prev Month Sales	Monthly Sales Growth
⊟ 2007	$10,697,642.89		
January	$675,656.58		
February	$615,633.57	$675,656.58	-8.88 %
March	$614,046.66	$615,633.57	-0.26 %
April	$707,348.69	$614,046.66	15.19 %
May	$966,623.91	$707,348.69	36.65 %
June	$987,545.18	$966,623.91	2.16 %
July	$996,175.98	$987,545.18	0.87 %
August	$883,280.80	$996,175.98	-11.33 %
September	$983,234.05	$883,280.80	11.32 %
October	$908,519.60	$983,234.05	-7.60 %
November	$1,172,632.83	$908,519.60	29.07 %
December	$1,186,945.05	$1,172,632.83	1.22 %
⊞ 2008	$12,802,000.68		
⊞ 2009	$13,768,349.90		

RegionCountryNa...

- Armenia
- Australia
- Bhutan
- Canada
- China
- Denmark
- France
- Germany

Figure 7-2. Calculating sales growth

In addition to these common data analytics, there are also times when you need to base your aggregations on measures that are non-additive, such as account balances or inventory. In these cases, you need to determine the last value entered and use that value to aggregate across the different time periods (see Figure 7-3).

StoreQuantity Colur												
Row Labels	200901	200902	200903	200904	200905	200906	200907	200908	200909	200910	200911	Grand Total
⊟Contoso 8GB Super-Slim MP3/Video Player M800 Pink	44	61	23	185	74	151	44	121	86	70	100	194
Contoso Catalog Store	22	61	23	29	24	32		53	30	46	42	42
Contoso North America Online Store	22			156	26	45		40	30	24	58	58
Contoso Ottawa No.1 Store					24	24						24
Contoso Ottawa No.2 Store								28	26			26
Contoso Toronto No.1 Store						27	22					22
Contoso Toronto No.2 Store						23	22					22

Figure 7-3. Aggregating inventory amounts

DAX contains many functions that help you create the various datetime-based analyses you may need. In the next section, you will see how to create a date table that is required to use many of the datetime-based functions.

Creating a Date Table

In order to use the built-in time intelligence functions in DAX, you need to have a date table in your model for the functions to reference. The only requirement for the table is that it needs a distinct row for each day in the date range at which you are interested in looking. Each of these rows needs to contain the full date of the day. The date table can, and often does, have more columns, but it doesn't have to.

There are several ways to create the date table. If you are retrieving data from a data warehouse, you can import a date dimension into the model and use it. If you don't have access to a date table, you can create it in the Power Pivot Model Designer. On the Design tab, select the Date Table drop-down and click New (see Figure 7-4).

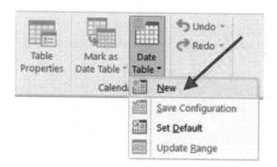

Figure 7-4. Creating a date table

This creates a date table called Calendar that contains a Date, Year, MonthNumber, Month, YYYY_MM, DayOfWeekNumber, and DayOfWeek fields (see Figure 7-5).

	Date	Year	MonthNumber	Month	YYYY-MM	DayOfWeekNumber	DayOfWeek
1	1/1/2003 12:00:00 AM	2003	1	January	2003-01	4	Wednesday
2	1/2/2003 12:00:00 AM	2003	1	January	2003-01	5	Thursday
3	1/3/2003 12:00:00 AM	2003	1	January	2003-01	6	Friday
4	1/4/2003 12:00:00 AM	2003	1	January	2003-01	7	Saturday
5	1/5/2003 12:00:00 AM	2003	1	January	2003-01	1	Sunday
6	1/6/2003 12:00:00 AM	2003	1	January	2003-01	2	Monday
7	1/7/2003 12:00:00 AM	2003	1	January	2003-01	3	Tuesday
8	1/8/2003 12:00:00 AM	2003	1	January	2003-01	4	Wednesday
9	1/9/2003 12:00:00 AM	2003	1	January	2003-01	5	Thursday
10	1/10/2003 12:00:00 AM	2003	1	January	2003-01	6	Friday
11	1/11/2003 12:00:00 AM	2003	1	January	2003-01	7	Saturday
12	1/12/2003 12:00:00 AM	2003	1	January	2003-01	1	Sunday

Figure 7-5. *The Calendar (date) table*

Once the table is created, you can adjust the start and end dates with Update Range under the Date Table drop-down (see Figure 7-6). The date range should span the range of dates contained in your data.

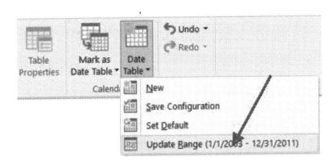

Figure 7-6. *Changing the range of the Calendar (date) table*

Once you have the table in the model, you need to mark it as the official date table (see Figure 7-7) and indicate which column is the unique key (see Figure 7-8). This tells the DAX query engine to use this table as a reference for constructing the set of dates needed for a calculation. For example, if you want to look at year-to-date sales, the query engine uses this table to get the set of dates it needs.

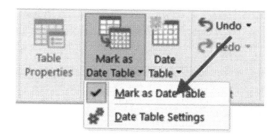

Figure 7-7. *Identifying the date table*

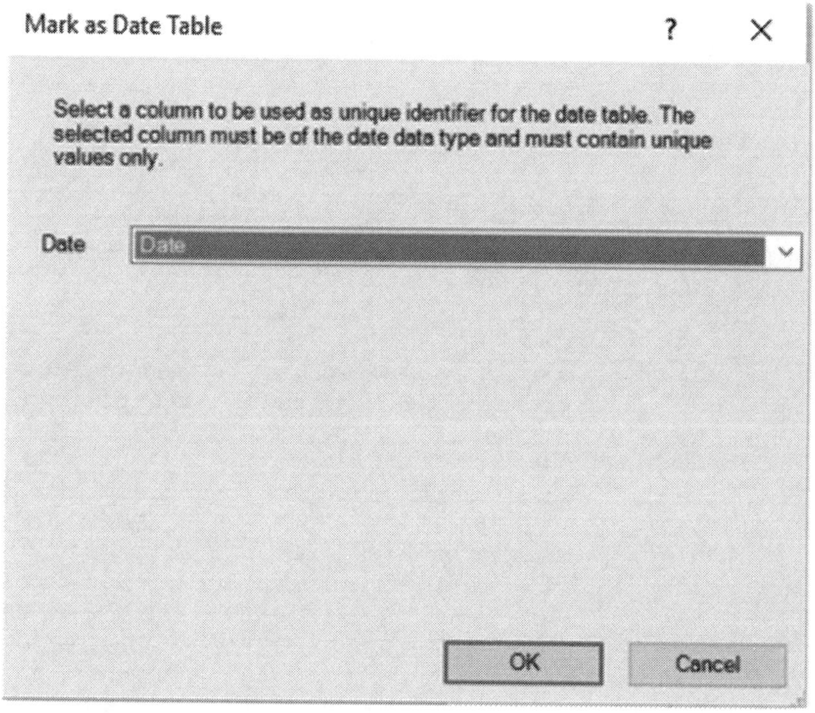

Mark as Date Table   ?   ✕

Select a column to be used as unique identifier for the date table. The
selected column must be of the date data type and must contain unique
values only.

Date   [Date   ▾]

                                    [OK   ]   [Cancel]

Figure 7-8. *Setting the date key*

There are many built-in time intelligent functions in DAX. Some of these functions, like FIRSTNONBLANK, return a single date. Some return a set of dates, such as PREVIOUSMONTH. And still others, like TOTALQTD, evaluate expressions over time. At this point, the DAX built-in time intelligence functions support the traditional calendar ending on December 31st. They also support a fiscal calendar that has a different year-end date and contains four quarters containing three months each. If you need to use a custom financial calendar, you must create your own custom calculations.

Now that you understand how to create and designate the date table in your model, it is time to look at implementing some of the common time intelligent functions to analyze your data.

Time Period–Based Evaluations

A common analysis often employed in data analytics is looking at period-to-date values. For example, you may want to look at sales year-to-date or energy consumption month-to-date. DAX provides the TOTALMTD, TOTALQTD, and TOTALYTD functions that make this very easy. For instance, the total year-to-date is defined as follows:

```
TOTALYTD(<expression>,<dates>[,<filter>][,<year_end_date>])
```

where expression is an expression that returns a scalar value. dates is the date table's key column. filter is an optional filter expression, and year_end_date is also optional—you can use it to indicate the year end of a fiscal calendar. The following expressions are used to calculate the sum of the sales and the sales year-to-date values.

```
Sum of Sales:=SUM(Sales[SalesAmount])
YTD Sales:=TOTALYTD([Sum of Sales],'Date'[Datekey])
```

If you want to calculate year-to-date sales for all products, use the following expression:

```
YTD Sales ALL Products:=TOTALYTD([Sum of Sales],'Date'[Datekey],ALL('Product'))
```

Figure 7-9 shows the measures in a pivot table. You can use these base measures to calculate further measures, such as percent of year-to-date sales and percent of all product sales.

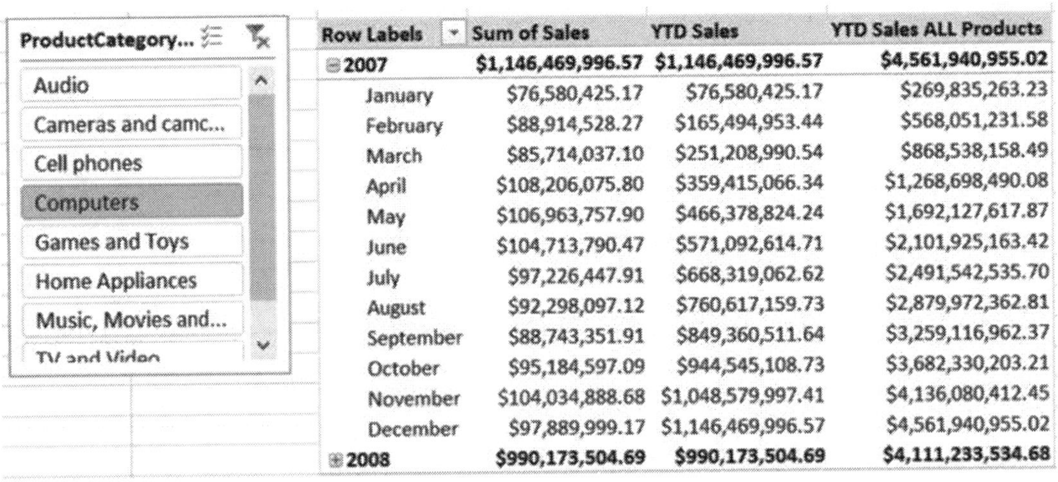

Row Labels	Sum of Sales	YTD Sales	YTD Sales ALL Products
⊟ 2007	$1,146,469,996.57	$1,146,469,996.57	$4,561,940,955.02
January	$76,580,425.17	$76,580,425.17	$269,835,263.23
February	$88,914,528.27	$165,494,953.44	$568,051,231.58
March	$85,714,037.10	$251,208,990.54	$868,538,158.49
April	$108,206,075.80	$359,415,066.34	$1,268,698,490.08
May	$106,963,757.90	$466,378,824.24	$1,692,127,617.87
June	$104,713,790.47	$571,092,614.71	$2,101,925,163.42
July	$97,226,447.91	$668,319,062.62	$2,491,542,535.70
August	$92,298,097.12	$760,617,159.73	$2,879,972,362.81
September	$88,743,351.91	$849,360,511.64	$3,259,116,962.37
October	$95,184,597.09	$944,545,108.73	$3,682,330,203.21
November	$104,034,888.68	$1,048,579,997.41	$4,136,080,412.45
December	$97,889,999.17	$1,146,469,996.57	$4,561,940,955.02
⊞ 2008	$990,173,504.69	$990,173,504.69	$4,111,233,534.68

ProductCategory...: Audio, Cameras and camc..., Cell phones, **Computers**, Games and Toys, Home Appliances, Music, Movies and..., TV and Video

Figure 7-9. *Calculating year-to-date values*

You can also use another set of functions—DATESMTD, DATESQTD, and DATESYTD—to create the same measures. Just as with the previous to-date measures, you need to pass the date key from the date table to the functions. The following expression uses the CALCULATE function with the DATESYTD filter to get the sales year-to-date measure:

```
YTD Sales 2:=CALCULATE([Sum of Sales],DATESYTD('Date'[Datekey]))
```

Using the CALCULATE function and the DATES functions is more versatile than the total-to-date functions because you can use them for any type of aggregation, not just the sum. The following expressions are used to calculate the average sales year-to-date. The results are shown in Figure 7-10.

```
Ave Sales:=AVERAGE([SalesAmount])
YTD Ave Sales:=CALCULATE([Ave Sales],DATESYTD('Date'[Datekey]))
```

 ProductCategory...	Row Labels	Ave Sales	YTD Ave Sales
Audio	⊟ 2007	$3,454.09	$3,454.09
Cameras and camc...	January	$2,921.80	$2,921.80
Cell phones	February	$3,460.11	$3,188.30
Computers	March	$3,282.68	$3,219.89
Games and Toys	April	$3,532.34	$3,307.98
Home Appliances	May	$3,428.33	$3,334.83
Music, Movies and...	June	$3,356.10	$3,338.71
TV and Video	July	$3,761.61	$3,394.22
	August	$3,607.93	$3,418.80
	September	$3,546.19	$3,431.68
	October	$2,971.18	$3,378.90
	November	$4,061.96	$3,436.23
	December	$3,657.66	$3,454.09
	⊞ 2008	$3,969.79	$3,969.79

Figure 7-10. *Calculating average year-to-date values*

Now that you know how to create time period–based calculations, you can use this to compare past performance with current performance. But first you need to know how to shift the date context to calculate past performance.

Shifting the Date Context

If you want to compare performance from one period to the same period in the past, say sales for the current month to sales for the same month a year ago, you need to shift the date context. DAX contains several functions that do this. One of the most versatile functions for shifting the date context is the PARALLELPERIOD function. As with the other time intelligence functions, you need to pass the key column of the date table to the function. You also need to indicate the number of intervals and the interval type of year, quarter, or month:

```
PARALLELPERIOD(<dates>,<number_of_intervals>,<interval>)
```

One thing to remember is that the PARALLELPERIOD function returns a set of dates that corresponds to the interval type. If you use the year, it returns a year of dates; the month interval returns a month's worth of dates. The following expression calculates the sales totals for the month of the previous year. Figure 7-11 shows the results of the calculation.

```
Month Sales Last Year:=Calculate([Sum of Sales],
PARALLELPERIOD('Date'[Datekey],-12,Month))
```

Row Labels	Sum of Sales	Month Sales Last Year
⊟ 2007	$571,204,151.10	
January	$33,937,209.25	
February	$39,627,318.77	
March	$43,055,837.85	
April	$45,152,238.05	
May	$49,678,655.61	
June	$49,431,542.53	
July	$53,458,586.99	
August	$50,771,841.27	
September	$49,242,024.87	
October	$47,437,924.07	
November	$54,262,312.57	
December	$55,148,659.27	
⊟ 2008	$600,175,898.67	$571,204,151.10
January	$41,172,371.61	$33,937,209.25
February	$44,356,169.32	$39,627,318.77
March	$44,067,571.51	$43,055,837.85
April	$53,070,715.43	$45,152,238.05
May	$53,183,905.20	$49,678,655.61
June	$51,653,752.92	$49,431,542.53
July	$56,149,796.74	$53,458,586.99
August	$49,966,766.60	$50,771,841.27

Figure 7-11. Calculating sales for a parallel period

Notice that if you drill down to the date level (see Figure 7-12), you still see the month totals for the month of the date for a year ago. As mentioned earlier, this is because the PARALLELPERIOD in this case always returns the set of dates for the same month as the row date for the previous year.

⊟ 2008	$600,175,898.67	$571,204,151.10
⊞ January	$41,172,371.61	$33,937,209.25
⊟ February	$44,356,169.32	$39,627,318.77
2/1/2008	$1,566,855.57	$39,627,318.77
2/2/2008	$1,463,784.54	$39,627,318.77
2/3/2008	$1,451,718.78	$39,627,318.77
2/4/2008	$1,373,878.11	$39,627,318.77
2/5/2008	$1,577,128.49	$39,627,318.77
2/6/2008	$1,401,943.35	$39,627,318.77
2/7/2008	$1,316,157.79	$39,627,318.77
2/8/2008	$1,640,352.74	$39,627,318.77
2/9/2008	$1,536,049.78	$39,627,318.77
2/10/2008	$1,544,487.02	$39,627,318.77
2/11/2008	$1,325,233.15	$39,627,318.77
2/12/2008	$1,621,591.76	$39,627,318.77
2/13/2008	$1,390,489.17	$39,627,318.77
2/14/2008	$1,484,512.08	$39,627,318.77

Figure 7-12. *Drilling to day level still shows month-level aggregation.*

Now that you can calculate the month sales of the previous year, you can combine it with current sales to calculate the monthly sales growth from one year to the next. Figure 7-13 shows the results.

```
YOY Monthly Growth:=([Sum of Sales]-[Month Sales Last Year])/[Month Sales Last Year]
```

Row Labels	Sum of Sales	Month Sales Last Year	YOY Monthly Growth
⊞ 2007	$571,204,151.10		#NUM!
⊟ 2008	$600,175,898.67	$571,204,151.10	5 %
January	$41,172,371.61	$33,937,209.25	21 %
February	$44,356,169.32	$39,627,318.77	12 %
March	$44,067,571.51	$43,055,837.85	2 %
April	$53,070,715.43	$45,152,238.05	18 %
May	$53,183,905.20	$49,678,655.61	7 %
June	$51,653,752.92	$49,431,542.53	4 %
July	$56,149,796.74	$53,458,586.99	5 %
August	$49,966,766.60	$50,771,841.27	-2 %
September	$49,627,897.65	$49,242,024.87	1 %
October	$46,947,843.65	$47,437,924.07	-1 %
November	$53,319,324.67	$54,262,312.57	-2 %
December	$56,659,783.37	$55,148,659.27	3 %

Figure 7-13. *Calculating year over year monthly growth*

Note that if there is no previous year sales, you get an error in the pivot table. You can control this by checking whether the month sales for last year is blank and inserting a blank value instead:

```
YOY Monthly Growth:=IF(
ISBLANK([Month Sales Last Year]),
BLANK(),
([Sum of Sales]-[Month Sales Last Year])/[Month Sales Last Year])
```

Another function commonly used to alter the date context is the DATEADD function. The DATEADD function is used to add a date interval to the current date context. You can add year, quarter, month, or day intervals:

```
DATEADD(<dates>,<number_of_intervals>,<interval>)
```

The following calculation is used to find the sum of the previous day sales using the DATEADD function as a filter:

```
Prev Day Sales:=Calculate([Sum of Sales],DATEADD('Date'[Datekey],-1,day))
```

Now that you know how to shift the date context, let's look at functions you can use in your filters that return a single date.

Using Single Date Functions

DAX contains a set of functions that return a single date. These are usually used when filtering the date context. For example, the FIRSTDATE function returns the first date in the column of dates passed to it. As an example, you can use this in combination with the DATESBETWEEN function to get the range of dates from the first day to the 15th day of the current date context set of dates:

```
DATESBETWEEN('Date'[FullDateAlternateKey]
,FIRSTDATE('Date'[FullDateAlternateKey])
,DATEADD(FIRSTDATE('Date'[FullDateAlternateKey]), 14, DAY))
```

This can then be used as a filter in the CALCULATE function to get the sales during the first 15 days of the period. The resulting pivot table is shown in Figure 7-14.

Row Labels ▾	TotalSales	First 15 Day Sales
⊟ 2005	$3,266,373.66	$198,963.36
⊞ July	$473,388.16	$198,963.36
⊞ August	$506,191.69	$245,773.41
⊞ September	$473,943.03	$224,025.27
⊞ October	$513,329.47	$274,285.55
⊟ November	$543,993.41	$307,175.05
11/1/2005	$20,731.50	
11/2/2005	$10,734.81	
11/3/2005	$13,931.52	
11/4/2005	$18,412.17	
11/5/2005	$21,990.44	
11/6/2005	$17,509.79	
11/7/2005	$26,446.09	
11/8/2005	$28,626.16	
11/9/2005	$14,313.08	
11/10/2005	$21,762.16	
11/11/2005	$21,469.62	
11/12/2005	$19,289.55	
11/13/2005	$27,709.76	
11/14/2005	$28,740.42	
11/15/2005	$15,508.00	

Figure 7-14. Calculating sales for the first 15 days of the month

If you are just looking at the monthly periods, you can use the functions STARTOFMONTH and ENDOFMONTH (there are ones for year and quarter also). The following expression is used to calculate the sum of the sales for the last 15 days of the month:

```
Last 15 Day Sales:=CALCULATE(SUM(InternetSales[SalesAmount]),
 DATESBETWEEN('Date'[FullDateAlternateKey]
 , DATEADD(ENDOFMONTH('Date'[FullDateAlternateKey]), -14, DAY)
,ENDOFMONTH('Date'[FullDateAlternateKey])))
```

Although the majority of measures you need to aggregate from a lower level to a higher level (for example, from days to months) are simple extensions of the base aggregate, at times you need to use special aggregations to roll up the measure. This type of measure is considered semi-additive and is covered in the next section.

Creating Semi-Additive Measures

You often encounter semi-additive measures when analyzing data. Some common examples are inventory and account balances. For example, to determine the total amount of inventory at a current point in time, you add the inventory of all stores. But to find the total inventory of a store at the end of the month, you don't add up the inventory for each day.

To deal with these situations, DAX contains the FIRSTNONBLANK and LASTNONBLANK functions. These functions return the first or last date for a non-blank condition. For example, the following expression determines the last non-blank date for the product inventory entries:

```
LASTNONBLANK ('Date'[DateKey],CALCULATE (SUM(Inventory[UnitsInStock]))
```

This is then combined with the CALCULATE function to determine the total units in stock:

```
Product Units In Stock:=CALCULATE(SUM(Inventory[UnitsInStock]),
  LASTNONBLANK('Date'[DateKey],
  CALCULATE(SUM(Inventory[UnitsInStock])))))
```

Now if you want to add up the units in stock across products, you can use the following expression:

```
Total Units In Stock:=SUMX(VALUES('Inventory'[ProductKey]),[Product Units In Stock])
```

Figure 7-15 shows the resulting pivot table. Note that the Total Units In Stock measure is additive across the products but non-additive across the dates.

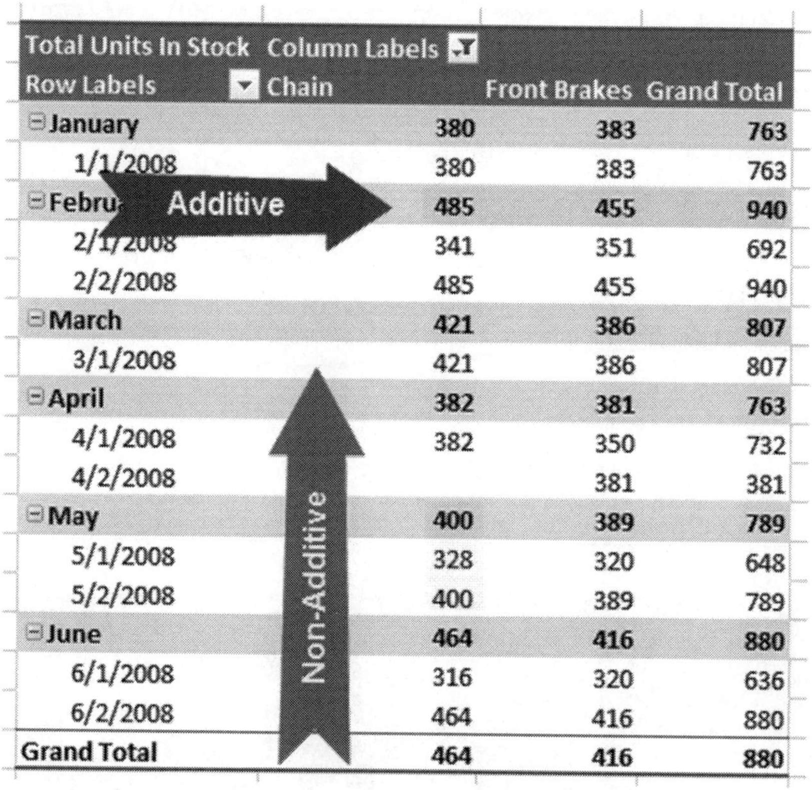

Total Units In Stock	Column Labels ▾		
Row Labels ▾	Chain	Front Brakes	Grand Total
⊟ January	380	383	763
1/1/2008	380	383	763
⊟ Febru **Additive** ➜	485	455	940
2/1/2008	341	351	692
2/2/2008	485	455	940
⊟ March	421	386	807
3/1/2008	421	386	807
⊟ April	382	381	763
4/1/2008	382	350	732
4/2/2008		381	381
⊟ May	400	389	789
5/1/2008	328	320	648
5/2/2008	400	389	789
⊟ June	464	416	880
6/1/2008	316	320	636
6/2/2008	464	416	880
Grand Total	464	416	880

Figure 7-15. Calculating units in stock

One of the advantages of DAX is that once you learn a pattern you can extend it to other scenarios. For example, you can employ the same techniques used in this inventory calculation when calculating measures in a cash flow analysis. The following calculation is used to calculate the ending balance:

```
Balance:=CALCULATE ( SUM ( Finance[Amount]),
  LASTNONBLANK ('Date'[DateKey],
    CALCULATE(SUM ( Finance[Amount])))))
```

In the previous examples, the inventory and balance were only entered as a row in the table when a change in inventory or balance occurred. Often the balance or inventory is entered every day, and the same value is repeated until there is a change. In these cases, you can use the DAX functions CLOSINGBALANCEMONTH, CLOSINGBALANCEQUARTER, and CLOSINGBALANCYEAR. These functions look at the last date of the time period and use that as the value for the time period. In other words, whatever the value is on the last day of the month is returned by the CLOSINGBALANCEMONTH function.

At this point, you should have a good grasp of how the various time functions work. In the following lab you will gain experience implementing some of these functions.

HANDS-ON LAB: IMPLEMENTING TIME INTELLIGENCE IN POWER PIVOT

In the following lab you will

- Create a date table.

- Use time intelligence functions to analyze data.

- Create a Month over Month Growth pivot table.

- Create an Inventory Level Report.

1. In the LabStarterFiles\Chapter7Lab1 folder, open the Chapter7Lab1.xlsx file. This file contains inventory and sales data from the Contoso test database.

2. Open the Power Pivot Model Designer in diagram view mode (see Figure 7-16). Notice there is no Date table. We could load one from the data source or create one in Excel.

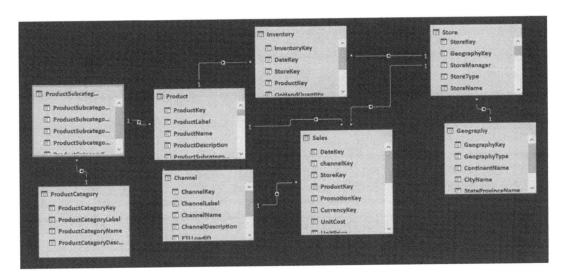

Figure 7-16. *The current Contoso data model*

3. To create the Date table, on the Design tab select the Date Table drop-down and click New. You will see a Calendar table added to the model.

4. Select the Date Table drop-down again and click the Update Range option. Change the Start Date to 1/1/2007.

5. You should see the table in the Data View window of the Power Pivot design window. Click the Design tab and select Mark As Date Table. Make sure the Calendar table is marked as the Date table and the Date column is selected as the unique identifier.

6. Create a relationship between the Sales table and Calendar table (see Figure 7-17).

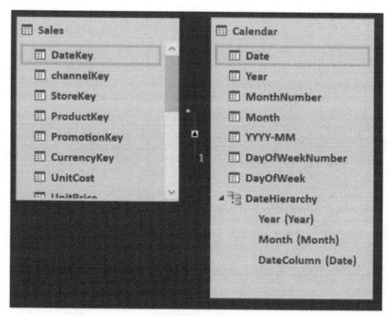

Figure 7-17. *Creating the relationship between the Sales and Date table*

7. Select the Sales table in the Data View window. Add the following measures and format them as currency:

```
Sum of Sales:=SUM(Sales[SalesAmount])
YTD Sales:=TOTALYTD([Sum of Sales],'Calendar'[Date])
MTD Sales:=TOTALMTD([Sum of Sales],'Calendar'[Date])
```

8. To test the measures, go to Sheet1 in Excel and click cell B2. On the Insert tab, select PivotTable. In the Create PivotTable window, select Use An External Data Source and click the Choose Connection button (see Figure 7-18).

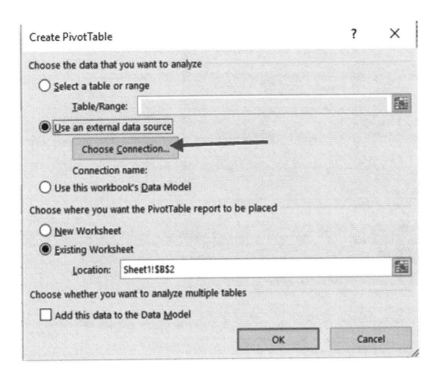

Figure 7-18. *Choosing an external data source*

9. In the Existing Connections window, select the Tables tab. In the Tables tab, select
    Tables In Workbook Data Model and click Open (see Figure 7-19). After selecting
    the connection, click OK in the Create PivotTable window.

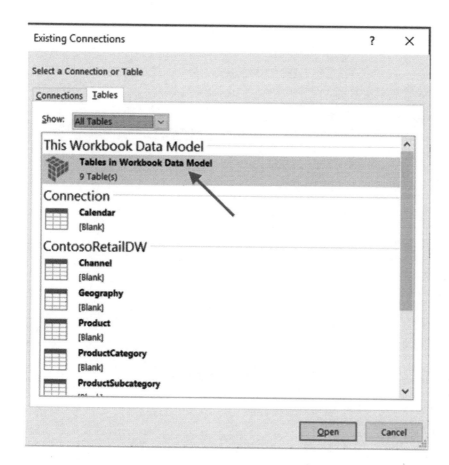

Figure 7-19. Selecting the data model connection

10. Add the measures Sum Of Sales, MTD Sales, and YTD Sales to the Values area and the DateHierarchy to the Rows area. In the Insert tab, select Slicer and choose the ChannelName. Investigate the data and verify that it is what you expected (see Figure 7-20).

Row Labels	Sum of Sales	YTD Sales	MTD Sales
⊟ 2007	$571,204,151.10	$571,204,151.10	$55,148,659.27
⊞ January	$33,937,209.25	$33,937,209.25	$33,937,209.25
⊞ February	$39,627,318.77	$73,564,528.02	$39,627,318.77
⊞ March	$43,055,837.85	$116,620,365.87	$43,055,837.85
⊞ April	$45,152,238.05	$161,772,603.92	$45,152,238.05
⊞ May	$49,678,655.61	$211,451,259.53	$49,678,655.61
⊞ June	$49,431,542.53	$260,882,802.06	$49,431,542.53
⊞ July	$53,458,586.99	$314,341,389.05	$53,458,586.99
⊞ August	$50,771,841.27	$365,113,230.32	$50,771,841.27
⊞ September	$49,242,024.87	$414,355,255.19	$49,242,024.87
⊞ October	$47,437,924.07	$461,793,179.26	$47,437,924.07
⊞ November	$54,262,312.57	$516,055,491.83	$54,262,312.57
⊞ December	$55,148,659.27	$571,204,151.10	$55,148,659.27
⊞ 2008	$600,175,898.67	$600,175,898.67	$56,659,783.37
⊞ 2009	$543,817,781.67	$543,817,781.67	$46,788,451.58
Grand Total	$1,715,197,831.44	$543,817,781.67	$46,788,451.58

ChannelName

Catalog

Online

Reseller

Store

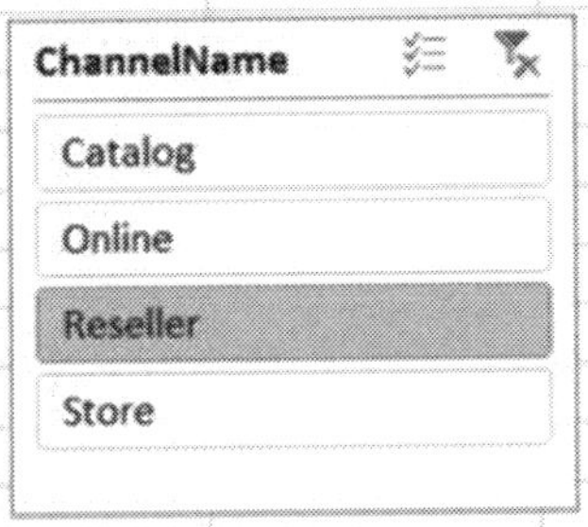

Figure 7-20. Verifying the year-to-date sales measure

11. Switch to the Sales table in the Data Model. Create a rolling three-month sales measure with the following expression. Format the measure as currency:

```
Rolling 3 Month Sales:=CALCULATE([Sum of Sales],
DATESINPERIOD('Calendar'[Date],LASTDATE('Calendar'[Date]),-3,MONTH))
```

12. Add the measure to the pivot table on Sheet1 and verify it is working as expected.

13. Next you want to compare sales growth from one month to the next. First create a previous month's sales measure:

```
Prev Month Sales:=CALCULATE([Sum of Sales],
PARALLELPERIOD('Calendar'[Date],-1,MONTH))
```

14. Next use the previous sales and current sales to create a sales growth measure. Format the measure as percent. Notice that you need to check to make sure the previous month sales exist. If it not, you need to return a blank value:

```
Monthly Sales Growth:=if(NOT(ISBLANK([Prev Month Sales])),
([Sum of Sales] - [Prev Month Sales])/[Prev Month Sales],BLANK())
```

15. Create a pivot table like the one shown in Figure 7-21 on Sheet2 in Excel to test your results.

Row Labels	Sum of Sales	Prev Month Sales	Monthly Sales Growth
⊟ 2007	$4,561,940,955.02	$4,136,080,412.45	10.30 %
⊞ January	$269,835,263.23		
⊞ February	$298,215,968.35	$269,835,263.23	10.52 %
⊞ March	$300,486,926.90	$298,215,968.35	0.76 %
⊞ April	$400,160,331.60	$300,486,926.90	33.17 %
⊞ May	$423,429,127.79	$400,160,331.60	5.81 %
⊞ June	$409,797,545.55	$423,429,127.79	-3.22 %
⊞ July	$389,617,372.27	$409,797,545.55	-4.92 %
⊞ August	$388,429,827.11	$389,617,372.27	-0.30 %
⊞ September	$379,144,599.56	$388,429,827.11	-2.39 %
⊞ October	$423,213,240.84	$379,144,599.56	11.62 %
⊞ November	$453,750,209.24	$423,213,240.84	7.22 %
⊞ December	$425,860,542.57	$453,750,209.24	-6.15 %
⊞ 2008	$4,111,233,534.68	$4,138,307,904.31	-0.65 %
⊞ 2009	$3,740,483,119.18	$3,808,534,878.67	-1.79 %
Grand Total	$12,413,657,608.89	$12,082,923,195.43	2.74 %

Figure 7-21. Testing the Monthly Sales Growth measure

16. To investigate semi-additive measures, you are going to create a pivot table that shows inventory counts. First, create a relationship between the Inventory and Calendar tables.

17. Add the following inventory count measure to the Inventory table:

```
Inventory Count:=SUM([OnHandQuantity])
```

18. To calculate the inventory over time, you need to find the last non-blank entry for the time period. The following formula will give you the value. The date range initial value is blank (prior to the first date), and the final date is the maximum date. You will use this formula as part of the formula in step 19:

```
LNB Date:=LASTNONBLANK(
DATESBETWEEN('Calendar'[Date],BLANK(),MAX('Calendar'[Date]))
,[Inventory Count])
```

19. Using the last non-blank filter and the CALCULATE function, you can calculate the last non-blank quantity for a product. Add the following measure to the Inventory table:

```
LNB Quantity:=CALCULATE([Inventory Count],
LASTNONBLANK(DATESBETWEEN('Calendar'[Date],
BLANK(),MAX('Calendar'[Date])),[Inventory Count]))
```

20. You can now add up the product quantity for products chosen. Add the following measure to the Inventory table:

```
Product Quantity:=SUMX(
VALUES(Product[ProductKey]),[LNB Quantity])
```

21. The final step is to add up the inventory across all the stores selected using the following measure:

```
Inventory Level:=SUMX(Values(Store[StoreKey]),[Product Quantity])
```

22. To test the measure, go to Sheet3 in Excel and create a pivot table like the one in Figure 7-22.

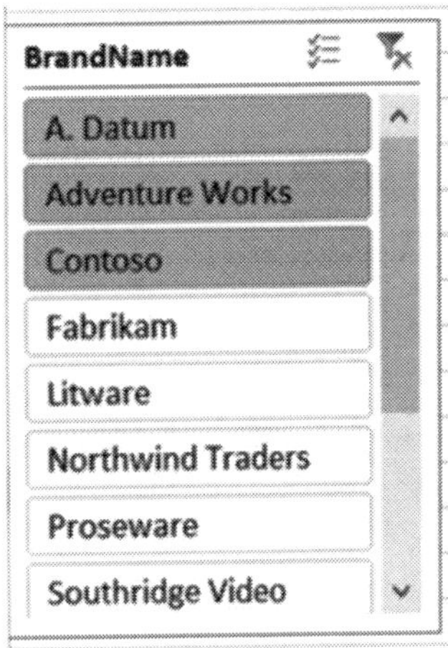

BrandName			Inventory Level Row Labels	Column Labels A. Datum	Adventure Works	Contoso	Grand Total
A. Datum			⊟ 2007	16227	14599	83012	113838
Adventure Works			⊞ January	6083	5188	29229	40500
Contoso			⊞ February	7464	6677	35158	49299
Fabrikam			⊞ March	7403	6853	34858	49114
Litware			⊞ April	9641	8782	45261	63684
Northwind Traders			⊞ May	10878	9869	51838	72585
Proseware			⊞ June	11689	10764	56310	78763
Southridge Video			⊞ July	13138	12328	67596	93062
			⊞ August	13579	12388	69190	95157
			⊞ September	13984	13171	74425	101580
			⊞ October	14289	13058	70748	98095
			⊞ November	17803	15755	91551	125109
			⊞ December	16227	14599	83012	113838
			⊞ 2008	23810	31818	165778	221406
			⊞ 2009	31391	46516	306776	384683
			Grand Total	31391	46516	306776	384683

Figure 7-22. *Testing the inventory measure*

Summary

This chapter provided you with the basics you need to successfully incorporate datetime-based analysis using Power Pivot and DAX. You should now understand how to shift the date context to compare measures based on parallel periods. You should also feel comfortable aggregating measures using the period-to-date DAX formulas. When you combine the concepts you learned in Chapter 6 and this chapter, you should start to recognize patterns in your analysis. Based on these patterns, you can identify the DAX template you need to solve the problem. Because not everyone will be familiar with creating pivot tables and pivot charts in Excel, Chapter 8 shows you the basics of how to create dashboards in Excel based on your model. If you are familiar with these concepts, you may want to skip ahead to Chapter 9.

CHAPTER 8

▓ ▓ ▓

Data Analysis with Pivot Tables and Charts

Once you have the data model created in Power Pivot, you need to create an interface for users to interact with the data model and perform data analysis using the model. You can use several programs to interface with the model depending on the type of analysis taking place; these include Power BI, Performance Point, and Reporting Services. Although all these tools are viable clients to use, one of the best client tools is Excel itself. Excel is a feature-rich environment for creating dashboards using pivot tables and pivot charts. Furthermore, it is very easy to share Excel files with colleagues or host the Excel workbook on SharePoint for increased performance and security. This chapter covers the basics of building an interface for analyzing the data contained in a Power Pivot model using pivot tables and pivot charts in Excel.

After completing this chapter, you will be able to

- Use pivot tables to explore the data.

- Filter data using slicers.

- Add visualizations to a pivot table.

- Use pivot charts to explore trends.

- Use multiple charts and tables linked together.

- Use cube functions to query the data model.

▓ **Note** This chapter contains references to color figures. If you are reading this book in print, or in a black-and-white e-book edition, you can find copies of color figures in the Source Code/Downloads package for the book at https://github.com/Apress/beginningpower-bi-2ed.

Pivot Table Fundamentals

One of the most widely used tools for analyzing data is the pivot table. The pivot table allows you to easily detect patterns and relationships from the data. For example, you can determine what products sell better during certain times during the year. Or you can see how marketing campaigns affect the sales of various products. Figure 8-1 shows the various areas of a pivot table.

© Dan Clark 2017
D. Clark, *Beginning Power BI*, DOI 10.1007/978-1-4842-2577-6_8

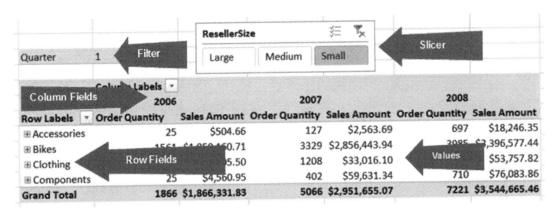

Figure 8-1. *The parts of a pivot table*

The row and column fields contain the attributes that you are interested in using to summarize the data. For example, the pivot table in Figure 8-1 is aggregating the values by product categories and years. The filter is used to filter the values in the pivot table by some attribute. The filter in Figure 8-1 is limiting the results to the first quarter of each year. The slicer works the same as the filter in this case, limiting the values to small resellers. Slicers have the added advantage of filtering multiple pivot tables and pivot charts.

To construct the pivot table, drag and drop the fields from the field list to the drop areas below the field list, as shown in Figure 8-2. If you just click the check box to select the fields, it will place text fields in the rows and any numeric values in the Values area. This can become quite annoying because it will place a field like Years in the Values area and treat it as a set of values to be summed. (Chapter 11 shows you how you can avoid this.)

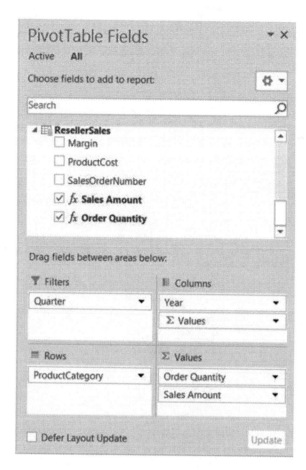

Figure 8-2. *Adding fields to the pivot table*

In order to add slicers to filter the pivot table, you need to go to the Insert tab in Excel and select the Slicer button. The next section looks at adding slicers and controlling multiple pivot tables with the same slicer.

Slicing the Data

To add a slicer to filter a pivot table, click the pivot table and on the Insert tab, select the Slicer button. You should see a pick list containing the fields in the Power Pivot data model (see Figure 8-3).

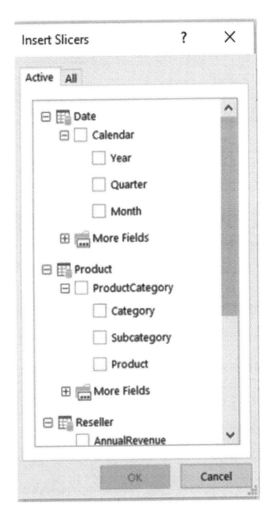

Figure 8-3. *Selecting the slicer field*

Because you had the pivot table selected when you inserted the slicer, it is automatically wired up to the pivot table. You can verify this by clicking the slicer and selecting the Slicer Tools Options tab (see Figure 8-4). You can use this tab to format the slicer and choose the Report Connections for the slicer.

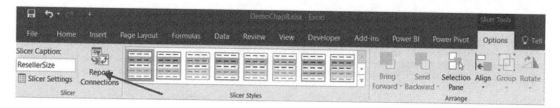

Figure 8-4. *Setting the slicer connections*

Figure 8-5 shows the Report Connections pick list for the slicer. Notice that the pivot table doesn't have to be on the same sheet as the slicer. The names of the pivot tables are the generic names given to them by Excel when they were created. As you add more pivot tables, it is a good idea to give them more meaningful names. If you click the pivot table and go to the PivotTable Tools Analyze tab, you will see a text box where you can change the name of the pivot table.

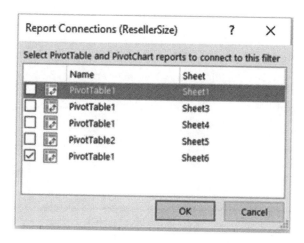

Figure 8-5. *Selecting connections for the slicer*

If you select the Slicer Settings button under the Slicer Tools Options tab, you launch the Slicer Settings window (see Figure 8-6) where you can change the name, caption, and sort order of the slicer. You can also choose how to show items with no data.

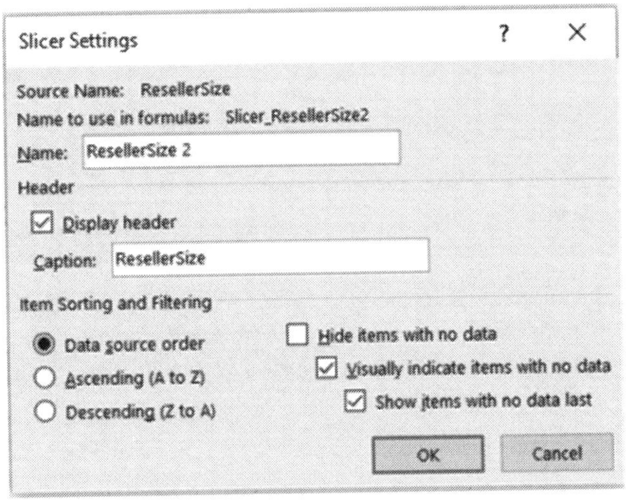

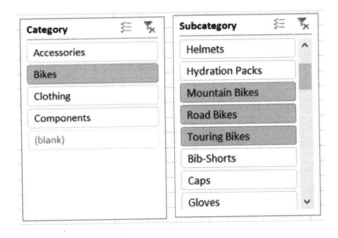

Figure 8-6. Changing the slicer settings

There are times when you need *cascading filters*, where one filter limits what can be chosen in the next filter. This is easy with slicers based on fields that are related in the model. When you select the related fields, the slicers are linked automatically for you. For example, Figure 8-7 shows a product category and product subcategory filter. If you select a product category, the corresponding product subcategories are highlighted.

Figure 8-7. Creating cascading filters using slicers

Adding Visualizations to a Pivot Table

To help identify trends, outliers, and provide insight into the data, you can add many types of visualizations to a pivot table. These include conditional formatting, data bars, and trend lines. Figure 8-8 shows a pivot table with data bars and conditional formatting.

Row Labels ▼	Order Quantity	Sales Amount	Margin
⊞ Accessories	2740	$60,086.05	$17,312.40
⊞ Bikes	4669	$3,699,096.26	($502,489.41)
⊞ Clothing	4967	$129,921.56	($3,853.94)
⊞ Components	5680	$1,453,875.07	$66,463.69
Grand Total	18056	$5,342,978.94	($422,567.26)

Figure 8-8. *Using conditional formatting and databars*

To create the visual formatting, select the data you want to format in the pivot table, and in the Home tab click the Conditional Formatting drop-down (see Figure 8-9). As you can see, you have a lot of options for creating conditional formatting. (In Figure 8-8 there is a Highlight Cells Rule that displays negative numbers in red.)

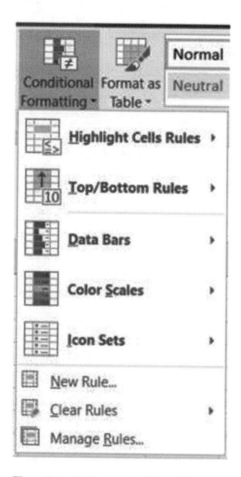

Figure 8-9. *Setting up conditional formatting*

Once you establish a rule, you can edit it by clicking the Manage Rules option and selecting the rule you want to edit. Figure 8-10 shows the various options you can set for a data bar formatting rule.

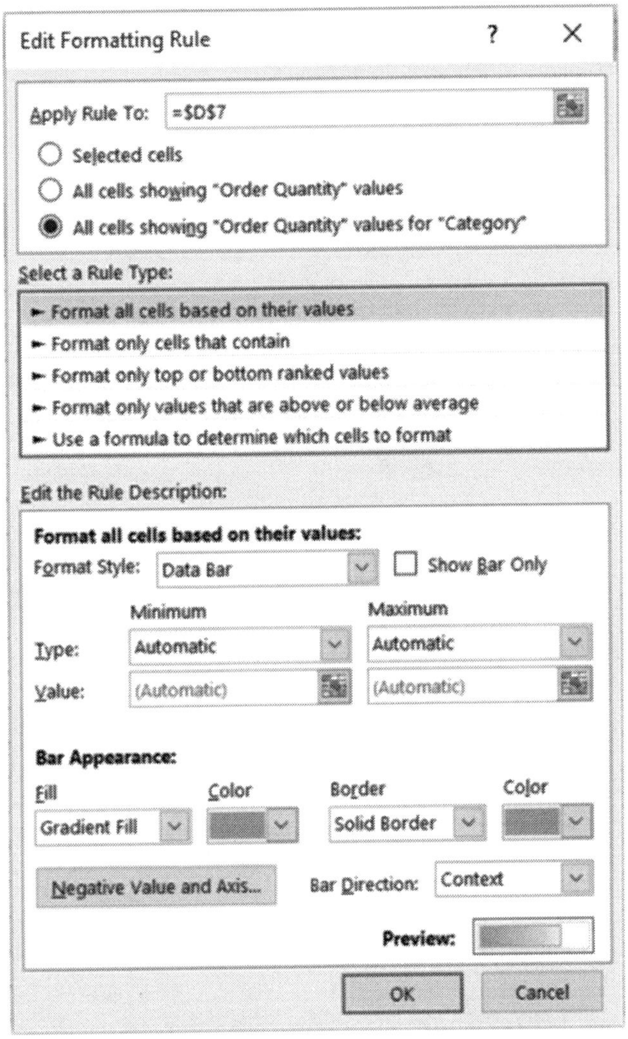

Figure 8-10. *Editing a data bar rule*

You can produce some interesting effects with the formatting rules. For example, the pivot table in Figure 8-11 shows a heat map used to quickly determine which months have good sales and which are bad.

Order Quantity	Column Labels ▼				
Row Labels ▼	Australia	Canada	France	Germany	United Kingdom
April	115	2861	628	541	750
August	415	5269	3252	1184	1350
December	901	3981	652	482	1505
February	110	2313	1444	504	562
January	103	1726	371	359	507
July	124	3794	890	756	1073
June	893	3827	625	427	1513
March	509	2428	376	286	1013
May	209	3824	2177	783	960
November	224	3885	2229	836	968
October	110	2848	659	615	829
September	1235	5005	1045	607	2163

Figure 8-11. *Creating a heat map with conditional formatting*

Another popular feature associated with pivot tables are spark lines. *Spark lines* are mini graphs that show the trend of a series of data. Figure 8-12 shows spark lines that display the sales trend across the four quarters of the year.

Year	2006 ▼				
Sum of SalesAmount	Column Labels ▼				
Row Labels ▼	1	2	3	4	Sales Trend
Large	$1,512,840.61	$1,673,185.81	$4,031,239.79	$2,895,748.58	
Medium	$690,013.60	$685,873.20	$1,253,354.23	$822,995.20	
Small	$1,866,331.83	$1,794,761.41	$3,595,645.41	$3,322,439.98	

Figure 8-12. *Using spark lines to show trends*

To create a spark line, highlight the values in the pivot table that contain the data and select the Sparklines button on the Insert tab. You then select the location of the spark line (see Figure 8-13). You have to choose between a line, a column, or a win/loss spark line.

Create Sparklines	? X
Choose the data that you want	
Data Range: C5:F5	
Choose where you want the sparklines to be placed	
Location Range: G5	
OK	Cancel

Figure 8-13. *Setting up a spark line*

Although adding visualizations to pivot tables can enhance your ability to analyze the data, many times the best way to spot trends and compare and contrast the data is through the use of charts and graphs. In the next section, you will see how charts and graphs are useful data analysis tools and how to add them to your analysis dashboards.

Working with Pivot Charts

Along with pivot tables, Excel has a robust set of charts and graphs available for you to use to analyze your data. Adding a pivot chart is very similar to adding a pivot table. On Excel's Insert tab, click the PivotChart drop-down. You have the option of selecting a single PivotChart or a PivotChart and PivotTable that are tied together (see Figure 8-14).

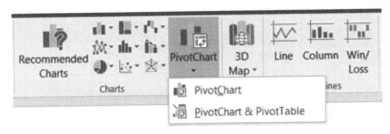

Figure 8-14. *Adding a pivot chart*

After selecting the pivot chart, you are presented with a window to select a data source and choose where you want to put the pivot chart (see Figure 8-15).

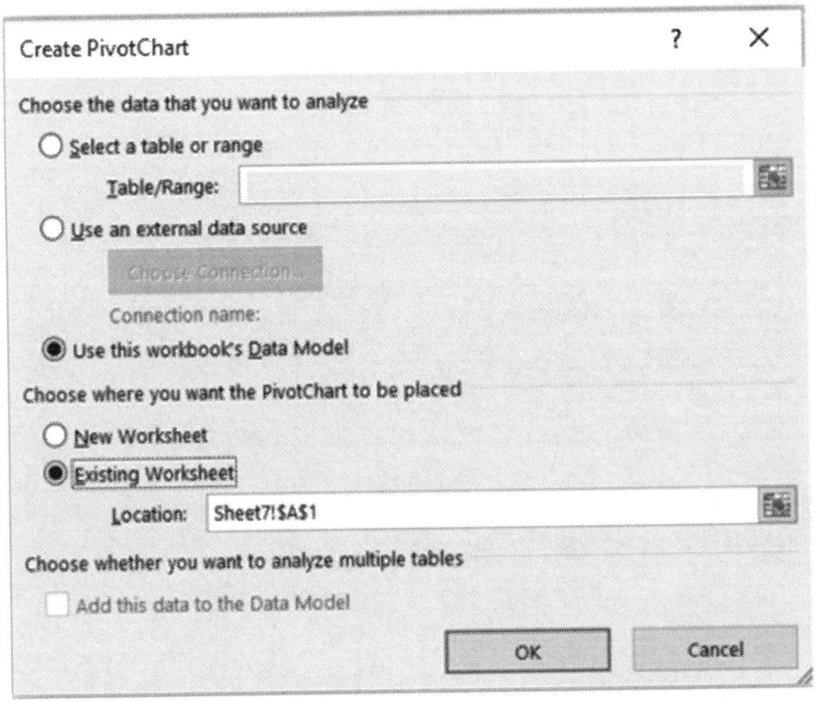

Figure 8-15. *Selecting a data source*

To select the Power Pivot model as the data source, click Use an external connection and click the Choose Connection button. In the Existing Connections window, select the Tables tab and select the Tables In Workbook Data Model (see Figure 8-16).

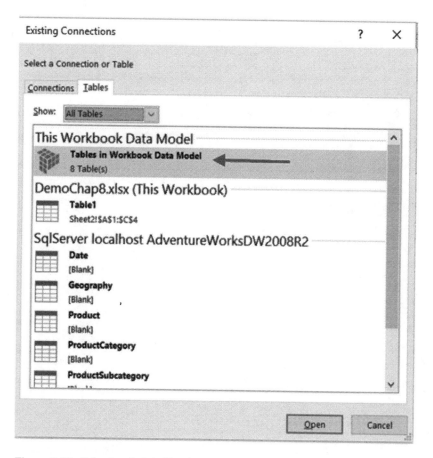

Figure 8-16. *Selecting the Workbook Data Model*

Once you select the data source, you are presented with a blank chart and the field selection box where you can drag and drop fields for the chart values and axis (see Figure 8-17).

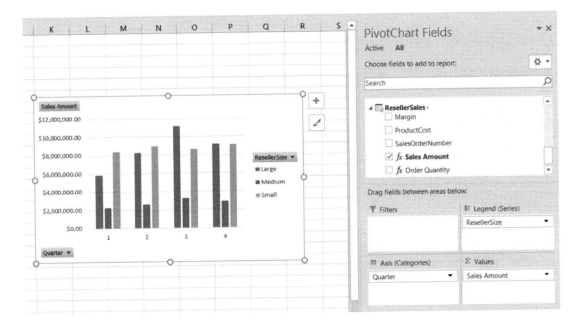

Figure 8-17. Creating a chart

By default, the chart is a column chart, but you can choose from many different types of charts. If you click the chart and select the PivotChart Tools Design tab, you can select the Change Chart Type button and choose from a variety of types (see Figure 8-18).

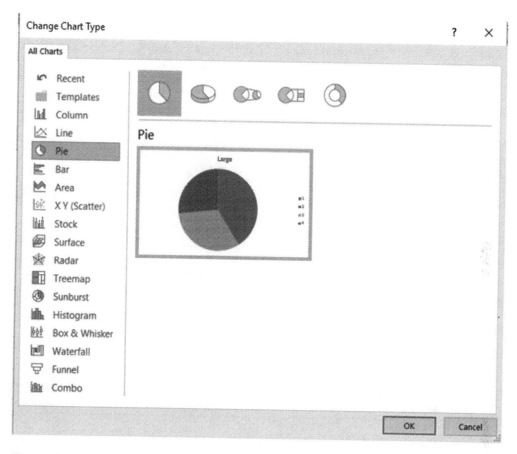

Figure 8-18. *Selecting a chart type*

Along with changing the chart type, the PivotChart Tools tabs offer you a vast assortment of design and formatting options you can use to customize the look and feel of your charts and graphs. It is definitely worth your time to play around with the tools and create various graphs to gain a better idea of the various options available.

Using Multiple Charts and Tables

When creating pivot tables and charts to display and make sense of the data, you often want to create a dashboard that easily allows you to determine performance. You may be interested in sales performance, network performance, or assembly-line performance. Dashboards combine visual representations, such as key performance indicators (KPIs), graphs, and charts, into one holistic view of the process. Although they are not technically considered dashboard tools, you can create some very compelling data displays using Excel with Power Pivot tables and charts that can then be displayed and shared in SharePoint.

When adding multiple charts and tables to a dashboard, you may want to link them together so they represent the same data in different ways. You also will probably want to control them with the same slicers so they stay in sync. The easiest way to do this is to add them using the Insert tab and selecting PivotChart & PivotTable (see Figure 8-19).

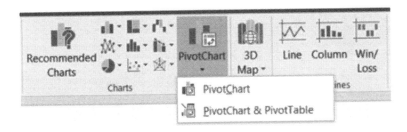

Figure 8-19. *Adding a pivot chart and a related pivot table*

Adding the pivot chart and pivot table in this way creates a link between them so that when you add a field to one, it adds the same field to the other. Also, when you add a slicer to the page, it automatically hooks up the slicer to both the pivot table and the pivot chart. Figure 8-20 shows a simple dashboard consisting of a linked pivot table, pivot chart, and slicer.

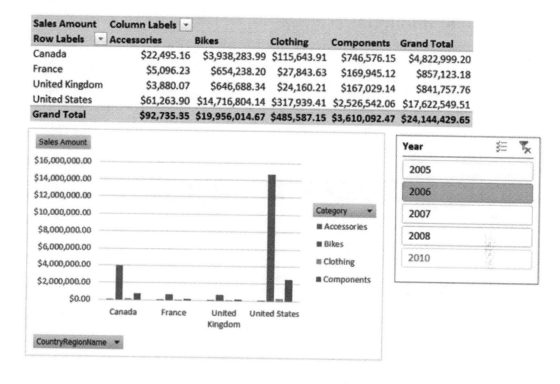

Sales Amount	Column Labels				
Row Labels	Accessories	Bikes	Clothing	Components	Grand Total
Canada	$22,495.16	$3,938,283.99	$115,643.91	$746,576.15	$4,822,999.20
France	$5,096.23	$654,238.20	$27,843.63	$169,945.12	$857,123.18
United Kingdom	$3,880.07	$646,688.34	$24,160.21	$167,029.14	$841,757.76
United States	$61,263.90	$14,716,804.14	$317,939.41	$2,526,542.06	$17,622,549.51
Grand Total	$92,735.35	$19,956,014.67	$485,587.15	$3,610,092.47	$24,144,429.65

Figure 8-20. *Creating a simple dashboard in Excel*

If you need to connect multiple charts together, open the Model Designer and select the PivotTable drop-down on the Home tab (see Figure 8-21). This also allows you to insert a flattened pivot table, which is useful for printing.

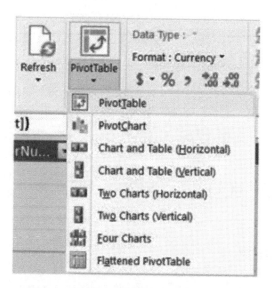

Figure 8-21. *Connecting multiple pivot charts*

Using Cube Functions

Using the built-in PivotChart and PivotTable layouts in Excel allows you to create compelling dashboards and provide great interfaces for browsing the data. There are times, though, when you may find yourself frustrated with some of the limitations inherent with these structures. For example, you can't insert your own columns inside the pivot table to create a custom calculation. You may also want to display the data in a non-tabular format for a customized report. This is where the Excel cube functions are really useful.

The Excel cube functions allow you to connect directly to the Power Pivot data model without needing to use a pivot table. The cube functions are Excel functions (as opposed to DAX functions) and can be found on the Excel Formulas tab under the More Functions drop-down (see Figure 8-22).

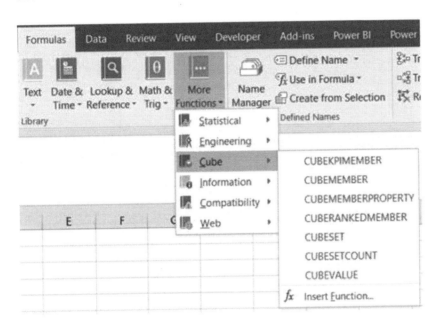

Figure 8-22. *Using cube functions to connect to the model*

The easiest way to see how these functions are used is to create a pivot table. On the PivotTable Tools Analyze tab, click the OLAP Tools drop-down and select the Convert To Formulas option (see Figure 8-23).

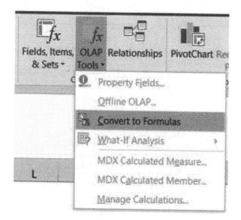

Figure 8-23. *Converting from a pivot table to cube functions*

Figure 8-24 shows the table after the conversion to cube functions. It uses the CUBEMEMBER function to return a member or *tuple* (ordered list) from the cube and the CUBEVALUE function to return an aggregated value from the cube.

		fx	=CUBEMEMBER("ThisWorkbookDataModel","[Product].[Category].&[Accessories]")						
	C	D	E	F	G	H	I		J
	Sales Amount	Column Labels							
	Row Labels	AU	CA	DE	FR	GB	US		Grand Total
	Accessories	$23,947.53	$118,127.35	$35,083.07	$48,031.73	$42,593.03	$303,515.23		$571,297.93
	Bikes	$1,323,820.73	$11,636,380.59	$1,543,015.65	$3,560,665.65	$3,405,747.21	$44,832,751.73		$66,302,381.56
	Clothing	$42,915.80	$378,947.63	$71,619.43	$128,092.22	$118,828.80	$1,037,436.95		$1,777,840.84
	Components	$203,651.31	$2,244,470.02	$334,269.89	$870,748.34	$711,839.79	$7,434,097.31		$11,799,076.66
	Grand Total	$1,594,335.38	$14,377,925.60	$1,983,988.04	$4,607,537.94	$4,279,008.83	$53,607,801.21		$80,450,596.98

Figure 8-24. *Using cube functions to retrieve values*

The following formula is used to return the column label for cell C4:

```
=CUBEMEMBER("ThisWorkbookDataModel","[Product].[Category].&[Accessories]")
```

The first parameter is the name of the connection to the data model, and the second parameter is the member expression.

The value in cell D4 is returned using the following formula:

```
=CUBEVALUE("ThisWorkbookDataModel",$C$2,$C4,D$3)
```

This formula uses cell references, but you can replace these with the cube functions contained in these cells:

```
=CUBEVALUE
(
    "ThisWorkbookDataModel",
    CUBEMEMBER("ThisWorkbookDataModel","[Measures].[Sales Amount]"),
    CUBEMEMBER("ThisWorkbookDataModel",
        "[Product].[Category].&[Accessories]"),
    CUBEMEMBER("ThisWorkbookDataModel",
        "[Geography].[CountryRegionCode].&[AU]")
)
```

Note that one of the parameters is the CUBEMEMBER function returning the aggregation you want the value of; the other parameters use the CUBEMEMBER to define the portion of the cube used in the aggregation.

You can now rearrange the values and labels to achieve the layout and formatting that you need (see Figure 8-25).

Sales	US	CA	GB
Total	$53,607,801	$14,377,926	$4,279,009
Bikes	$44,832,752	$11,636,381	$3,405,747
Components	$7,434,097	$2,244,470	$711,840
Total	$52,266,849	$13,880,851	$4,117,587
Others			
Accessories	$303,515	$118,127	$42,593
Clothing	$1,037,437	$378,948	$118,829

Figure 8-25. Rearranging the data

HANDS-ON LAB: CREATING THE BI INTERFACE IN EXCEL

In the following lab you will

- Add conditional formatting to a pivot table.

- Create a chart to help analyze data.

- Link together pivot tables and pivot charts.

- Use cube functions to display model data.

1. In the LabStarterFiles\Chapter8Lab1 folder, open the Chapter8Lab1.xlsx file. This file contains inventory and sales data from the test AdventureWorksDW database.

2. In Excel Sheet1, insert a Power Pivot table using the PivotTable button on the Insert tab. Select the Use An External Data Source and click the Choose Connection button. On the Tables tab of the Existing Connections window, select Tables In Workbook Data Model (see Figure 8-26).

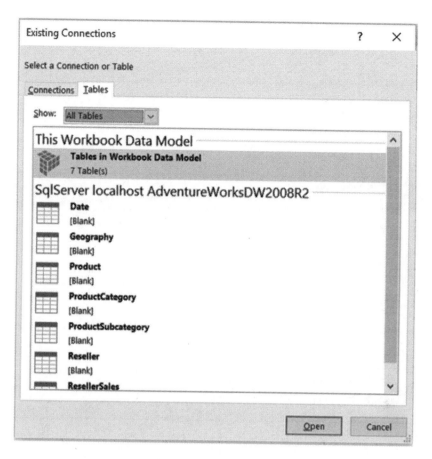

Figure 8-26. *Selecting the connection*

3. Add TotalQuantity, TotalSales, and TotalMargin from the ResellerSales table to the Values drop area in the Field List window. Add the Calendar hierarchy to the Row Labels drop area.

4. Note that some of the margins are negative. To bring attention to the negative values, you are going to format them in red.

5. Select a TotalMargin cell in the pivot table. On the Home tab, click the Conditional Formatting drop down. Select the Highlight Cells, Less Than option. Format the cells that are less than 0 with red text (see Figure 8-27).

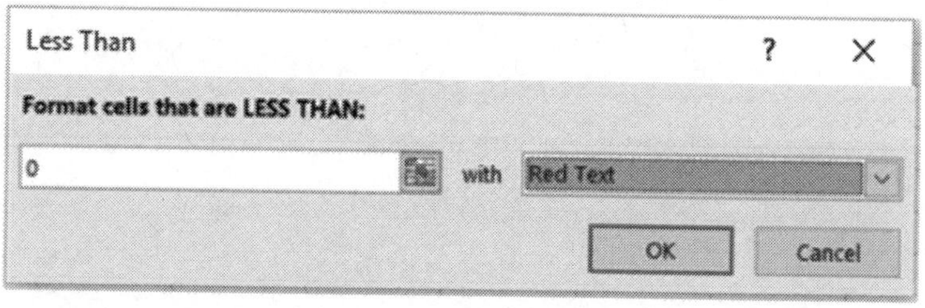

Figure 8-27. *Setting conditional formatting*

6. When finished, you should see an icon next to the selected cell. Click it and select the All Cells Showing TotalMargin Values option.

7. Select one of the TotalSales cells. This time, select the Data Bars under the Conditional Formatting drop-down. Select one of the gradient styles. After selecting the data bar, you should see a small icon next to the values. Click it and select the All Cells Showing TotalSales Values.

8. Your Pivot table should look similar to Figure 8-28. Expand the years and note that the formatting shows up for the quarters, months, and years.

Row Labels	▼	TotalQuantity	TotalSales	TotalMargin
⊞ 2005		10835	$8,065,435.31	$328,927.08
⊞ 2006		58241	$24,144,429.65	$323,401.79
⊟ 2007		100172	$32,202,669.43	($168,557.73)
⊞ 1		12307	$5,266,343.51	$193,324.41
⊞ 2		19466	$6,733,903.82	$298,556.44
⊟ 3		39784	$10,926,196.09	($710,603.34)
July		9871	$2,665,650.54	($181,857.11)
August		15139	$4,212,971.51	($250,821.21)
September		14774	$4,047,574.04	($277,925.03)
⊞ 4		28615	$9,276,226.01	$50,164.75
⊞ 2008		45130	$16,038,062.60	($13,288.53)
Grand Total		214378	$80,450,596.98	$470,482.60

Figure 8-28. Adding data bars to the pivot table

9. Open Sheet2 and on the Insert tab, select the PivotChart drop-down. From the drop-down, chose the pivot chart. Insert the chart on the current sheet using the Tables In Workbook Data Model connection.

10. In the Field List window, add the TotalSales from the ResellerSales table to the Values drop area and add the CountryRegionName from the Geography table to the Axis Fields drop area. You should see a column chart showing sales by country (see Figure 8-29).

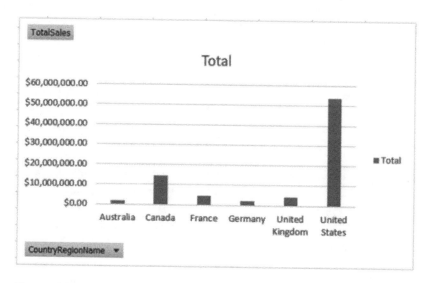

Figure 8-29. *Adding a column chart*

11. Select the column chart. You should see the PivotChart Tools tabs. In the Design tab, you can change the chart colors, layout, and chart type.

12. The Format tab lets you format the shapes and text in the chart. The Analyze tab lets you show/hide the field buttons.

13. Rename the title of the chart to *Sales By Country*. Hide the field buttons and delete the legend.

14. Right-click the vertical axis and select Format Axis. Under Axis Options, change the Display Units to Millions. Under the Number node, change the Category to Currency with zero decimal places. Your chart should look similar to Figure 8-30.

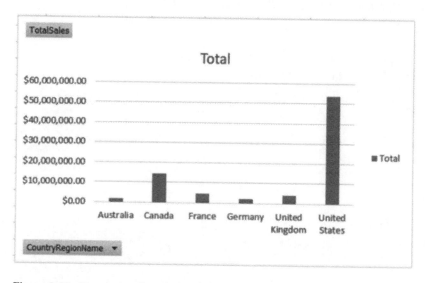

Figure 8-30. *Formatting the column chart*

15. Sometimes you want to see a data chart and a data table together. To do this, go to the Power Pivot Model Designer and on the Home tab, select the PivotTable drop-down. From the drop-down, chose the Chart And Table (Horizontal). Insert the chart and table on a new sheet.

16. Change the chart type to a pie chart. On the Field List window for the chart, add the TotalSales field to the Values drop area and the CountryRegionCode to the Axis Fields drop area.

17. Change the title of the chart to Sales By Country and remove the field button.

18. Change the Chart Layout on the Design tab to show values as % of total (see Figure 8-31).

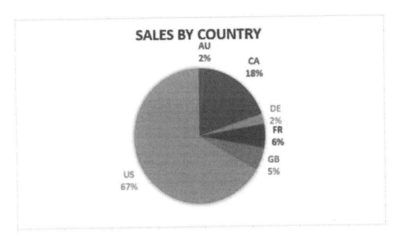

Figure 8-31. *Creating the sales pie chart*

19. Click the pivot table to bring up its Field List window. Add the ResellerSales TotalSales to the Values drop area. Add the Product Subcategory to the Row Labels drop area.

20. With the pie chart selected, insert a slicer for the product category and one for the year (see Figure 8-32). Verify that the slicers filter the pie chart but not the pivot table.

Figure 8-32. *Inserting the slicers*

21. Select the Year slicer and on the Slicer Tools Options tab, click the Report Connections button. Add the pivot table located on the same sheet as the pie chart. Repeat this for the category slicer.

22. Verify that the slicers filter both the chart and the pivot table. Your dashboard should look similar to Figure 8-33.

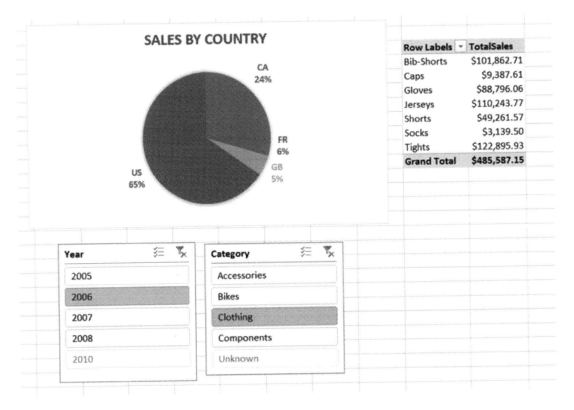

Figure 8-33. *Creating a dashboard*

23. Add a new sheet to the workbook. You are going to use cube functions to calculate the top product and top reseller in total sales. The final result should look similar to Figure 8-34.

	A	B	C	D
1		TotalSales		
2		Top Reseller	Brakes and Gears	$877,107.19
3		Top Products	Mountain-200 Black, 38	$3,105,726.66

Figure 8-34.

24. Add the following code in B1 to select the TotalSales measure:

```
=CUBEMEMBER("ThisWorkbookDataModel","[Measures].[TotalSales]")
```

25. In B2, use the following function to get the set of resellers ordered by TotalSales descending—you will use this set to select the top reseller:

```
=CUBESET("ThisWorkbookDataModel",
    "[Reseller].[ResellerName].children","Top Reseller",2,B1)
```

26. In B3, use this function to get the set of products ordered by TotalSales descending:

```
=CUBESET("ThisWorkbookDataModel",
    "[Product].[Product].children","Top Products",2,B1)
```

27. In C2, use the CUBERANKEDMEMBER function to get the top reseller from the set returned by the function in B2:

```
=CUBERANKEDMEMBER("ThisWorkbookDataModel",B2,1)
```

28. In C3, use the CUBERANKEDMEMBER function to get the top product from the set returned by the function in B3:

```
=CUBERANKEDMEMBER("ThisWorkbookDataModel",B3,1)
```

29. In D2, use the CUBEVALUE function to get the total sales of the top reseller found in C2. Notice you have to concatenate the name of the reseller found in C2 to the [Reseller].[ResellerName] attribute in the Power Pivot model:

```
=CUBEVALUE("ThisWorkbookDataModel",
    "[Reseller].[ResellerName].&["& C2 &"]","[Measures].[TotalSales]")
```

30. Using a similar CUBEVALUE function, you can get the total sales value for the top product:

```
=CUBEVALUE("ThisWorkbookDataModel",
    "[Product].[Product].&[" &C3&"]","[Measures].[TotalSales]")
```

Summary

As you saw in this chapter, Excel is a feature-rich environment for creating dashboards using pivot tables and pivot charts. At this point, you should feel comfortable creating pivot tables and pivot charts using your workbook model as a data source. You also used Excel cube functions to query the model directly without needing to use a pivot table. Although this chapter covered the basics to get you started, you have a lot more to learn about Excel and how it can help you analyze your data. I encourage you to dig deeper into these features.

The next chapter looks at another useful tool for self-service data analysis: Power BI. Power BI provides a rich interactive interface for users to explore the data. Although Excel is a great tool for business analysts, it can be difficult to share your results with the rest of the business. This is where Power BI shines. You can build models, reports, and dashboards that are hosted and delivered through the web. They can easily be viewed on mobile devices and can be accessed anywhere there is an Internet connection. The best part is Power BI uses the same tools to get data and build models you have used in Excel: Power Query and Power Pivot.

PART II

**Building Interactive Reports
and Dashboards with Power BI
Desktop**

CHAPTER 9

■ ■ ■

Introducing Power BI Desktop

As you have seen in the previous chapters, Excel is an excellent tool for developing analytic solutions. It works quite well for individual analysis and sharing the results among a small group of consumers. But where it is lacking is when you need to share the results of your analysis with a broader audience. This is where the Power BI portal and Power BI Desktop come in to play. The Power BI portal is where you can host, share, and secure interactive dashboards and reports with others. Power BI Desktop is where you create the model and visuals on which the dashboards in the portal are based. The great thing about Power BI Desktop is that it uses the same tools you've been using in Excel. It uses Power Query to get, clean, and shape the data. It then uses a model designer similar to Power Pivot to construct a tabular model on top of which you create interactive visuals.

This chapter introduces you to using Power Query and Model Designer in Power BI Desktop. Hopefully this will be a familiar experience and be fairly intuitive after working with these tools in Excel.

After reading this chapter you will be familiar with the following:

- Setting up the Power BI environment

- Getting, cleaning, and shaping data

- Creating table relationships

- Adding calculations and measures

- Incorporating time-based analysis

Setting Up the Power BI Environment

Power BI Desktop is a free tool used to create visual analytic dashboards that can be hosted in the Power BI portal or in SQL Server Reporting Services 2016 server. You can download it from the Power BI website at `https://powerbi.microsoft.com/en-us/desktop/`. If you sign up for the Power BI portal or have an Office 365 subscription, you can log into the portal and download the tool (see Figure 9-1).

© Dan Clark 2017
D. Clark, *Beginning Power BI*, DOI 10.1007/978-1-4842-2577-6_9

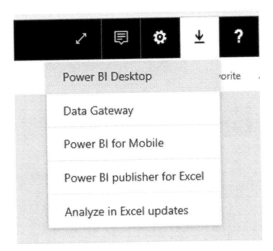

Figure 9-1. *Downloading Power BI Desktop*

Once you download Power BI Desktop, click Run to begin the install. Follow the installation wizard, which is fairly straightforward. After the install, launch Power BI Desktop. Click the File tab ➤ Options and Settings ➤ Options to set up the various options for your development environment (see Figure 9-2).

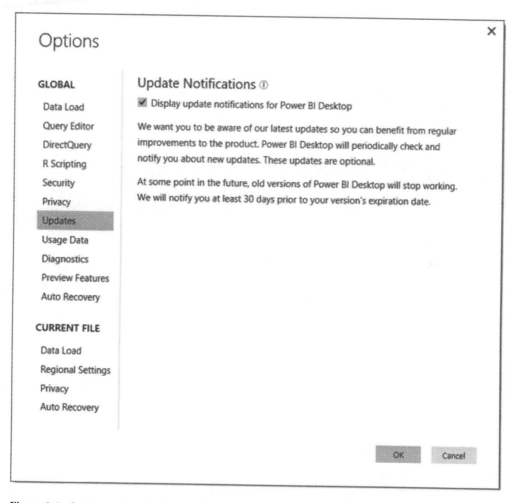

Figure 9-2. *Setting options for Power BI Desktop*

One thing to be aware of is that Microsoft has been releasing monthly updates that include new features. Make sure you get notified and install these updates when they are released. You can check which version you have installed by selecting the Diagnostics tab in the Options window. If you are like me and want to play with upcoming features that are still in development, you can turn them on in the Preview Features tab in the Options window.

Now that you have installed and set up the Power BI Desktop development environment, you are ready to get some data.

Getting, Cleaning, and Shaping Data

The Power Query interface in Power BI Desktop is very similar to the Power Query interface used in Excel (discussed in Chapter 3). As discussed in that chapter, the first step in creating a data analytics solution is importing data. When you open Power BI Desktop and start a new report project, you will see a Home tab where you can start importing the data (see Figure 9-3).

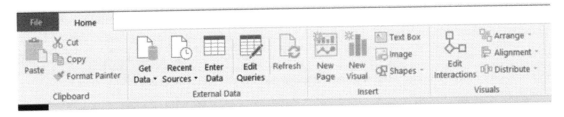

Figure 9-3. *The Home tab in Power BI Desktop*

If you select the Get Data drop-down in the External Data area of the tab, you can see the variety of data sources available to you. You can get data from the Web, files, databases, and a variety of other sources (see Figure 9-4).

Figure 9-4. Some of the many data sources available in Power BI Desktop

The type of data source you choose will dictate what information you need to supply to gain access to the data source. For example, a SQL Server database requires logon credentials, whereas a CSV file requires the file path. Once you connect to a data source, a window will launch displaying a sample of the data. Figure 9-5 shows the data contained in a CSV file.

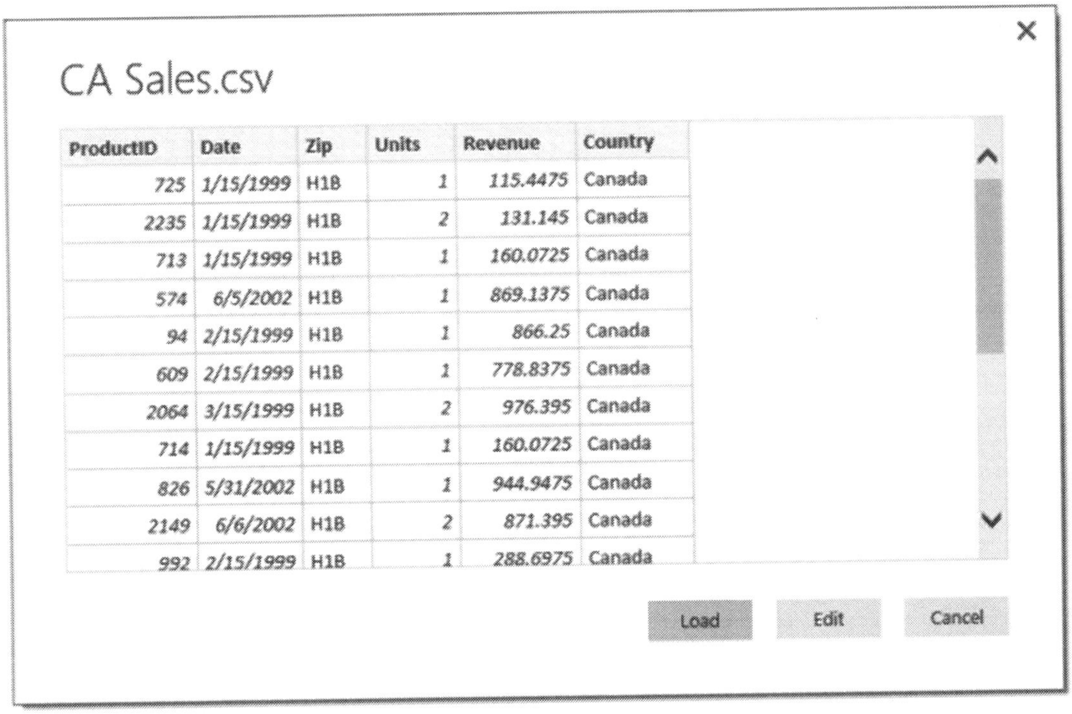

CA Sales.csv

ProductID	Date	Zip	Units	Revenue	Country
725	1/15/1999	H1B	1	115.4475	Canada
2235	1/15/1999	H1B	2	131.145	Canada
713	1/15/1999	H1B	1	160.0725	Canada
574	6/5/2002	H1B	1	869.1375	Canada
94	2/15/1999	H1B	1	866.25	Canada
609	2/15/1999	H1B	1	778.8375	Canada
2064	3/15/1999	H1B	2	976.395	Canada
714	1/15/1999	H1B	1	160.0725	Canada
826	5/31/2002	H1B	1	944.9475	Canada
2149	6/6/2002	H1B	2	871.395	Canada
992	2/15/1999	H1B	1	288.6975	Canada

Load   Edit   Cancel

Figure 9-5. *Data from a CSV file*

After previewing the data, you can either load it directly into the data model or edit the query before loading the data. Clicking Edit will launch the familiar Power Query Editor where you can transform, cleanse, and filter the data before importing it into the data model (see Figure 9-6).

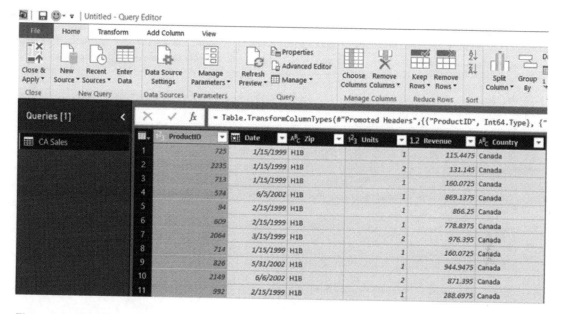

Figure 9-6. *The Power Query Editor*

Some common transformations you will perform are removing duplicates, replacing values, removing error values, and changing data types. When you launch the Query Editor window, you will see several steps may have been applied for you, depending on the data source. For example, Figure 9-7 shows data from a CSV file. In the applied steps list, you can see Promoted Headers and Changed Type have been applied.

Figure 9-7. *Steps added to the query*

Often you need to replace values from source systems so that they are consistent. For example, some rows have a country abbreviation, and some have the full name. You can easily replace these values as the data is imported by selecting the column and then selecting the Replace Values transformation in the menu. This launches a window to enter the values to find and what to replace them with (see Figure 9-8).

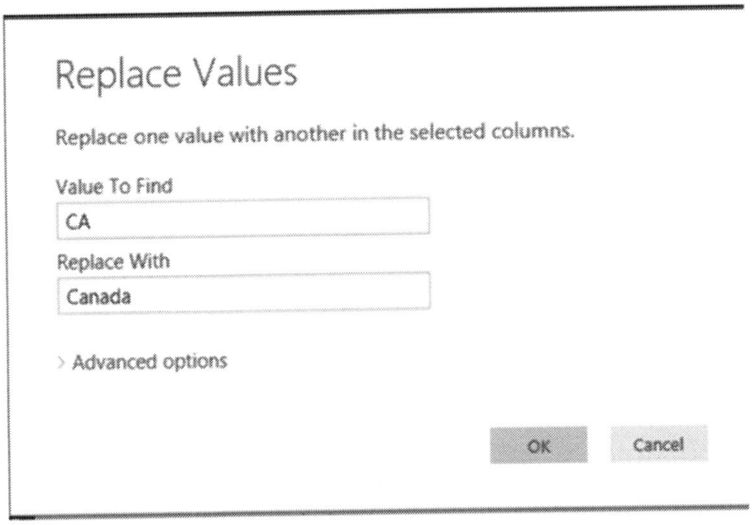

Figure 9-8. Replacing values in a column

As you apply the data transformations and filtering, the Query Editor lists the steps you have applied. This allows you to organize and track the changes made to the data. You can rename, rearrange, and remove steps by right-clicking the step in the list (see Figure 9-9).

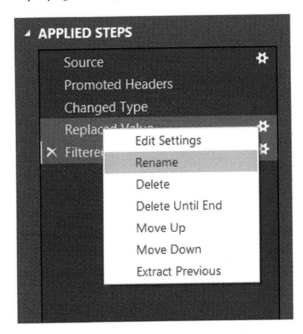

Figure 9-9. Managing the query steps

Sometimes a source may provide you with data in a column that needs to be split up among several columns. For example, you may need to split the city and state, or the first name and last name. To do this, select the column in the Query Editor and on the Home tab choose Split Column. You can either split the column by a delimiter or by the number of characters (see Figure 9-10).

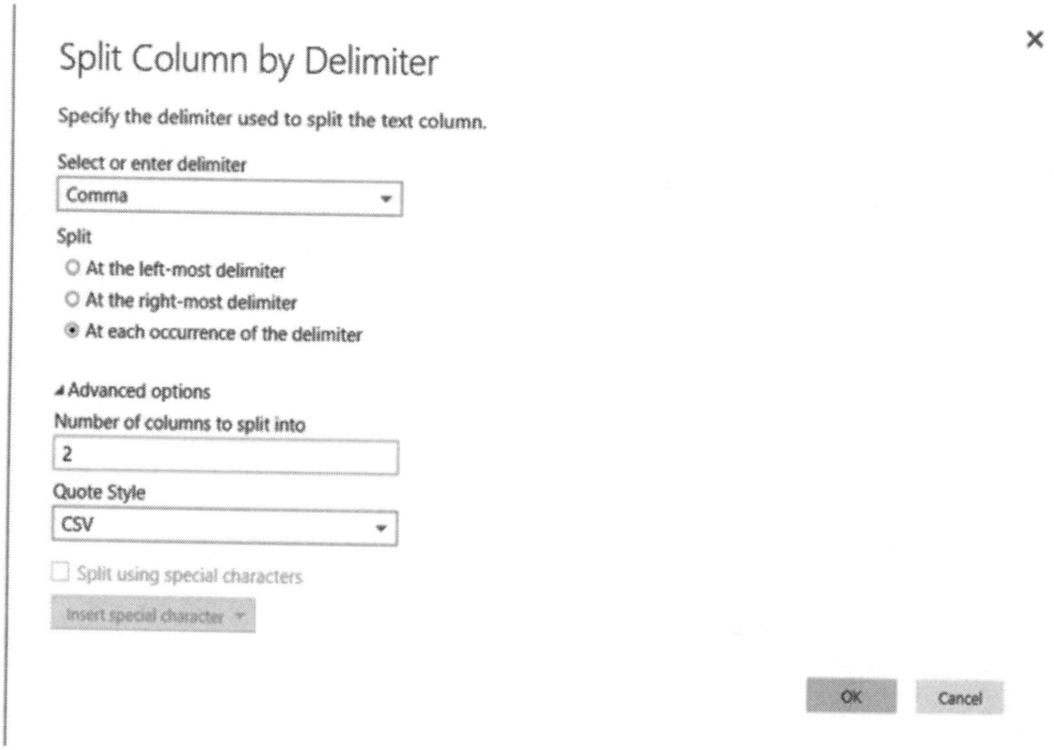

Figure 9-10. Splitting a column using a delimiter

Another common scenario is the need to group and aggregate data. For example, you may need to roll the data up by month or sales territory, depending on the analysis. To aggregate and group the data in the Query Editor, select the column you want to group by and select the Group By transform in the Home tab. You are presented with a Group By Editor window (see Figure 9-11).

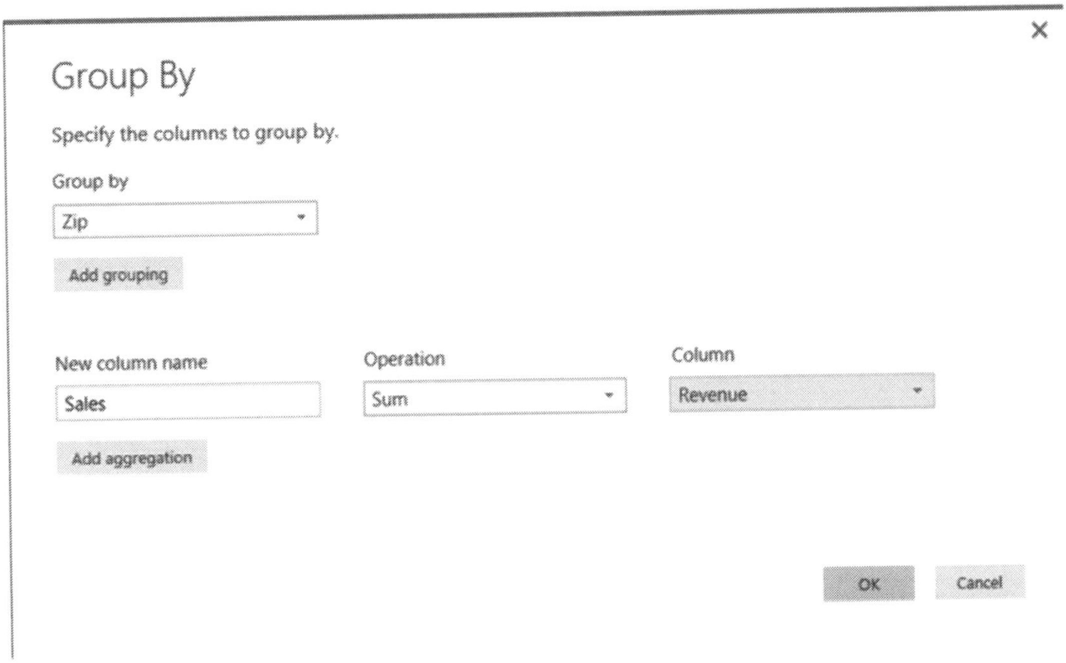

Figure 9-11. Grouping data in Power Query

These are just a few of the data-shaping features exposed by the Power Query Editor. (For a more detailed discussion of Power Query, refer to Chapters 3 and 13.)

Once you have cleaned and shaped the data, you can select the Close & Apply option on the Home tab. This will load the tables into the data model and close the Power Query Editor. You are now ready to work with the data model to create table relations, calculated columns, and measures.

Creating Table Relationships

After the data tables are imported into the data model, you are ready to create the relationships between the tables. As discussed in Chapter 4, typically you want to set up your model in a star schema where the fact table is in the center of the star, and the dimension tables are related to the fact table by keys (see Figure 9-12).

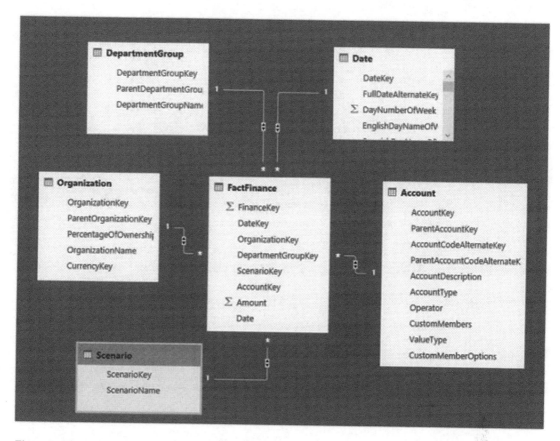

Figure 9-12. *A typical star schema*

The fact table contains numbers that you need to aggregate. For example, in the finance table you have the amount, which is a monetary value that needs aggregated. In a sales fact table, you may have sales amount and item counts. In a human resources system, you might have hours worked. The dimension tables contain the attributes that you are using to categorize and roll up the measures. For example, the financial measures are classified as profit, loss, and forecasted. You want to roll the values up to the department and organization level and you want to compare values between months and years.

To create a relationship between two tables in the Power BI model, you open up the Power BI Desktop and switch to the Relationships view (see Figure 9-13). By default, Power BI Desktop will try to auto-detect new relationships when data is loaded. This works well if the data comes from a database where the relationships have already been defined. If your data comes from many different sources, you may want to turn this off under the File ➤ Options ➤ Data Load settings.

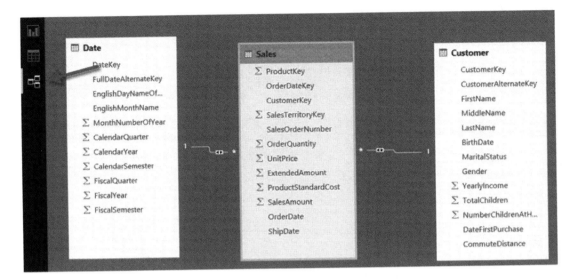

Figure 9-13. Switching to the Relationships view

To manage the relationships between the tables, select the Manage Relationships button in the Home tab. This launches the Manage Relationships window where you can create new relationships, edit existing relationships, and delete existing relationships (see Figure 9-14).

Figure 9-14. Managing table relationships

Clicking the Edit button presents you with the Edit Relationship window (see Figure 9-15). This is where you set the tables and key columns used that define the relationship along with the cardinality and cross filter direction. Cardinality can be many-to-one, one-to-one, or one-to-many. This indicates how rows match in the tables. For example, one customer can have many sales, but a sale can only match one customer. A one-to-one relationship example could be a product table and a product marketing table. For every product listed in the main table, there is a corresponding row in the product marketing table containing a product description and image.

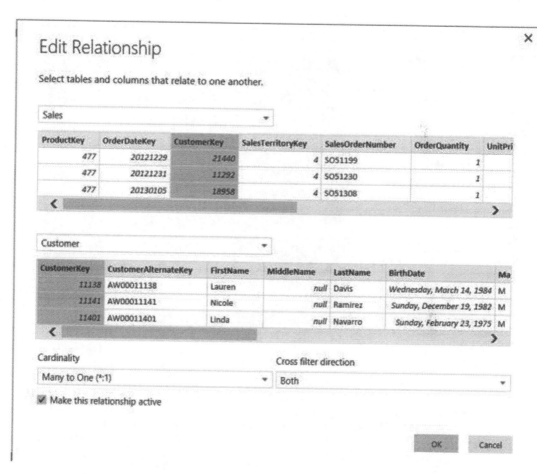

Figure 9-15. *Editing a table relationship*

Figure 9-16 shows the resulting relationship in the Relationship view. If you click the relationship arrow, the two key columns of the relationship are highlighted. You can also see there is a one-to-many relationship between the Customer table and the Sales table. The *many* side is indicated by the * symbol.

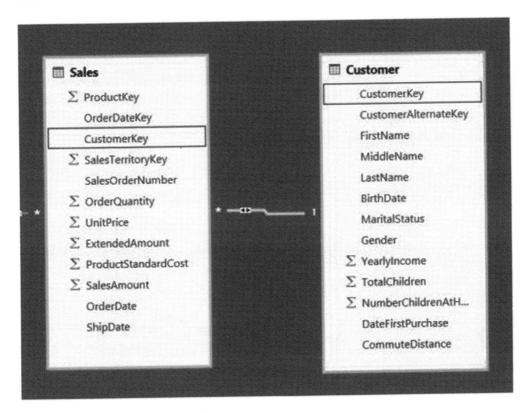

Figure 9-16. *Viewing a relationship in the Relationship view*

The two arrows on the relationship line indicate cross filtering works in both directions. When you create a filter on the Customer table, it will also filter the corresponding rows of the Sales table. In addition, applying a filter on the Sales table will apply the filter through to the Customer table. This is important when you have a many-to-many relationship between two tables. Figure 9-17 shows a many-to-many relationship between the Product table and the Customer table.

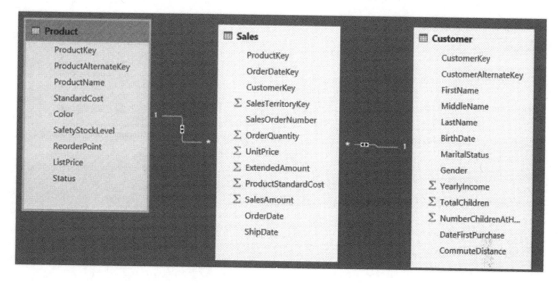

Figure 9-17. *Filtering across multiple tables*

After setting up the relationships between the tables in the model, you are ready to add any calculations and measures that will aid in the data analysis.

Adding Calculations and Measures

As you saw in Chapters 5 and 6, one of the most important aspects of creating a solid data model involves adding calculated columns and measures that aid in the analysis of the data. For example, you may need to calculate years of service for employees or concatenate first and last names. Just like Power Pivot in Excel, Power BI Desktop uses DAX to create calculated columns and measures.

To create a calculated column, select the Data view tab in the Power BI Desktop editor. Next, select the table to add the calculated column to, click the New Measure drop-down on the Home tab, and choose the New Column option (see Figure 9-18).

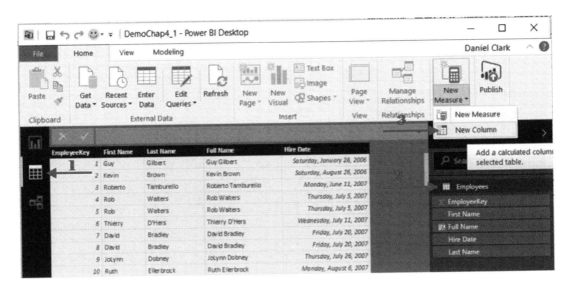

Figure 9-18. *Adding a calculated column*

In the formula bar, enter the DAX formula for the column and select the check mark to complete entering the formula (see Figure 9-19). One slight difference between Power Pivot in Excel and the Power BI Desktop is that you include the name of the column in the formula bar.

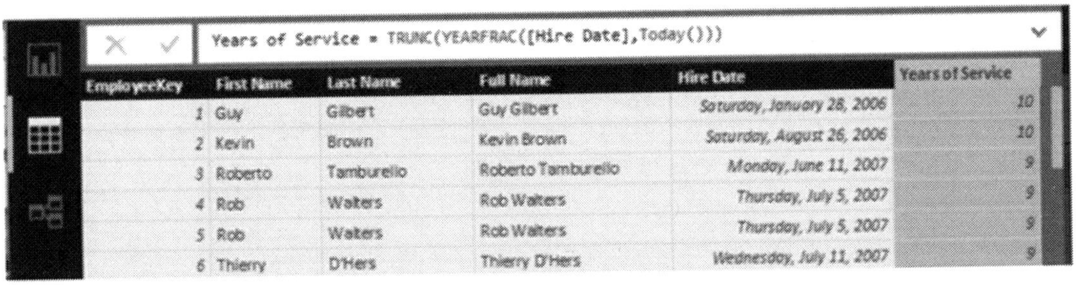

Figure 9-19. *Entering the DAX formula*

To create a measure, you go through the same process as creating a calculation, except choose the New Measure option (refer to Figure 9-18). After selecting the New Measure, you will see Measure = added to the formula bar. Enter the DAX code to create the measure. For example, entering the following code will create a measure called Sales (see Figure 9-20).

```
Sales = Sum([SalesAmount])
```

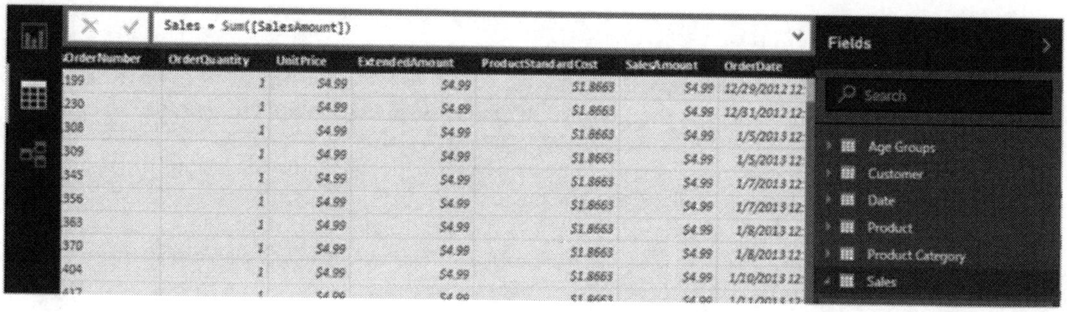

Figure 9-20. *Creating a measure*

The difference between a calculated column and a measure is that calculated columns are pre-calculated and stored in the model. Measures are calculated when filters are applied to them and are recalculated every time different filters are applied. So, the more calculated columns you have, the greater the size of your Power BI Desktop file, and the more measures you have, the greater the memory needed to update the report. Remember, though, that the tabular model is based on an in-memory analytics engine and columnar storage (discussed in Chapter 1). It is designed to load all the data into memory and make calculations on the fly. As such, you are better off limiting the amount of calculated columns in favor of measures.

Context plays an important role when creating measures in the tabular model. Unlike static reports, Power BI reports are designed for dynamic analysis by the client. When the user interacts with the report, the context changes, and the values are recalculated. Knowing how the context changes and how it affects the results is essential to being able to build and troubleshoot DAX formulas.

As discussed in Chapter 6, there are three types of context you need to consider: row, query, and filter. The row context comes into play when you are creating a calculated column. It includes the values from all the other columns of the current row as well as the values of any table related to the row. Query context is the filtering applied to a measure in a visual. When you drop a measure into a visual, the DAX query engine examines any filters applied and returns the value associated with the context. Filter context is added to the measure using filter constraints as part of the formula. The filter context is applied in addition to the row and query contexts. You can alter the context by adding to it, replacing it, or selectively changing it using filter expressions. For example, you could use the following formula to calculate sales of all products:

```
All Sales = CALCULATE(Sum(Sales[SalesAmount]),ALL('Product'))
```

The filter context would clear any product filter implemented by the query context. You could then use this measure to create a more complex measure, like percentage of all product sales:

```
Sales Ratio = Divide([Sales],[All Sales],0)
```

A common type of data analysis involves comparing measures over time, and that involves importing or creating a date table, as you will see next.

Incorporating Time-based Analysis

As discussed in Chapter 7, one of the most common types of data analysis is comparing values over time. For example, you may want to look at sales this quarter compared to sales last quarter or month-to-date (MTD) help desk tickets compared to last month. DAX contains many functions that help you create the various datetime based analysis you may need. For example, you can use the following expressions to calculate the sum of the sales and the sales year-to-date (YTD) values:

```
Total Sales = SUM([SalesAmount])
YTD Sales = TOTALYTD([Total Sales],'Date'[Datekey])
```

In order to use the built-in time intelligence functions in DAX, you need to have a date table in your model for the functions to reference. The only requirement for the table is that it needs a distinct row for each day in the date range you are interested in looking at. Each of these rows needs to contain the full date of the day. The date table can and often does have more columns, but it doesn't have to. You can either import a date table from the source if one is available or use the DAX Calendar function. To use the Calendar function, on the Modeling tab click the New Table button. In the formula bar, enter the CALENDAR function with the appropriate date range or the CALENDARAUTO function, which looks at the model and determines the correct date range (see Figure 9-21).

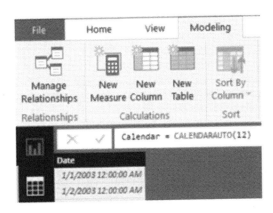

Figure 9-21. *Creating a date table*

After creating the date table, you can use DAX to create additional calculated columns such as month, year, and weekday. The final step is to create a relationship between the date table and the table that contains the values you want to analyze.

Now that you are familiar with using Power Query and the Model Designer in Power BI Desktop, it's time to get your hands dirty and complete the following hands-on lab. This lab will help you become familiar with working with the Power BI Desktop editor.

HANDS-ON LAB: CREATING THE DATA MODEL IN POWER BI DESKTOP

In the following lab you will

- Import data.

- Clean and shape the data.

- Create table relationships.

- Add calculated columns and measures.

1. If not already installed, download and install Power BI Desktop from
   https://powerbi.microsoft.com/en-us/desktop/.

2. Open Power BI Desktop and dismiss the startup screen. On the Home tab, select
   Edit Queries.

3. In the Query Editor, click the New Source drop-down and choose the CSV option.
   Navigate to the SF311Calls.csv in the LabStarterFiles\Chapter9Lab1 folder. Open
   the file and click OK to open it up in the Query Editor. You should see the Query
   Editor window with San Francisco call center data, as shown in Figure 9-22.

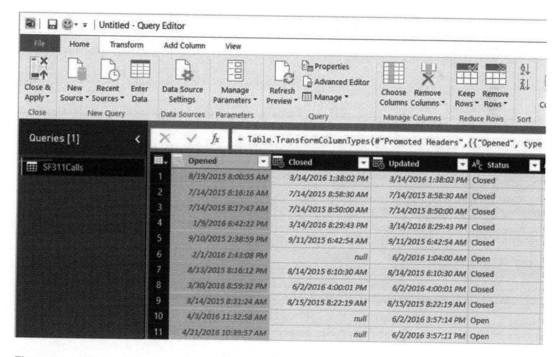

Figure 9-22. The Query Editor window with call center data

4. In the Applied Steps list, if the Query Editor didn't automatically add the transform to set the first row as headers, add it now.

5. Check the types of each column to see whether the Query Editor updated the Opened, Closed, and Updated columns to a datetime data type. The rest of the columns should be the text data type.

6. Filter the data so that it doesn't include data from the Test Queue, zzRPD, and zzTaxi Commission agencies (see Figure 9-23).

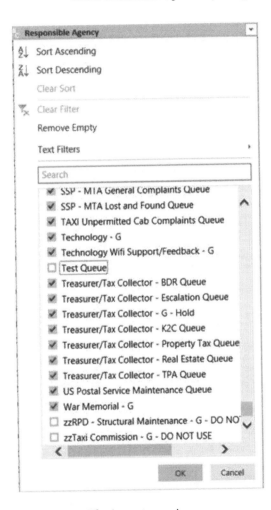

Figure 9-23. Filtering out agencies

7. Select the Opened column and filter the rows so that Opened is after 12/31/2014.

8. Select the Opened column again and on the Add Column tab select the Time drop-down. Select Hour and then Start Of Hour. Rename the new column to Hour Opened.

9. Change the data types of the Opened and Closed columns to Date (no time) and the Hour Opened to the Time data type.

10. In the Home tab, select the New Source drop-down and choose the CSV option. Navigate to the file Categories.csv in the LabStarterFiles\Chapter9Lab1 folder. Open the file and click OK to open it in the Query Editor.

11. Under the Transform tab, select Use First Row As Headers.

12. Select the SF311Calls query and merge it with the Categories query using the Category column (See Figure 9-24).

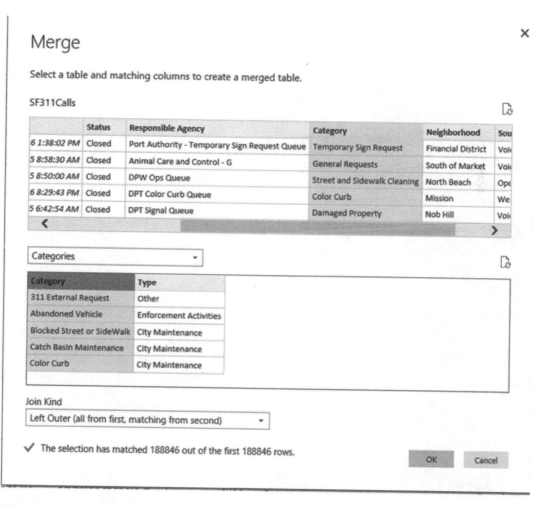

Figure 9-24. *Merging queries*

13. Expand the resulting column and select the Type field (see Figure 9-25).

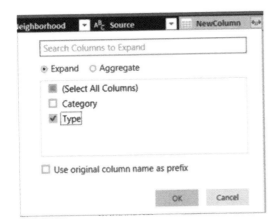

Figure 9-25. *Expanding the new column*

14. In the query list, right-click on the Categories query and uncheck the Enable Load option (see Figure 9-26).

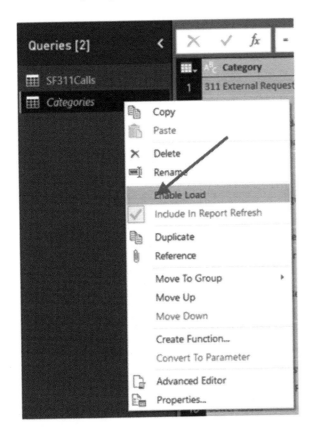

Figure 9-26. *Disabling the load to the model*

15. On the Home tab, select Close & Apply.

16. To create a date table on the Modeling tab, click the New Table button. In the formula bar, enter the following code:

```
Date = CALENDAR(Date(2015,01,01),Date(2016,09,31))
```

17. In the Data view, select the Date table. Change the Date column's data type to Date and format it to show MM/dd/yyyy.

18. Create a calculated column for Year, Month No, Month, and Day using the following code:

```
Year = [Date].[Year]
Month No = [Date].[MonthNo]
Month = [Date].[Month]
Day = FORMAT([Date],"ddd")
```

19. Sort the Month column by the Month No column and hide the Month No in Report view.

20. Switch to the Relationship view and create a relationship between the SF311Calls table and the Date table using the Date Opened and Date columns (see Figure 9-27).

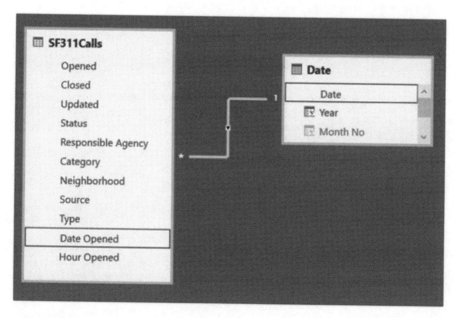

Figure 9-27. Creating a relationship between tables

21. In the Data view, select the SF311Calls table. Add a Days Open column using the following formula:

```
Days Open = DATEDIFF([Opened],if(ISBLANK([Closed]),max
('Date'[Date]),[Closed]),DAY)
```

22. Add the following measures to the SF311Calls table:

```
Number of Cases = COUNTROWS('SF311Calls')
Previous Month Number of Cases = Calculate([Number of Cases],
PARALLELPERIOD('Date'[Date],-1,MONTH))
```

23. Save the file as Chapter9Lab1 and close Power BI Desktop.

Summary

This chapter introduced you to Power BI Desktop. In particular, you now know how to get and shape data and build a data model using Power BI Desktop. Most of the concepts were a review of topics covered in previous chapters. The purpose of this chapter was for you to gain familiarity with using Power BI Desktop and discovering how similar it is to working in the Excel BI toolset. In the next chapter, you will look at creating interactive reports in Power BI Desktop. This is where Excel and Power BI diverge. Power BI has a very rich set of interactive visuals you can use to view and gain insight into the data. These visuals can then be deployed to the Power BI portal, where they can be used to create powerful dashboards and shared with others.

CHAPTER 10

■ ■ ■

Creating Reports with Power BI Desktop

In the last chapter, you saw how to import, clean, and shape data using Power BI Desktop. In addition, you created the data model and augmented it with calculated columns and measures. In this chapter you will investigate some of the common visualizations used to create reports in Power BI Desktop. You will become familiar with how to control visual interactions, along with report filtering. You will build standard visualizations such as column, bar, and pie charts. In addition, you will look at line and scatter charts. Finally, you will investigate how to use maps to analyze data geographically.

After completing this chapter, you will be able to

- Create tables and matrices.

- Construct bar, column, and pie charts.

- Build line and scatter charts.

- Create map-based visualizations.

■ **Note** For copies of color figures, go to Source Code/Downloads at `https://github.com/Apress/beginning-power-bi-2ed`.

Creating Tables and Matrices

Although it is one of the most basic types of data visualization, a *table* is still one of the most useful ways to look at your data. This is especially true if you need to look up detailed information. To create a visual on the report page, select the Report view. In this view, you will see a Visualizations toolbox and a Fields list on the right side of the designer (see Figure 10-1).

© Dan Clark 2017
D. Clark, *Beginning Power BI*, DOI 10.1007/978-1-4842-2577-6_10

Figure 10-1. *The Visualization toolbox*

Selecting the table visualization will reveal a Values drop area where you will drag fields from the Fields list and drop them into the Values area. This will create a table with the fields as columns. Figure 10-2 shows a table displaying customer contact information.

Full Name	AddressLine1	City	State/Province	Country/Region	Phone
Aaron Adams	4116 Stanbridge Ct.	Downey	California	United States	417-555-0154
Aaron Alexander	5021 Rio Grande Drive	Kirkland	Washington	United States	548-555-0129
Aaron Allen	6695 Black Walnut Court	Sooke	British Columbia	Canada	648-555-0141
Aaron Baker	8054 Olivera Rd.	Renton	Washington	United States	488-555-0125
Aaron Bryant	2325 Candywood Ct	Redwood City	California	United States	754-555-0137
Aaron Butler	9761 Darnett Circle	Lebanon	Oregon	United States	466-555-0180
Aaron Campbell	3310 Harvey Way	Bellflower	California	United States	187-555-0177
Aaron Carter	3450 Rio Grande Dr.	Woodland Hills	California	United States	180-555-0167
Aaron Chen	4633 Jefferson Street	Los Angeles	California	United States	969-555-0160
Aaron Coleman	3393 Alpha Way	Santa Monica	California	United States	914-555-0128
Aaron Collins	6767 Stinson	Santa Cruz	California	United States	170-555-0177
Aaron Diaz	9413 Maria Vega Court	Melton	Victoria	Australia	1 (11) 500 555-0130
Aaron Edwards	663 Contra Loma Blvd.	Beverly Hills	California	United States	355-555-0115
Aaron Evans	5623 Detroit Ave.	Daly City	California	United States	150-555-0128
Aaron Flores	8225 Northridge Road	Edmonds	Washington	United States	831-555-0184
Aaron Foster	4461 Centennial Way	Newton	British Columbia	Canada	477-555-0181
Aaron Gonzales	4247 Bellows Ct	Novato	California	United States	647-555-0136
Aaron Gonzalez	1431 Semillon Circle	Grossmont	California	United States	628-555-0119

Figure 10-2. Customer contact information

When you combine a table with the automatic filtering you get with Power BI, this becomes a great way to look up customers based on their demographic data. When you select the table in the view, you will see a Filters area in the Visualizations toolbox (see Figure 10-3). The fields in the table will show up automatically in the table filter list. To add a field to the filter list that you want to filter on but don't want to show up in the table, just drag the field from the Fields list to the Filters area. Along with visual level filters, you can filter all visuals on a page and all visuals on all pages of the report.

Figure 10-3. *Filtering a table*

If you click the Format tab in the Visualizations toolbox (signified by a paint roller), you will see a pretty extensive set of formatting options available (see Figure 10-4). Figure 10-5 shows a formatted table using one of the built-in styles.

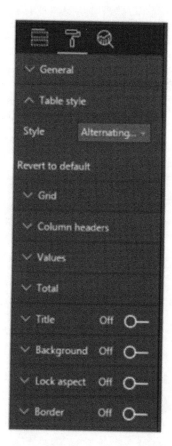

Figure 10-4. *Table formatting options*

Full Name	AddressLine1	City	State/Province	Country/Region	Phone
Aaron Adams	4116 Stanbridge Ct.	Downey	California	United States	417-555-0154
Aaron Alexander	5021 Rio Grande Drive	Kirkland	Washington	United States	548-555-0129
Aaron Allen	6695 Black Walnut Court	Sooke	British Columbia	Canada	648-555-0141
Aaron Baker	8054 Olivera Rd.	Renton	Washington	United States	488-555-0125
Aaron Bryant	2325 Candywood Ct	Redwood City	California	United States	754-555-0137
Aaron Butler	9761 Darnett Circle	Lebanon	Oregon	United States	466-555-0180
Aaron Campbell	3310 Harvey Way	Bellflower	California	United States	187-555-0177
Aaron Carter	3450 Rio Grande Dr.	Woodland Hills	California	United States	180-555-0167
Aaron Chen	4633 Jefferson Street	Los Angeles	California	United States	969-555-0160
Aaron Coleman	3393 Alpha Way	Santa Monica	California	United States	914-555-0128
Aaron Collins	6767 Stinson	Santa Cruz	California	United States	170-555-0177
Aaron Diaz	9413 Maria Vega Court	Melton	Victoria	Australia	1 (11) 500 555-0130
Aaron Edwards	663 Contra Loma Blvd	Beverly Hills	California	United States	355-555-0115

Figure 10-5. *A formatted table*

221

Unfortunately, at the time of this writing, you can't implement any conditional formatting, such as showing negative values in red. But new features are added monthly, so that may show up soon.

A matrix is similar to a table in that it contains rows and columns, but instead of showing detail-level records, it aggregates data up by the fields displayed in the row and column headers. When you create a pivot table in Excel, it is essentially a matrix. You can format a matrix just like the table. You also have the option to show or hide the totals. Figure 10-6 shows a matrix with the row totals tuned on and the column totals turned off.

Year	Quarter	Specialty Bike Shop	Value Added Reseller	Warehouse
2011	1	$357,680.11	$1,199,250.53	$1,992,095.75
	2	$484,307.26	$1,489,610.61	$2,053,162.46
	3	$716,261.89	$2,285,904.14	$1,949,919.95
	4	$450,750.76	$2,348,904.76	$2,864,954.49
	Total	$2,009,000.02	$7,323,670.04	$8,860,132.65
2012	1	$727,802.20	$3,417,922.30	$4,142,979.63
	2	$456,549.73	$3,193,907.21	$2,906,114.44
	3	$360,229.08	$3,071,804.48	$2,382,046.55
	4	$462,170.37	$3,312,605.14	$3,759,500.42
	Total	$2,006,751.39	$12,996,239.12	$13,190,641.03
2013	1	$740,099.94	$4,074,733.82	$5,727,827.66
	2	$782,759.64	$3,738,212.53	$4,135,685.28
	3	$660,560.24	$3,636,572.44	$3,347,546.96
	4	$515,396.78	$2,980,561.30	$3,234,877.56
	Total	$2,698,816.59	$14,430,080.10	$16,445,937.47
Total		$6,714,568.00	$34,749,989.26	$38,496,711.15

Figure 10-6. *Matrix showing sales amount by quarter and reseller type*

One feature missing from the current implementation of the matrix is the ability to expand and collapse by the various row and column headers. Hopefully this will be added soon.

In addition to wanting to see aggregated values in a matrix, you often want to show these values using a visual representation such as a bar, column, or pie chart. The next section looks at creating those.

Constructing Bar, Column, and Pie Charts

Some of the most common data visualizations used to compare data are the bar, column, and pie charts. A bar chart and a column chart are very similar. The bar chart has horizontal bars where the x-axis is the value of the measure, and the y-axis contains the categories you are comparing. For example, Figure 10-7 shows a bar chart comparing sales by country.

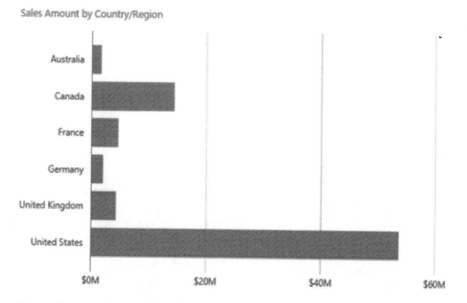

Figure 10-7. *Bar chart comparing sales by country*

The column chart switches the axes so that the measure amounts are on the y-axis and the categories are on the x-axis. For example, the bar chart in Figure 10-7 can just as easily be displayed as a column chart, as shown in Figure 10-8.

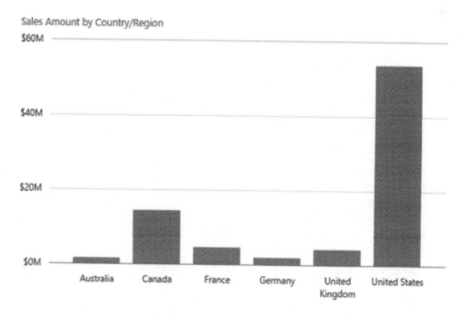

Figure 10-8. *A column chart comparing sales by country*

There are three types of bar or column charts to choose from: stacked, 100% stacked, and clustered. Figure 10-8 is a stacked column chart that doesn't have a field for the legend. If you drag the Year field to the Legend drop area, it changes the visualization to the one shown in Figure 10-9. Note that the values for each year are stacked on top of each other.

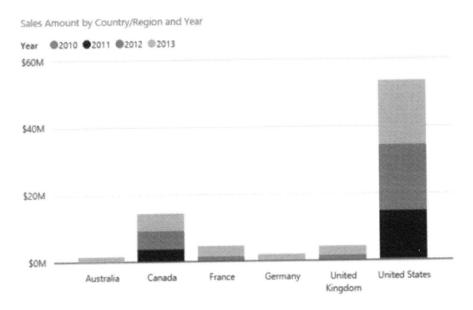

Figure 10-9. *Creating a stacked column chart*

Although the stacked column chart shows absolute values, you can change it to a 100% stacked chart to show relative values in terms of percentages. In Figure 10-10, the Country field is moved to the legend and the Year field is placed on the axis. It also has data labels set as Visible for easier comparisons.

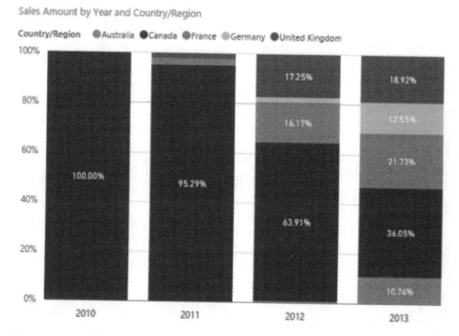

Figure 10-10. *Creating a 100% stacked column chart*

A clustered column chart moves the columns for the various countries side by side instead of stacking them on top of one another. Figure 10-11 shows the same information as Figure 10-9 but as a clustered column chart.

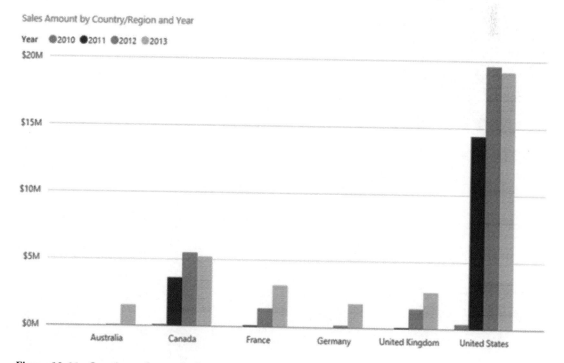

Figure 10-11. *Creating a clustered column chart*

With Power BI Desktop, you have lots of control over the layout of the charts. On the Format tab in the Visualization toolbox, you can control things such as Title, Legend, and Data colors (see Figure 10-12).

Figure 10-12. *Controlling the legend layout and data colors*

A nice feature associated with the bar and column charts is the ability to add reference lines to aid in the data analysis. If you select the Analytics tab in the Visualizations toolbox (see Figure 10-13), you see the various lines you can add. Figure 10-14 shows a column chart with the average line displayed.

Figure 10-13. *Adding reference lines to a chart*

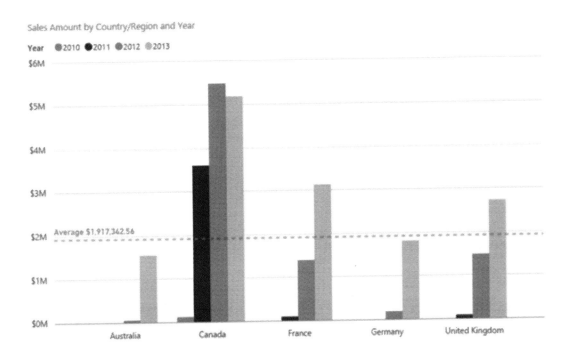

Figure 10-14. *Displaying the average reference line*

As with most visualizations, in Power View you get automatic filtering and sorting capabilities. For example, if you select the chart and click the ellipses in the upper right corner of the chart, you get the option to change the sorting by sales amount instead of by country name (see Figure 10-15).

Figure 10-15. *Changing the sorting of a column chart*

Pie charts are similar to stacked column or stacked bar charts in that they allow you to compare the measures for members of a category and also the total for the category. Figure 10-16 shows a pie chart comparing sales of different types of resellers.

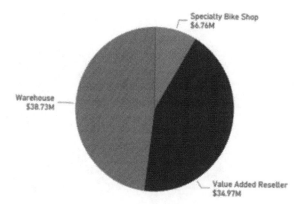

Sales Amount by Business Type

Figure 10-16. *Comparing data using a pie chart*

Just as with column and bar charts, you have lots of control over the layout of the pie chart, including data labels, data colors, and positioning of the title and the legend.

Although bar, column, and pie charts are great for comparing aggregated data for various categories, if you want to spot trends in the data, line and scatter charts are a better choice. You will investigate these types of charts next.

Building Line and Scatter Charts

A line chart is used to look at trends across equal periods. The periods are often time units consisting of hours, days, months, and so on. The time periods are plotted along the x-axis, and the measurement is plotted along the y-axis. Figure 10-17 shows order quantity by month. Each line represents a different year. Using this chart, you can easily spot trends, such as order quantities being up in 2013 while the overall trend is very similar to 2012.

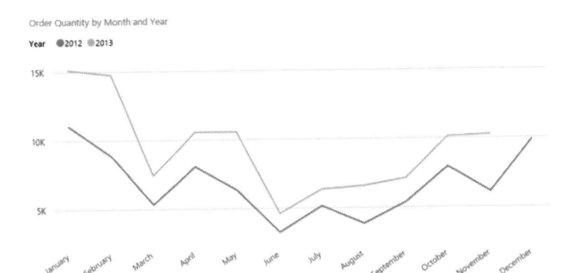

Figure 10-17. *Spotting trends using a line chart*

If you need to compare trending of two measures at the same time, you can use a scatter chart. Scatter charts plot one measure along the y-axis and the other along the x-axis. To create a scatter chart, select a category field and two numeric fields—for example, reseller name (category), sales amount (numeric), and sales profit (numeric). Figure 10-18 shows the resulting scatter chart.

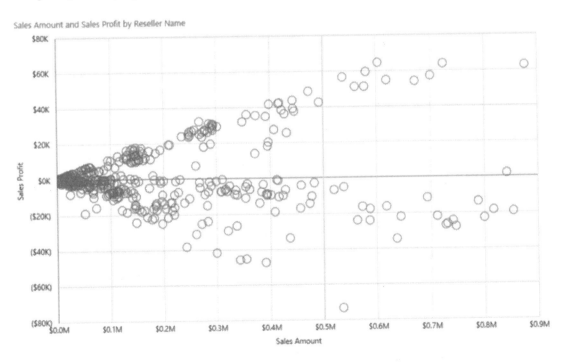

Figure 10-18. *Comparing data in a scatter chart*

Using a scatter chart, you can easily spot trends and outliers that don't follow the trend.

If you look at the Field drop area for the scatter chart (see Figure 10-19), you see both Size and Legend drop areas. You can add another measure to the Size drop box and another category to the Legend drop box.

Figure 10-19. *Adding size and color to a scatter chart*

Once you add the size axis to the scatter chart, it becomes a bubble chart. Figure 10-20 shows a bubble chart where the size of the bubble represents the number of employees of the reseller, and the color represents the reseller's business type.

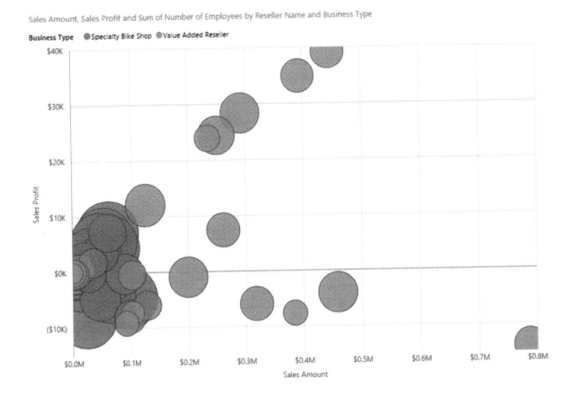

Figure 10-20. *Comparing data in a bubble chart*

If you take a look at the drop area for the scatter chart, you should see another drop box labeled Play Axis. You can drop a time-based field in this box, which results in a play axis being placed below the scatter chart. A *play axis* allows you to look at how the measures vary over time. It allows you to play, pause, and retrace the changes as you perform your analysis. If you click one of the bubbles in the chart, you can see a trace of the changes that occurred over the time period. Figure 10-21 shows a bubble chart that can be used to analyze how sales for different countries compare over time.

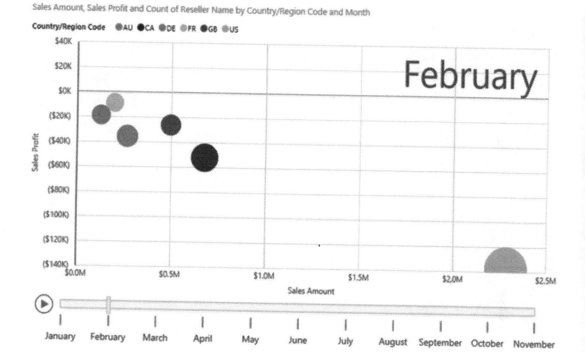

Figure 10-21. *Adding a play axis to a bubble chart*

In addition to the standard visualizations for comparing data, Power BI Desktop allows you to look at data geographically using maps. You will see how to create map-based visualizations in the next section.

Creating Map-Based Visualizations

One of the nice features of Power BI is that it can use map tiles to create visualizations. If your data contains a geographic field such as city, state/province, and country, it's very easy to incorporate the data into a map. You can tell whether a field can be geo-located by a globe icon in the field list (see Figure 10-22).

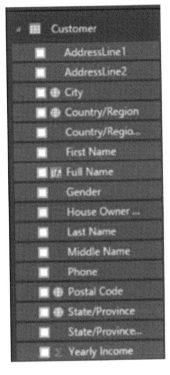

Figure 10-22. *The globe icon indicates fields that can be mapped.*

There are currently two types of maps in Power BI: map and filled map. When you use a map, the locations show up on the map as bubbles with sizes indicating the value of the measure. Figure 10-23 shows number of customers by city, where the map is zoomed in to the Bay Area in Northern California.

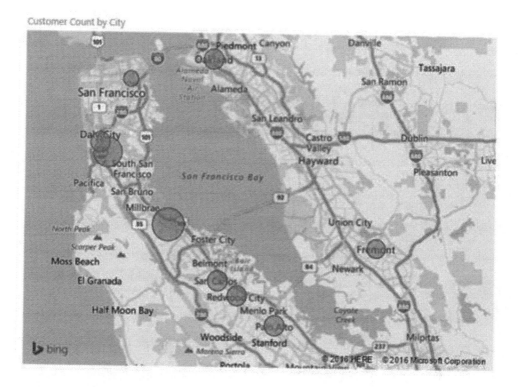

Figure 10-23. *Viewing data on a map*

If you look at the Field drop areas of the map, you should see Longitude and Latitude drop boxes; this feature allows you to create precise location points on the map. There is also a Legend drop area where you can drop a category field. That will convert the bubbles on the map into pie charts showing each category (see Figure 10-24).

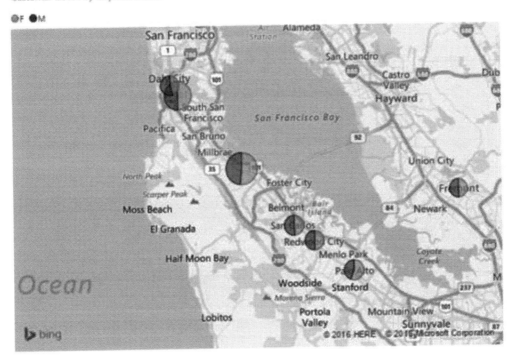

Figure 10-24. *Adding a category to the map*

A filled map uses geo-spatial areas rather than bubbles on the map. Common areas used are continent, country, region, state, city, or county. Figure 10-25 shows the number of customers in the Western states of the United States. The darker the shading, the larger the number of customers for the state.

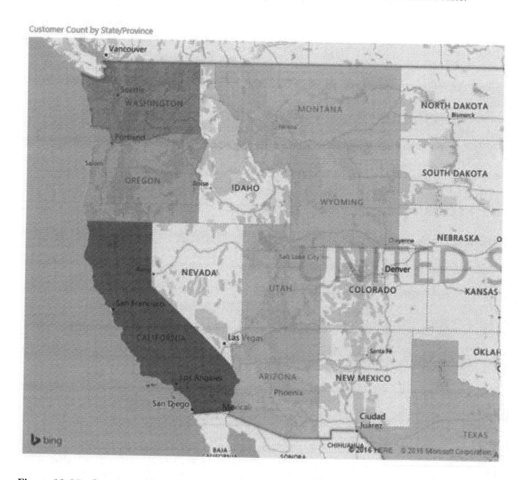

Figure 10-25. *Creating a filled map*

Another type of map (that is currently in preview but should be released by the time this book is published) is the shape map. Shape map visuals are based on ESRI/TopoJSON maps. They give you the ability to use custom maps that you can create, such as geographical, seating arrangements, floor plans, and more. Figure 10-26 shows the number of customers in various San Francisco neighborhoods.

Figure 10-26. Using custom shapes

Up to this point, you have created each of the visualizations as a standalone chart or graph. One of the strengths of Power BI is its ability to tie these visualizations together to create interactive reports for data exploration.

Linking Visualizations in Power BI

A great feature of Power BI is that if the data model contains a link between the data used to create the various visualizations, Power BI will use the relationship to implement interactive filtering. *Interactive filtering* is when the process of filtering one visualization automatically filters a related visualization. For example, Figure 10-27 shows a bar chart that displays sales for the different product categories from the Adventure Works sample database and a column chart that shows various countries' sales.

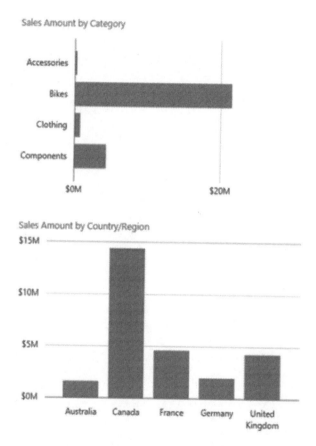

Figure 10-27. *Adding related visualizations to the same page*

Because the Sales table is related to the SalesTerritory table and the Product table, if you select one of the Product category bars, it will highlight the bar chart to show sales for that category (see Figure 10-28).

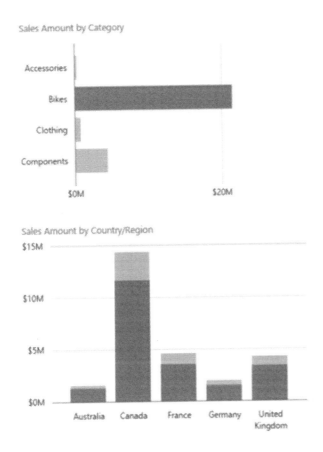

Figure 10-28. *Interactive filtering of related visualizations*

The filtering works both ways, so you can click one of the columns in the lower chart, and it will filter the top chart to show sales for that country. This interactive filtering works for most types of visualizations available in Power BI. Figure 10-29 shows a bubble chart and a table. When you click a bubble, the table is filtered to show the detail records that make up the bubble values.

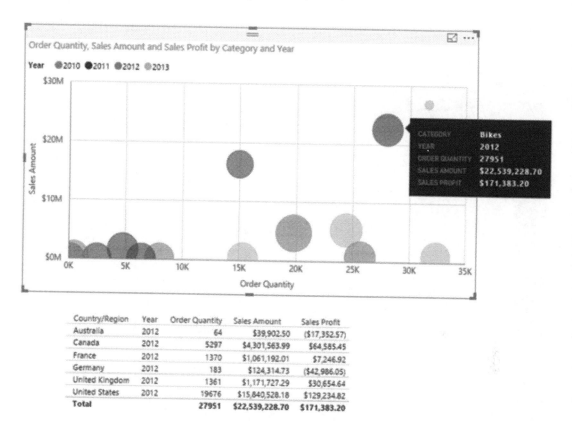

Country/Region	Year	Order Quantity	Sales Amount	Sales Profit
Australia	2012	64	$39,902.50	($17,352.57)
Canada	2012	5297	$4,301,563.99	$64,585.45
France	2012	1370	$1,061,192.01	$7,246.92
Germany	2012	183	$124,314.73	($42,986.05)
United Kingdom	2012	1361	$1,171,727.29	$30,654.64
United States	2012	19676	$15,840,528.18	$129,234.82
Total		27951	$22,539,228.70	$171,383.20

Figure 10-29. Filtering to show the details that make up the bubble values

You can control the visual interactions between visuals by selecting a visual and then clicking the Format tab. The other visuals on the page will then display three icons (see Figure 10-30). Clicking the first one will cause it to filter, clicking the second will cause it to highlight as in Figure 10-28, and clicking the third icon will turn off the interaction.

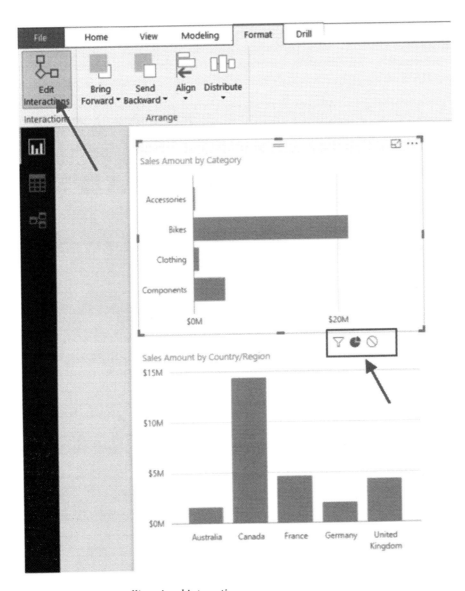

Figure 10-30. Controlling visual interaction

Along with built-in visual interaction, another powerful feature of Power BI visuals is the ability to drill down and up through hierarchies, the topic of the next section.

Drilling Through Visualizations

One of the nice features built-in to most Power BI visualizations is the ability to drill down and up through the various detail levels. This is useful when you have hierarchies such as month, quarter, and year, or products, categories, and subcategories. To enable drilling, just place the different levels of the hierarchy in the appropriate well, depending on the visual. Figure 10-31 shows a hierarchy placed in the Axis well of a columnar chart. You can control the drill through actions using the icons at the top of the chart.

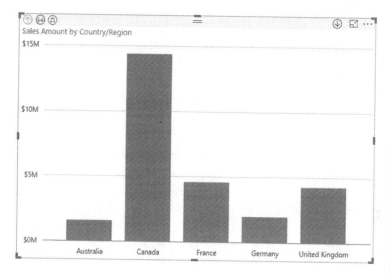

Figure 10-31. Enabling drilling on a column chart

You can also control the drill-through action under the Visual Tools ➤ Drill tab (see Figure 10-32). You have the option of showing the next level or expanding to the next level. For example, if you select Show Next Level and select Canada, it will drill through to show provinces in Canada. If you select expand to the next level, it will show all states/provinces for all countries.

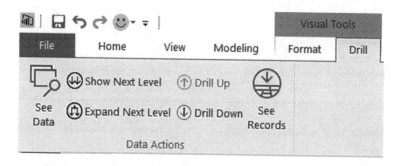

Figure 10-32. Controlling drill-through actions

Now that you have seen how to create some of the visualizations available in Power BI, it is time to get some hands-on experience by creating a few.

HANDS-ON LAB: CREATING VISUALIZATIONS IN POWER BI DESKTOP

In the following lab you will

- Create standard visuals.

- Create a map-based visualization.

- Explore visual interactions.

1. In the LabStarterFiles\Chapter10Lab1 folder, open the Chapter10Lab1.pbix file. This file contains 311 call center data for San Francisco.

2. On the left side of the designer, select the Report view. You should see a blank report page.

3. In the Visualizations toolbox, select the Table visualization. Create a table that lists Type of request, Ave Days Open CY, and Ave Days Open PY.

4. Filter the table to only show cases where the Status is closed. Format the table with alternating rows and change the font size to 10. Your table should look similar to Figure 10-33.

Type	Ave Days Open CY	Ave Days Open PY
City Maintenance	5.38	7.16
Enforcement Activities	8.48	11.48
Other	4.40	9.09
Property Damage Reports	12.22	31.58
Service Requests	7.34	24.96
Total	7.32	15.15

Figure 10-33. Creating a table

5. Click an empty area of the report page and select the 100% Stacked bar chart from the Visuals toolbox.

6. Add the Number of Cases to the Values well, the Type to the Axis well, and the Year to the Legend well.

7. Change the data colors to gold and orange and turn on the data labels. Change the data labels to black. Your chart should be similar to Figure 10-34.

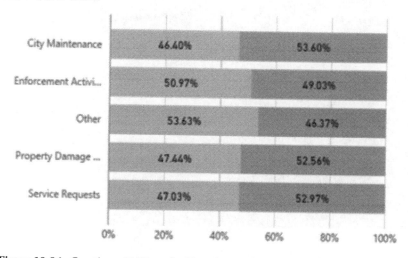

Figure 10-34. *Creating a 100% stacked bar chart*

8. Select a blank area of the page and click the Treemap visual in the toolbox. Add the Number of Cases to the Values well and the Neighborhood to the Group well.

9. Note that when you hover over the neighborhood areas, the tooltip shows the neighborhood and the number of cases. You can also add additional information to the tooltip. Add the Ave Days Open to the Tooltips well. Your final chart should look similar to Figure 10-35.

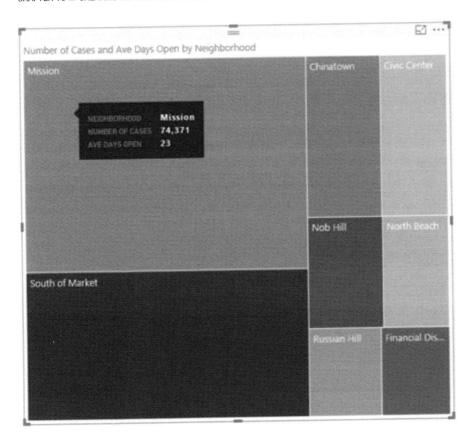

Figure 10-35. Creating a tree map

10. If you click one of the neighborhood blocks, you should see that the table and bar chart are filtered by the neighborhood. In this case, we want to turn off the filtering for the table.

11. With the tree map selected, go to the format tab under the Visual Tools tab and Click the Edit Interactions button. You should see the icons above the table to turn on and off filtering (see Figure 10-36). Turn off filtering for the table.

Type	Ave Days Open CY	Ave Days Open PY
City Maintenance	5.36	7.09
Enforcement Activities	7.74	13.01
Other	3.86	8.83
Property Damage Reports	12.95	31.73
Service Requests	6.69	19.89
Total	6.83	13.52

Figure 10-36. Turning off filtering

12. Click the Edit Interactions button on the Format tab to turn off the edit mode. Test the filtering by clicking the areas in the tree map. The bar chart should filter, but the table should not.

13. Click the plus sign (+) in the lower right corner of the designer to add a new report page.

14. On the new page, add a line chart that shows the Week Ending Date on the axis and Number of Cases as the values. By default, the date becomes a date hierarchy when it is dropped in the Axis well. Change this to show just the Week Ending Date (see Figure 10-37).

Figure 10-37. *Showing just the date and not the hierarchy*

15. Click the Analytics icon (the magnifying glass in Figure 10-37) and add a trend line to the graph.

16. Click a blank area of the page and select a slicer from the Visual toolbox. Add the Week Ending Date to the Fields well. Use the slicer to adjust the date range in the graph (see Figure 10-38).

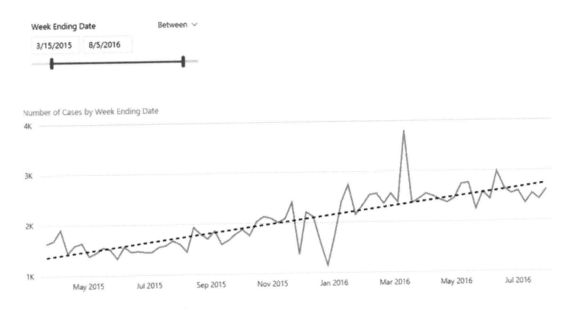

Figure 10-38. *Adjusting the date range of the graph*

17. To create a map-based visualization, add a new report page. Select the Map visual in the Visualization toolbox (the globe icon). From the NeighborhoodLatLon table, drag the Latitude and Longitude fields to the Latitude and Longitude field wells.

18. Drag the Neighborhood field to the Legend well. From the SF311Calls table, drag the Number of Cases field to the Size well. Your map should look similar to Figure 10-39.

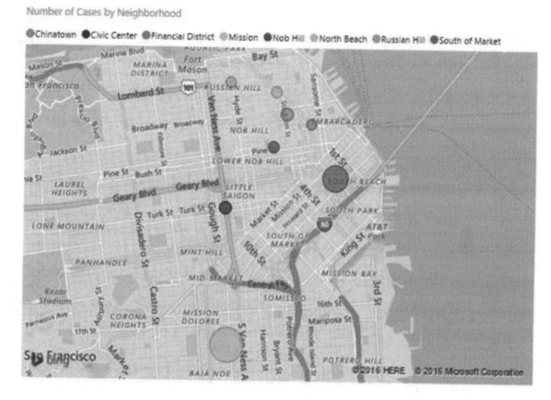

Figure 10-39. Mapping the number of cases for each neighboorhood

19. Experiment with mapping other fields and zooming to different areas of the map. When done, save your changes and exit Power BI Desktop.

Summary

In this chapter you have seen how to create various visualizations in Power BI Desktop. You created basic bar, line, and tree map charts. In addition, you saw how to present measures tied to a geo-spatial field on a map. You also saw how to control visual interactions and drill through functionality in your reports. You are now ready to deploy these reports to the Power BI portal. Once deployed, you will create interactive dashboards based on the reports and expose these to others.

CHAPTER 11

■ ■ ■

Publishing Reports and Creating Dashboards in the Power BI Portal

Now that you know how to create reports in Power BI Desktop, it's time to publish your reports for others to use. In this chapter, you will see how to publish reports created in Power BI Desktop to the Power BI Service (portal). Once the reports are published, you will create dashboards and share them with colleagues. In addition, you will set up an automated data refresh schedule.

After completing this chapter, you will be able to

- Create a user-friendly model.

- Publish Power BI Desktop files to the Power BI Service.

- Add tiles to a dashboard.

- Share dashboards.

- Refresh data in published reports.

Creating a User-Friendly Model

Before publishing your models and reports for others to use, it is very important that users of your Power BI models have a pleasant experience as they build and explore the various visualizations in Power BI. One of the most useful things you can do is rename the tables and fields so they make sense to business users. You may often find that the names of the fields in the original source are abbreviated or have cryptic names that only make sense to the database developers.

Another good idea is to only expose fields that users find meaningful. It is always wise to hide any non-business key values that are used to relate the tables in the model. To hide a column from clients of the model, right-click the column and select Hide in Report View (this will turn the column grey in the Model Designer). Figure 11-1 shows hiding a EmployeeKey field that has no business relevance.

© Dan Clark 2017
D. Clark, *Beginning Power BI*, DOI 10.1007/978-1-4842-2577-6_11

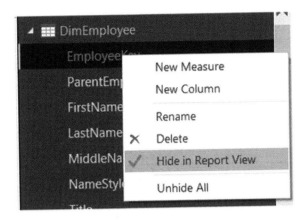

Figure 11-1. Hiding fields in report view

It's also a good idea to check the data type and format of the fields in the model. Depending on the data source, fields may be exported as text fields and need to be changed in the model. This is particularly true when it comes to date fields. You can use the Model tab in the data view of Power BI Desktop to set the data type and format of the fields.

As you look at the field list in the data view, notice the icons in front of the fields. The calculator icon indicates that the field is a measure created in the Power BI model. The summation symbol indicates that the field is numeric and will be aggregated when dragged to the Fields drop area. By default, the aggregate is a summation, which may not be what the aggregate needed. In some cases, you don't want to aggregate a number; for example, in the date table the year field is not meant to be aggregated. You can control this behavior in the Power BI model by setting the Summarize By drop-down on the Modeling tab (see Figure 11-2).

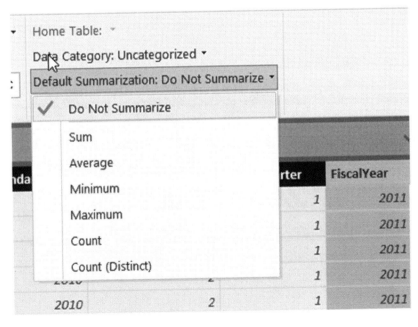

Figure 11-2. Setting default summarizations for fields

Another setting available on the Modeling tab of Power BI Desktop is the data category setting for the fields. This comes into play for location types like city, zip codes, and countries. When Power BI knows the column is a location type, it can use the field to implement a visualization using Bing mapping layers. The other data categories that are useful to set are the image and web URLs. When you set these, Power BI will know these are hyperlinks and format them appropriately (see Figure 11-3).

Figure 11-3. *Setting the data category for a field*

Now that you have the model and reports developed in Power BI Desktop, you are ready to deploy them to the Power BI portal.

Publishing Power BI Desktop Files to the Power BI Service

Now that you are ready to deploy the model and reports created in Power BI Desktop to the Power BI Service, make sure you are signed up for the service. If you are not signed up for the service through your organization, you can sign up for a free account at https://powerbi.microsoft.com/en-us/. Once you have signed up for the account, you can log into the portal through https://app.powerbi.com. Once logged in, you should see a blank canvas organized under a My Workspace heading. Click the upper left icon to show the navigation pane (see Figure 11-4).

Figure 11-4. *The Power BI portal*

In the navigation pane, there are headings for dashboards, reports, and datasets. There is also a button for getting data (see Figure 11-5).

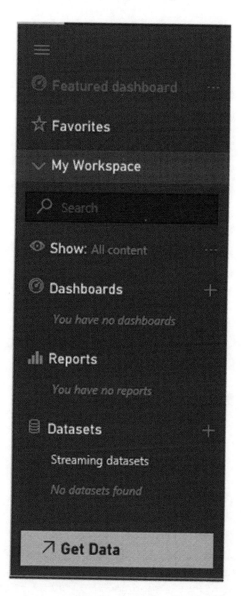

Figure 11-5. *The navigation pane in Power BI*

After clicking the Get Data button, you can either select predefined content packs, files, or databases (see Figure 11-6). Because you are publishing a Power BI Desktop file, choose the Files option.

Figure 11-6. *Selecting a data source*

After selecting the file, the next step is selecting the location of the file. It can be a local file, a file stored in OneDrive, or a file stored in SharePoint (see Figure 11-7).

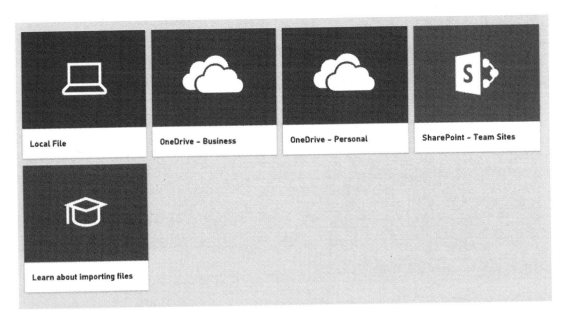

Figure 11-7. *Selecting the file location*

Once you select the file, it is imported into the Power BI Service, and you will see a new dataset, report, and dashboard listed in the Navigation pane. Selecting the dataset will present Report Designer, which is essentially the same as the report view in Power BI Desktop. You or a colleague can use this designer to create new reports. Selecting the report will show the report pages you developed in Power BI Desktop (see Figure 11-8). The report is in view mode and is fully interactive. You can switch to edit mode and update the report.

■ **Note**   Any changes to the report are not reflected back to the original Power BI Desktop file. You can export the report as a Power BI Desktop file, but it is a completely separate file from the original file uploaded to the Power BI portal.

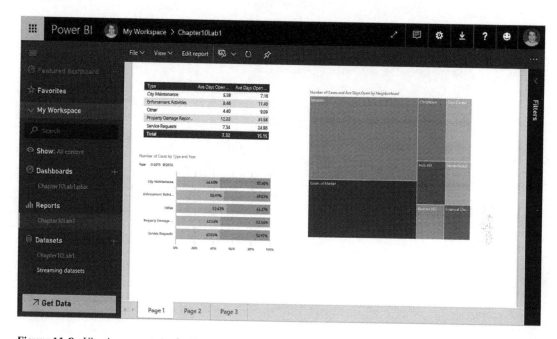

Figure 11-8. Viewing reports in the Power BI portal

Selecting the dashboard will show a dashboard with an empty tile. There are two ways to add tiles to your dashboard: you can create a new visual by using a natural language query or pin a visualization from a report. In the next section you will start adding tiles to the dashboard.

Adding Tiles to a Dashboard

Once you have deployed your reports to the Power BI portal, you can use the report visuals to create your dashboards. When you select a visual in the report, you will see a pin icon in the upper right corner of the visual (see Figure 11-9).

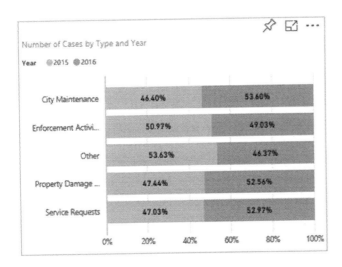

Figure 11-9. *Selecting a visual to add to a dashboard*

When you click the pin, you are presented with a Pin to dashboard window (see Figure 11-10). You have the option of pinning the visual to an existing dashboard or creating a new one.

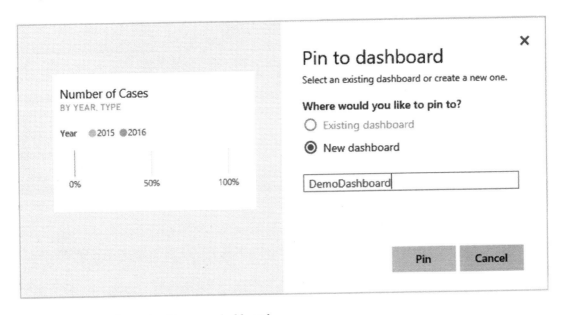

Figure 11-10. *Pinning a visual to a new dashboard*

Once you have pinned the visual to the dashboard, you can navigate to the dashboard to see the new visual (see Figure 11-11).

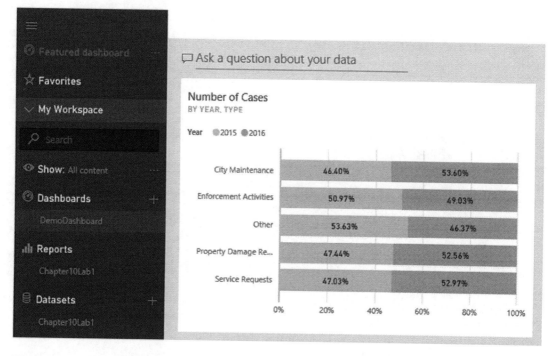

Figure 11-11. *Viewing the dashboard*

If you click the visual in the dashboard, you will drill through to the underlying report where the visual was pinned from.

In addition to pinning visuals to dashboards from reports, you can ask a question to create a visual in the dashboard. Clicking Ask a question about your data at the top of the dashboard will take you to the Q&A entry screen (see Figure 11-12).

< Exit Q&A

💬 Ask a question about your data

CHAPTER10LAB1:

| previous month number of cases | SF311 calls | ave days open | dates | date hierarchy | week ending date |

| ave days open PY | neighborhood lat lons | closed | number of cases |

Figure 11-12. *Asking questions about the data*

The Q&A screen shows the key words and phrases you can use in your question. Figure 11-13 shows using the Q&A window to create a bar chart showing 311 calls opened by type. Once you create the visual, you will see the Visualizations and Fields toolboxes. You can use these to format, filter, or change the type of the visual. When you're done designing the visual, you can pin it to the dashboard.

259

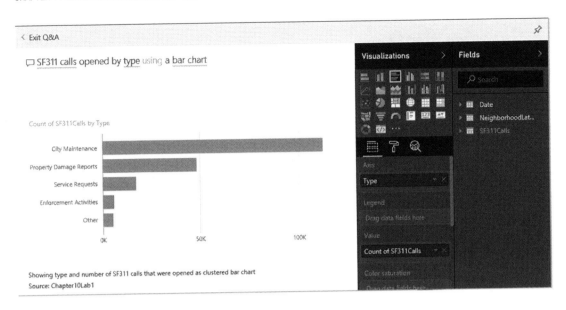

Figure 11-13. *Creating a bar chart using Q&A*

If you don't want to expose the Q&A window to users of your dashboard, you can turn this feature off in the Dashboard Settings (see Figure 11-14).

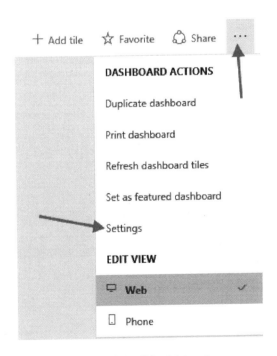

Figure 11-14. *Turning off the Q&A option*

In addition to adding visuals to the dashboard, you can add media tiles to the dashboard, including text, images, video, and web content. Clicking the Add tile link in Figure 11-14 launches the Add tile window where you can select the media type you want to add (see Figure 11-15).

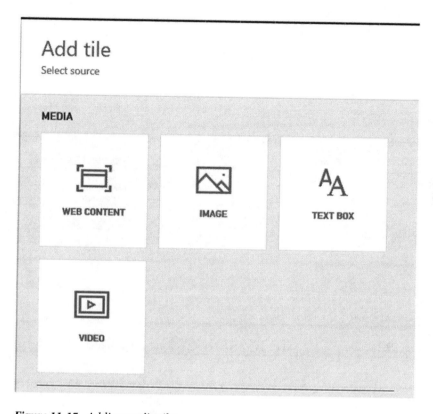

Figure 11-15. Adding media tiles

Once you have added the tiles to the dashboard, you can rearrange and resize the tiles. Figure 11-16 shows a completed dashboard containing a text tile, a web content tile, and two visual tiles.

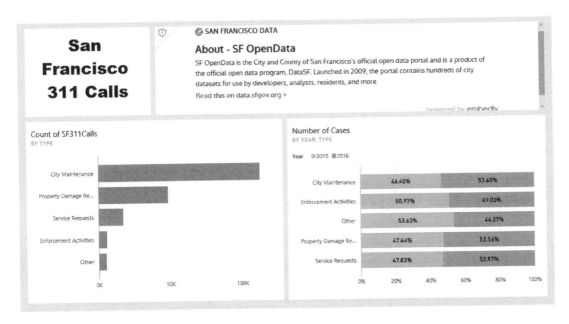

Figure 11-16. *A completed dashboard*

Now that you have created a dashboard, you are ready to share it with your colleagues.

Sharing Dashboards

You can share dashboards with colleagues both in and outside your organization as long as they have signed up for the Power BI Service. When you share a dashboard, users can view and interact with the dashboard but they cannot edit it or create their own copies. To share the dashboard, click the Share link in the upper right corner of the dashboard (refer to Figure 11-14). Using the Share dashboard window, enter the email address of the users you want to share it with. You can also control whether they can share the dashboard and whether to send them an email indicating that the dashboard has been shared with them (see Figure 11-17).

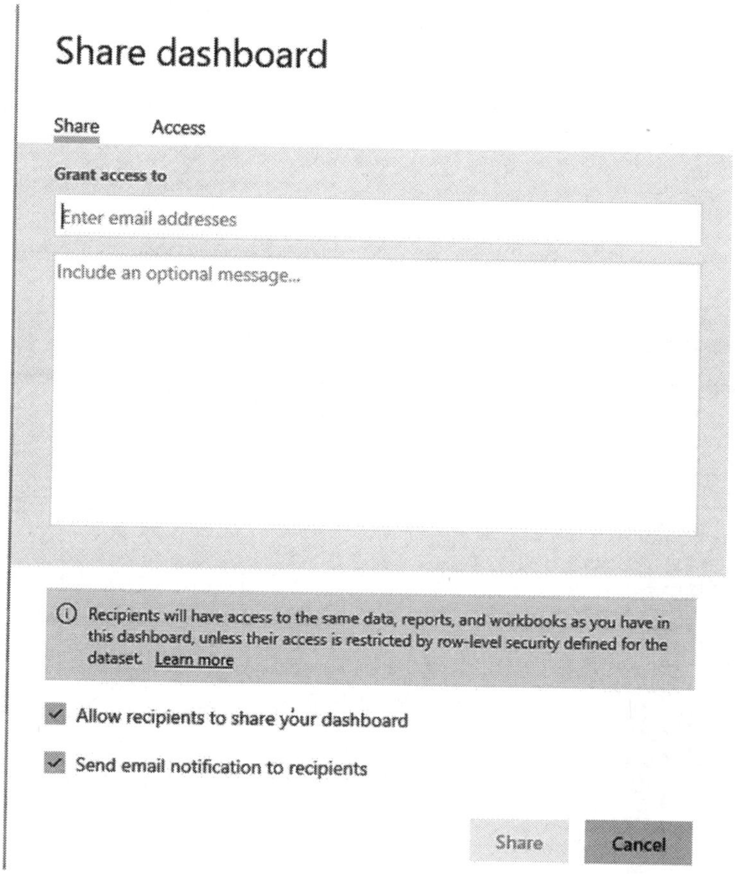

Share dashboard

Share   Access

Grant access to

Enter email addresses

Include an optional message...

ⓘ Recipients will have access to the same data, reports, and workbooks as you have in this dashboard, unless their access is restricted by row-level security defined for the dataset. Learn more

☑ Allow recipients to share your dashboard

☑ Send email notification to recipients

Share   Cancel

Figure 11-17. *Sharing a dashboard*

Once the dashboard is shared, recipients will see the dashboard with a shared icon in their Power BI portal (see Figure 11-18).

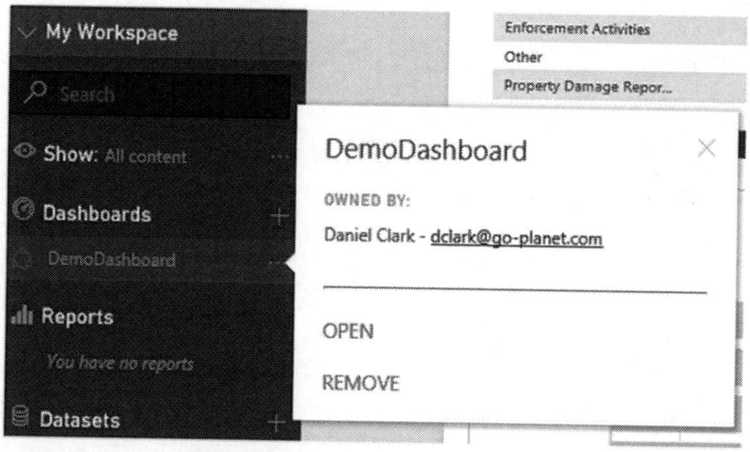

∨ **My Workspace**

🔍 Search

👁 **Show:** All content

◉ **Dashboards**   +

    DemoDashboard

▬ **Reports**

    You have no reports

🗄 **Datasets**   +

Enforcement Activities
Other
Property Damage Repor...

DemoDashboard   ✕

OWNED BY:

Daniel Clark - dclark@go-planet.com

OPEN

REMOVE

Figure 11-18. *A shared dashboard*

One thing to be aware of is that although the underlying reports don't show up in the navigation pane, users can view them by clicking the visuals in the dashboard.

Although sharing dashboards is useful for exposing dashboards to end users, many times you'll want to collaborate with colleagues and allow them to make changes to the reports and dashboards. This is where Power BI *groups* are very useful. Because Power BI groups are based on Office 365 groups, group members must be in the same Office 365 tenant. Group members must also have a Power BI Pro license (currently $10/month). When you create a group, a group workspace is created where members can create and edit reports and dashboards.

To get to your group workspaces, expand the workspace node in the navigation pane (see Figure 11-19).

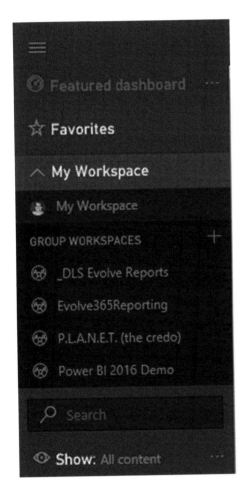

Figure 11-19. *Using group workspaces*

If you need to expose your reports to the general public, you can publish the report to the web. When viewing the report in the portal, click File ➤ Publish to web (see Figure 11-20).

Figure 11-20. Publishing a report to the web

When publishing to the web, you can either provide a link where it will be open in its own web page or host it in an iframe as part of another web page (see Figure 11-21).

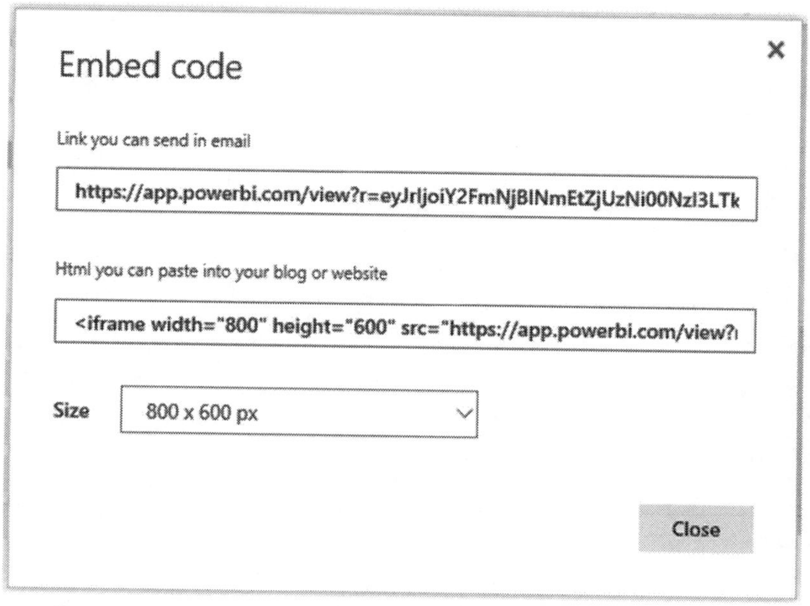

Figure 11-21. Getting a public link to a report

Now that you have seen how to publish and share your reports and dashboards, it's time to see how to keep the data up to date.

Refreshing Data in Published Reports

Keeping your data fresh in your reports and dashboards is critical for making informed decisions and investigating trends. How you refresh the data depends on the source and its volatility. Some data doesn't change much and can be refreshed weekly or monthly. Some sources can be updated daily or hourly, whereas others may need to be as close to live as possible. You need to carefully consider the business requirement for refreshing the data. Often a business user will claim they need live data without weighing the complexity and overhead this requires.

Although I'm not going to cover every data-source scenario, you should be aware of a few common ones. If your data source is a file on OneDrive, by default the data is refreshed hourly. You can turn this off and opt for a manual refresh if you want. If your data source is a web service like Salesforce or Microsoft Project Online, the data is automatically refreshed at a rate that depends on the provider. If your data is from a database in the cloud such as SQL Azure, you can schedule a data refresh. If you are connecting to an on-premises database, you will need to install a data gateway before you can schedule a data refresh.

To schedule a data refresh, in the navigation pane in the Power BI portal select a dataset and click the ellipses to the right of the dataset node. In the pop-up menu (see Figure 11-22), you can choose to do a manual refresh or set up a scheduled refresh.

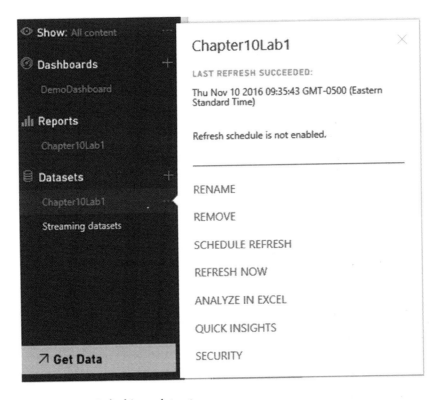

Figure 11-22. *Refreshing a dataset*

When you choose Schedule Refresh, you will see a window where you can set up the refresh frequency. You can set up a daily refresh and indicate what times to refresh the data (see Figure 11-23). You can also set up a weekly refresh and indicate what days of the week to refresh the data.

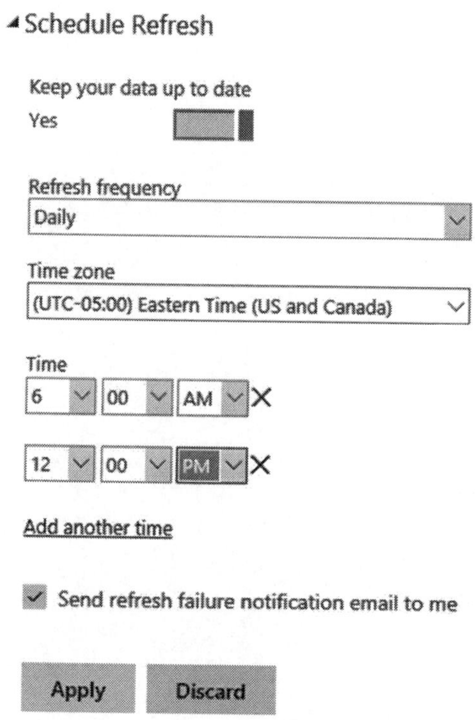

◢ Schedule Refresh

Keep your data up to date
Yes

Refresh frequency
Daily

Time zone
(UTC-05:00) Eastern Time (US and Canada)

Time
6 ∨ 00 ∨ AM ∨ ✕

12 ∨ 00 ∨ PM ∨ ✕

Add another time

☑ Send refresh failure notification email to me

Apply   Discard

Figure 11-23. *Setting up a refresh schedule*

If you are connecting to an on-premise dataset, you will need to install a gateway. Clicking the down arrow in the upper right corner of the Power BI portal displays a menu where you can choose to install a data gateway (see Figure 11-24).

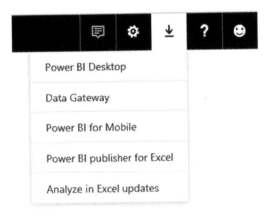

Figure 11-24. *Installing a data gateway*

Once the gateway is installed, click the sprocket icon and select the Manage gateways link (see Figure 11-25).

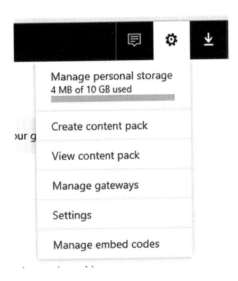

Figure 11-25. *Managing gateways*

In the Gateway Settings window, select Add date sources to use the gateway. In the Data Source Settings window, name the data source and select the type of data source (see Figure 11-26).

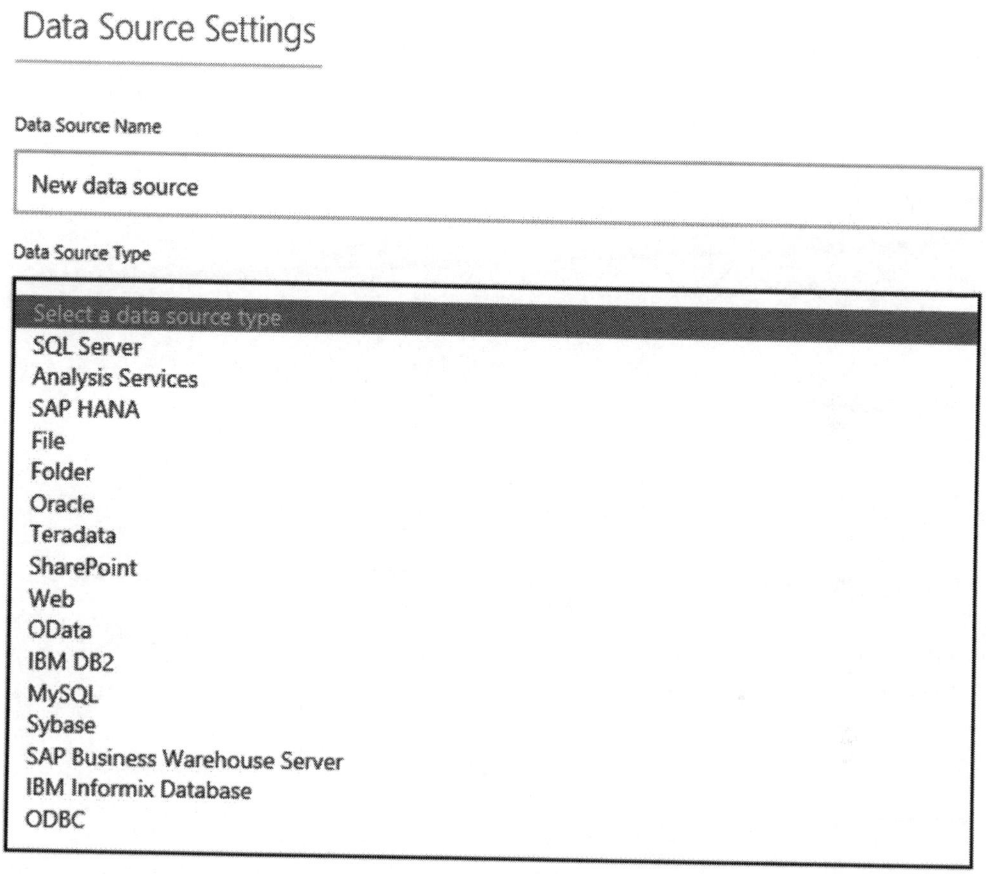

Data Source Settings

Data Source Name

New data source

Data Source Type

Select a data source type
SQL Server
Analysis Services
SAP HANA
File
Folder
Oracle
Teradata
SharePoint
Web
OData
IBM DB2
MySQL
Sybase
SAP Business Warehouse Server
IBM Informix Database
ODBC

Figure 11-26. *Adding a data source to the gateway*

After selecting a data source type, you need to provide a connection string and credentials. Figure 11-27 shows setting up a connection to a local file.

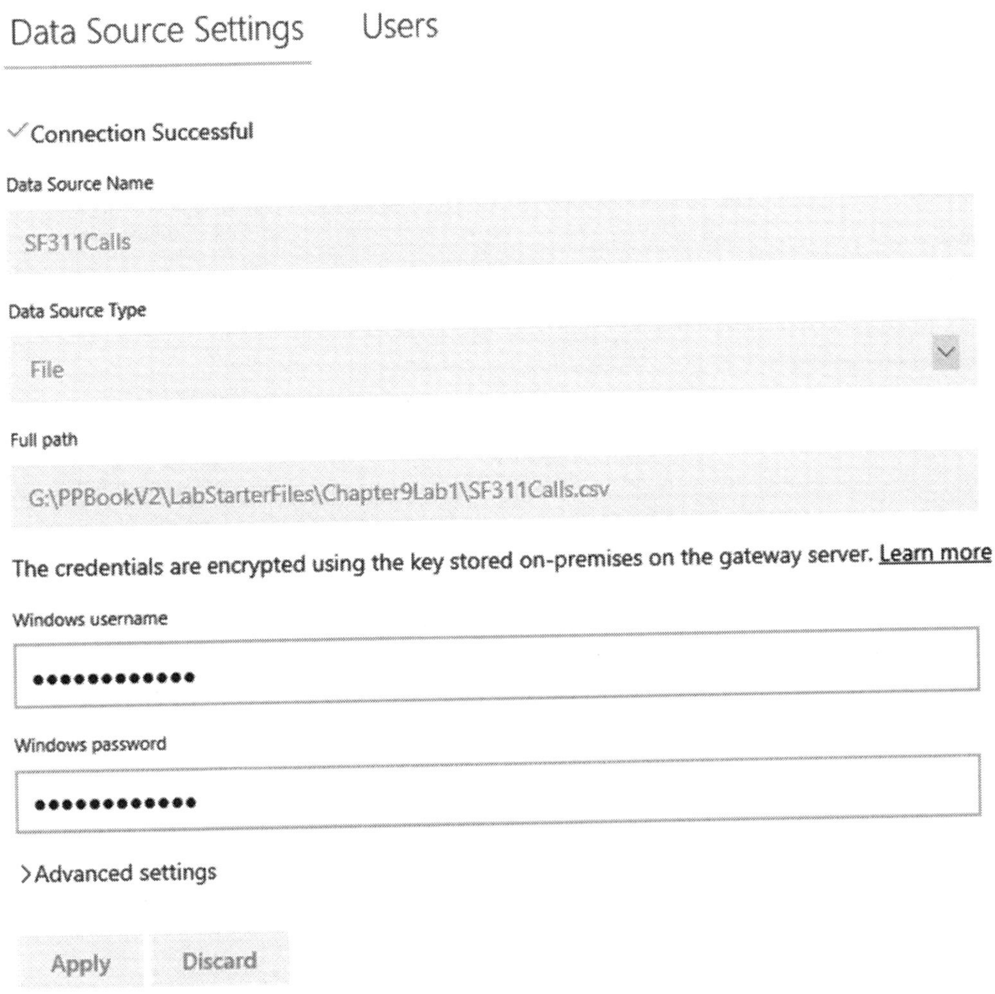

Data Source Settings   Users

✓ Connection Successful

Data Source Name

SF311Calls

Data Source Type

File

Full path

G:\PPBookV2\LabStarterFiles\Chapter9Lab1\SF311Calls.csv

The credentials are encrypted using the key stored on-premises on the gateway server. Learn more

Windows username

●●●●●●●●●●●●

Windows password

●●●●●●●●●●●●

> Advanced settings

Apply   Discard

Figure 11-27. *Connecting to a local file*

Now that you have seen how to create, publish and share your reports on the Power BI portal, it's time to get some hands-on experience publishing reports and creating dashboards.

HANDS-ON LAB: CREATING DASHBOARDS ON THE POWER BI PORTAL

In the following lab you will

- Publish a report to the portal.

- Create a dashboard on the portal.

- Set up a data refresh schedule.

1. In the LabStarterFiles\Chapter11Lab1 folder, open the Chapter11Lab1.pbix file. This file contains sales data from Northwind Traders. You should see a basic report, as shown in Figure 11-28.

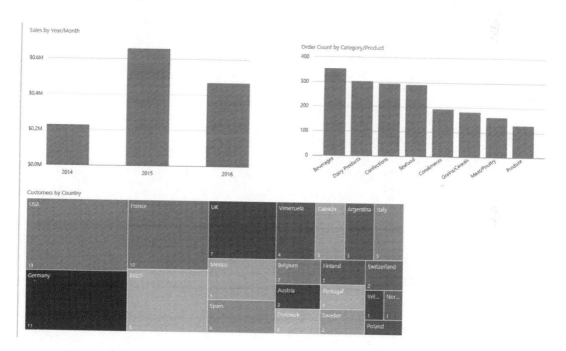

Figure 11-28. *Sample sales report*

2. If you are not signed in to the Power BI Service, click File ➤ Sign In (see Figure 11-29).

Figure 11-29. *Sign in to the Power BI Service*

3. After signing in, click the Publish button on the Home tab. Select My Workspace as the destination.

4. Once published, click the link to open the report in Power BI (see Figure 11-30).

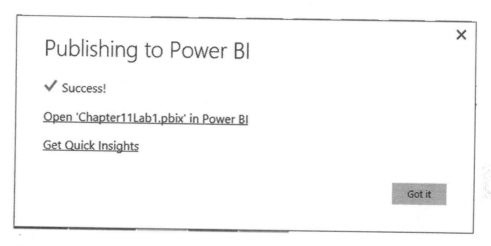

Figure 11-30. *Opening the report in Power BI*

5. In the report view, hover over the Sales by Year/Month chart. You should see a pin icon in the upper right corner (see Figure 11-31).

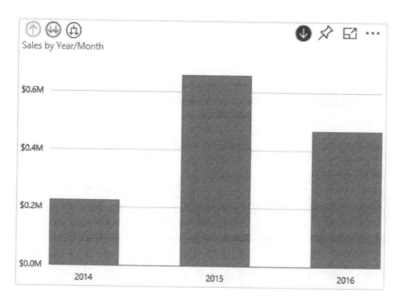

Figure 11-31. *Pinning a tile to a dashboard*

6. In the Pin to dashboard window, select a new dashboard and name it Northwind Sales (see Figure 11-32).

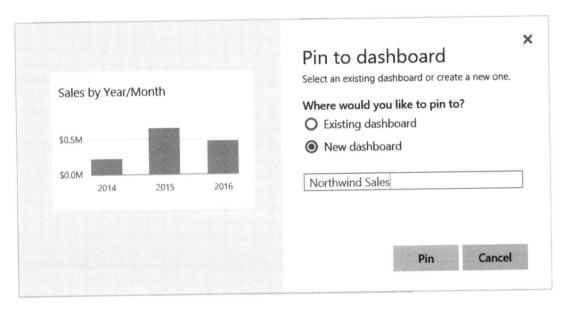

Figure 11-32. Creating a new dashboard

7. Add the Order Count by Category/Product to the Northwind Sales dashboard.

8. Expand the navigation pane and select the Northwind Sales dashboard (see Figure 11-33).

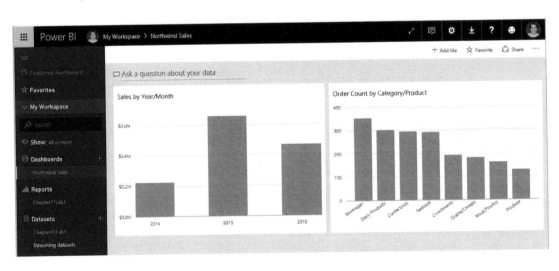

Figure 11-33. Viewing the dashboard

9. Click the Ask a question about your data link. Enter *Product that is discontinued by category sorted by unit in stock descending*. You should see a table as shown in Figure 11-34. Pin this table to the dashboard.

< Exit Q&A

💬 Product that is discontinued by category sorted by unit in stock descending

Product...	ProductName	UnitsInStock ▼	UnitsOnOrd...	ReorderLev...	Discontinued	Category ▼
9	Mishi Kobe Niku	29	0	0	True	Meat/Poultry
28	Rössle Sauerkraut	26	0	0	True	Produce
42	Singaporean Hokkien Fried Mee	26	0	0	True	Grains/Cereals
24	Guaraná Fantástica	20	0	0	True	Beverages
17	Alice Mutton	0	0	0	True	Meat/Poultry
29	Thüringer Rostbratwurst	0	0	0	True	Meat/Poultry
53	Perth Pasties	0	0	0	True	Meat/Poultry
5	Chef Anton's Gumbo Mix	0	0	0	True	Condiments

Figure 11-34. Using Q&A to create a table

10. Exit the Q&A window to go back to the dashboard. Hover the mouse pointer over the new tile and click the ellipses in the upper right corner. A menu is displayed, as shown in Figure 11-35.

Figure 11-35. Displaying a tile menu

11. Click the tile icon to display the Tile details window. Change the title and put a check mark in Display last refresh time, as shown in Figure 11-36.

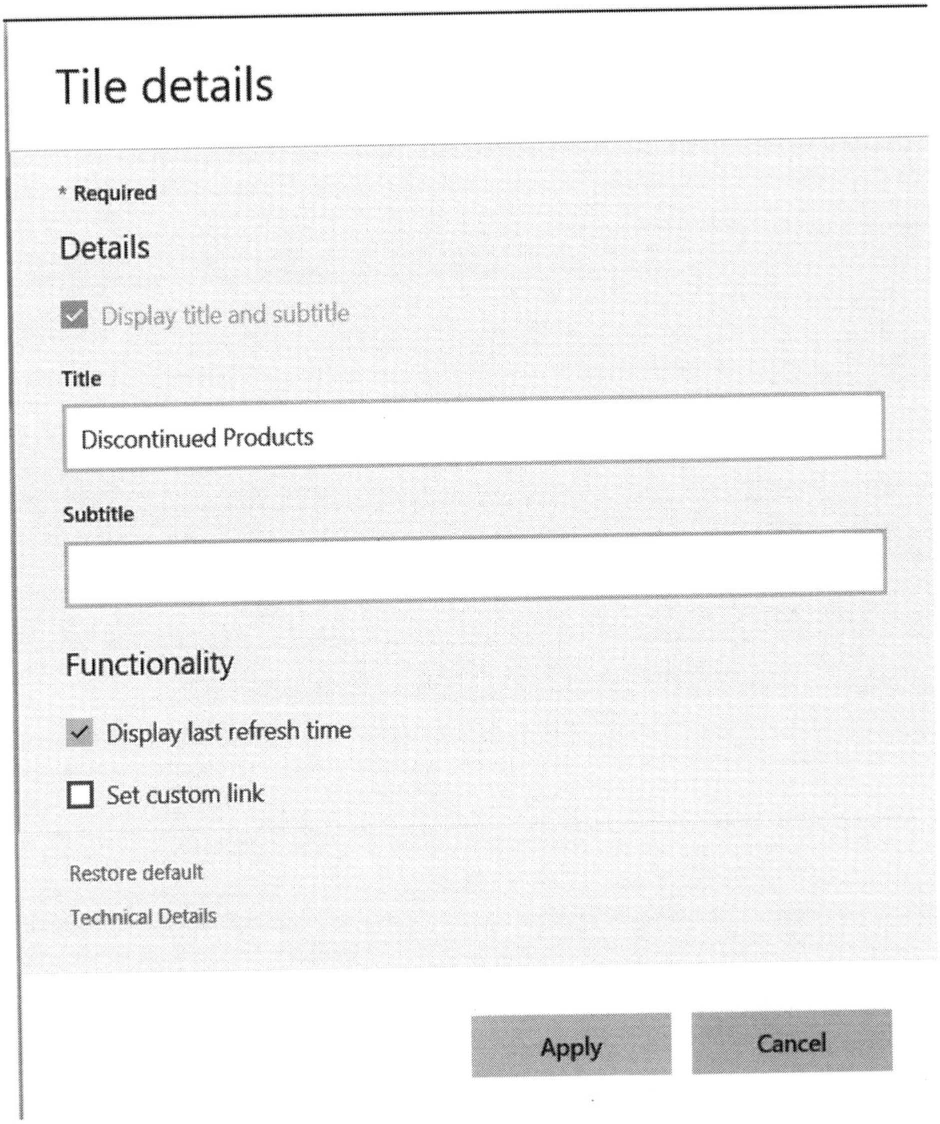

Tile details

* Required

Details

☑ Display title and subtitle

Title

Discontinued Products

Subtitle

Functionality

☑ Display last refresh time

☐ Set custom link

Restore default

Technical Details

Apply   Cancel

Figure 11-36. Editing the tile details

12. Add a text box tile and rearrange and resize the tiles so that your final dashboard looks similar to Figure 11-37.

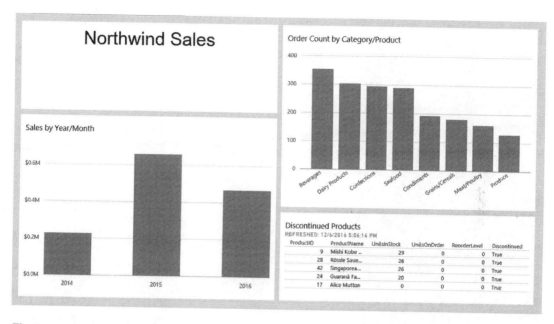

Figure 11-37. *The final dashboard*

13. To set up a refresh schedule, in the navigation pane click the ellipses to the right of the dataset and click Schedule Refresh in the menu (see Figure 11-38).

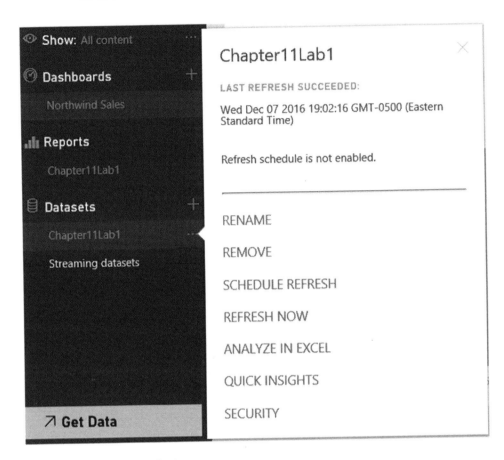

Figure 11-38. Displaying the dataset menu

14. In the resulting window, expand the Data source credentials node and the Schedule Refresh node (see Figure 11-39).

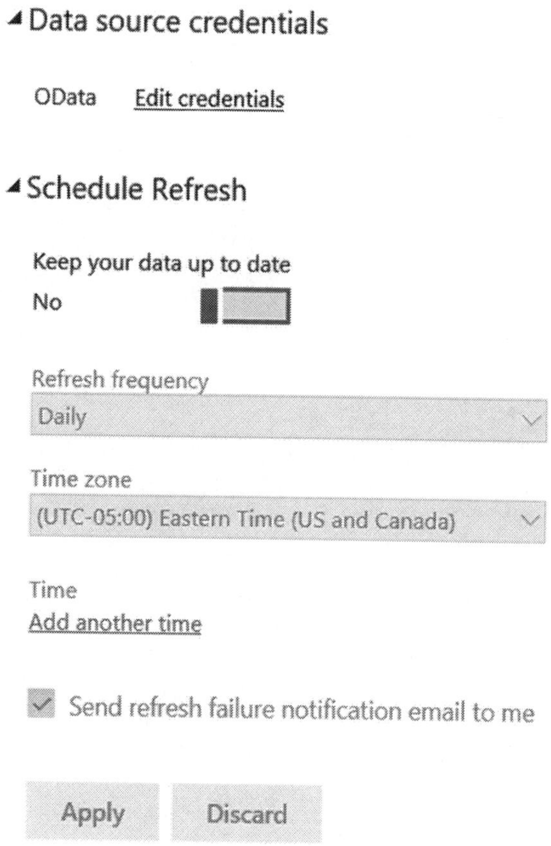

◢ Data source credentials

OData   <u>Edit credentials</u>

◢ Schedule Refresh

Keep your data up to date

No

Refresh frequency

Daily

Time zone

(UTC-05:00) Eastern Time (US and Canada)

Time
<u>Add another time</u>

☑ Send refresh failure notification email to me

Apply   Discard

Figure 11-39. Scheduling data refresh

15. Before scheduling the refresh, click the Edit credentials link under the Data source credentials node. Make sure Authentication method is set to Anonymous (see Figure 11-40).

Configure Chapter11Lab1
url
http://services.odata.org/Northwind/Northwind.svc
Authentication method
Anonymous
Sign in
Cancel

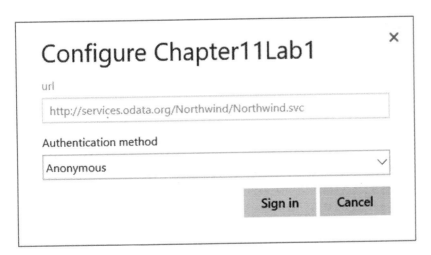

Figure 11-40. *Editing the data source credentials*

16. Create a refresh schedule that runs daily at 7:00 a.m. (see Figure 11-41).

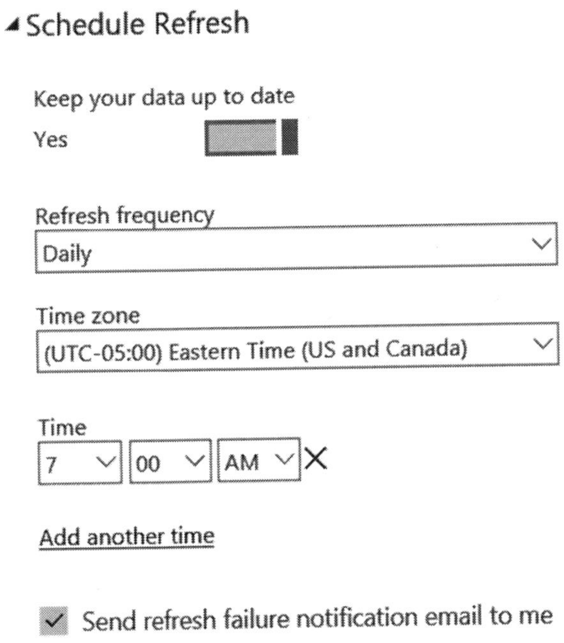

Schedule Refresh
Keep your data up to date
Yes
Refresh frequency
Daily
Time zone
(UTC-05:00) Eastern Time (US and Canada)
Time
7
00
AM
Add another time
Send refresh failure notification email to me

Figure 11-41. *Creating a daily refresh*

Summary

In this chapter you have seen how to publish reports created in Power BI Desktop to the Power BI Service (portal). You created dashboards and saw how to share them with colleagues. You also learned how to set up an automated data refresh schedule.

In the next chapter, you will look at several realistic case studies to solidify the concepts of the previous chapters. By working through these case studies, you will be able to gauge which areas you have mastered and which you need to study further.

■ ■ ■

Creating a Complete Solution

So far in this book, you've gained experience working with each of the pieces of Microsoft's self-service BI toolset. You've used Power Query, Power Pivot, Excel, and the Power BI Desktop. This chapter provides you with several use cases to solidify the concepts of the previous chapters. By working through these use cases, you will gauge which areas you have mastered and which you need to spend more time studying. Because this is sort of like your final exam, I have deliberately not included step-by-step instructions as I did for earlier exercises. Instead, I have given you general directions that should be sufficient to get you started. If you get stuck, refer back to the previous chapters to remind yourself of how to accomplish the task.

This chapter contains the following use cases:

- Reseller sales analysis
- Sales quota analysis
- Sensor analysis

Use Case 1: Reseller Sales Analysis

In this scenario, you work for a bike equipment company and have been asked to analyze the sales data. You need to build a dashboard to compare monthly store sales. An added constraint is that you only want to compare resellers who have been open for at least a year when you make the comparison.

Load the Data

Create a new Excel workbook named StoreSalesAnalysis.xlsx. In the Chapter12Labs folder, find the UseCase1 folder, which contains a StoreSales.accdb Access database. This database houses the sales data you need to analyze. Using this as a data source, import the data tables and columns listed in Table 12-1 using Power Pivot in Excel (covered in Chapter 2).

© Dan Clark 2017
D. Clark, *Beginning Power BI*, DOI 10.1007/978-1-4842-2577-6_12

Table 12-1. *Store Sales Tables and Columns to Import*

Source Table	Friendly Name	Columns
dbo_DimDate	Date	FullDate, MonthName, MonthNumberOfYear, CalendarQuarter, CalendarYear
dbo_DimGeography	Location	GeographyKey, City, StateProvinceCode, StateProvinceName, CountryRegionCode, EnglishCountryRegionName, PostalCode
dbo_DimProduct	Product	ProductKey, ProductSubcategoryKey, EnglishProductName, StandardCost, ListPrice, DealerPrice
dbo_DimProductCategory	Category	ProductCategoryKey, EnglishProductCategoryName
dbo_DimProductSubcategory	Subcategory	ProductSubcategoryKey, EnglishProductSubcategoryName, ProductCategoryKey
dbo_DimReseller	Reseller	ResellerKey, GeographyKey, BusinessType, ResellerName, YearOpened
dbo_FactResellerSales	ResellerSales	ProductKey, ResellerKey, SalesOrderNumber, SalesOrderLineNumber, OrderQuantity, UnitPrice, ExtendedAmount, TotalProductCost, SalesAmount, OrderDate

Create the Model

After importing the tables, create the table relationships using the appropriate keys. Your model should now look similar to Figure 12-1.

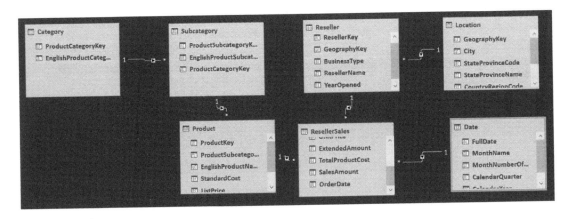

Figure 12-1. *Store sales model*

Rename the table columns and show or hide the columns from client tools according to the information listed in Table 12-2.

Table 12-2. *Table and Column Properties*

Table	Column	New Name	Hide from Client
Date	FullDate	Full Date	
	MonthName	Month	
	MonthNumberOfYear	Month Number	X
	CalendarQuarter	Calendar Quarter	
	CalendarYear	Calendar Year	
Product	ProductKey	—	X
	SubcategoryKey	—	X
	StandardCost	Standard Cost	
	ListPrice	List Price	
	DealerPrice	Dealer Price	
Reseller	ResellerKey	—	X
	GeographyKey	—	X
	BusinessType	Reseller Type	
	ResellerName	Reseller Name	
	YearOpened	Year Opened	
Location	GeographyKey	—	X
	StateProvinceCode	State Province Code	
	StateProvinceName	State Province	
	CountryRegionCode	Country Code	
	EnglishCountryRegionName	Country	
	PostalCode	Postal Code	
ResellerSales	ProductKey	—	X
	ResellerKey	—	X
	SalesOrderNumber	Order Number	
	SalesOrderLineNumber	Order Line Number	
	OrderQuantity	Quantity	
	UnitPrice	Unit Price	
	ExtendedAmount	Extended Amount	
	TotalProductCost	Product Cost	
	SalesAmount	Sales Amount	
	OrderDate	-	X

In the Date table, create a calendar hierarchy of Year - Quarter - Month. Mark the table as the Date table with the Full Date column as the key. Sort the Month column by the Month Number column. Format the Full Date column to only show the date and not the time.

Create Calculated Columns

Using the DAX RELATED function, create a calculated column in the Product table for Product Subcategory and Product Category. If the ProductSubcategoryKey is blank, fill in the Category and Subcategory columns with "Misc".

```
[Category]
=IF(ISBLANK([ProductSubcategoryKey]),"Misc",
    RELATED(Category[EnglishProductCategoryName]))

[Subcategory]
=IF(ISBLANK([ProductSubcategoryKey]),"Misc",
    RELATED(Subcategory[EnglishProductSubcategoryName]))
```

Hide the Category and Subcategory tables from any client tools. Finally, create a hierarchy with the Product Category and Product Subcategory columns named Prd Cat.

Create Measures

Add the following measures to the ResellerSales table:

```
Month Sales:=TOTALMTD(SUM([Sales Amount]),'Date'[Full Date])

Prev Month Sales:=CALCULATE(Sum([Sales Amount]),PREVIOUSMONTH('Date'[Full Date]))

Monthly Sales Growth:=[Month Sales] - [Prev Month Sales]

Monthly Sales Growth %:=DIVIDE([Monthly Sales Growth],[Prev Month Sales],0)
```

Test your measures by creating a pivot table, as shown in Figure 12-2.

Row Labels	Month Sales	Prev Month Sales	Monthly Sales Growth	Monthly Sales Growth %
⊞ 2013	$1,702,944.54		$1,702,944.54	0.00 %
⊞ 2014	$2,185,213.21	$1,702,944.54	$482,268.67	28.32 %
⊟ 2015	$3,510,948.73	$2,185,213.21	$1,325,735.52	60.67 %
⊟ 1	$1,563,955.08	$2,185,213.21	($621,258.13)	-28.43 %
January	$1,317,541.83	$2,185,213.21	($867,671.38)	-39.71 %
February	$2,384,846.59	$1,317,541.83	$1,067,304.76	81.01 %
March	$1,563,955.08	$2,384,846.59	($820,891.51)	-34.42 %
⊞ 2	$1,987,872.71	$1,563,955.08	$423,917.63	27.11 %
⊞ 3	$4,047,574.04	$1,987,872.71	$2,059,701.33	103.61 %
⊞ 4	$3,510,948.73	$4,047,574.04	($536,625.31)	-13.26 %
⊞ 2016		$3,510,948.73	($3,510,948.73)	-100.00 %

Figure 12-2. *Viewing the measures in a pivot table*

Now you need to create a measure to determine whether a store was open for at least a year for the month you are calculating the sales for. In the Reseller table, add the following measures:

```
Years Open:=Year(FIRSTDATE('Date'[Full Date])) - Min([Year Opened])
```

```
Was Open Prev Year:=If([Years Open]>0,1,0)
```

Create a pivot table to test your measures, as shown in Figure 12-3. Remember that the measures only make sense if you filter by year.

Row Labels	Years Open	Was Open Prev Year
A Bicycle Association	23.00	1
A Bike Store	28.00	1
A Cycle Shop	-2.00	0
A Great Bicycle Company	27.00	1
A Typical Bike Shop	16.00	1
Acceptable Sales & Service	10.00	1
Accessories Network	14.00	1
Acclaimed Bicycle Company	19.00	1
Ace Bicycle Supply	6.00	1
Action Bicycle Specialists	6.00	1
Active Cycling	0.00	0
Active Life Toys	1.00	1
Active Systems	10.00	1
Active Transport Inc.	8.00	1
Activity Center	27.00	1
Advanced Bike Components	24.00	1

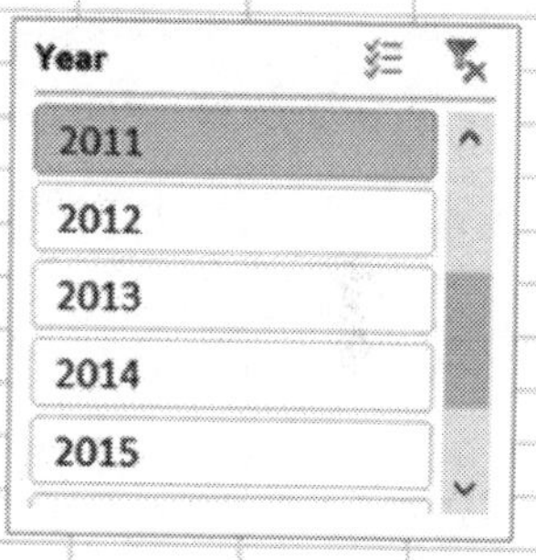

Year: 2011, 2012, 2013, 2014, 2015

Figure 12-3. Testing the measures

Now you can combine these measures so that you are only including resellers who have been in business for at least a year at the time of the sales. Create the following measures:

```
Month Sales Filtered:=Calculate([Month Sales],FILTER(Reseller,[Was Open Prev Year]=1))
```

```
Prev Month Sales Filtered:=CALCULATE([Prev Month Sales],
    Filter(Reseller,[Was Open Prev Year]=1))
```

```
Monthly Sales Growth Filtered:=[Month Sales Filtered]-[Prev Month Sales Filtered]
```

```
Monthly Sales Growth Filtered %:=DIVIDE([Monthly Sales Growth Filtered],
    [Prev Month Sales Filtered],0)
```

Test your new measures by creating a Power Pivot table, as shown in Figure 12-4. You should see a difference between the filtered and the nonfiltered measures.

Row Labels	Month Sales	Month Sales Filtered	Monthly Sales Growth %	Monthly Sales Growth Filtered %
⊞ 2013	$1,702,944.54	$1,639,241.75	0.00 %	0.00 %
⊟ 2014	$2,185,213.21	$2,176,877.61	28.32 %	30.37 %
⊟ 1	$1,455,280.41	$1,406,985.25	-14.54 %	-15.74 %
January	$713,116.69	$658,066.68	-58.12 %	-60.59 %
February	$1,900,788.93	$1,897,013.80	166.55 %	188.27 %
March	$1,455,280.41	$1,406,985.25	-23.44 %	-25.83 %
⊞ 2	$1,001,803.77	$993,947.29	-31.16 %	-29.36 %
⊞ 3	$2,885,359.20	$2,872,092.51	188.02 %	188.96 %
⊞ 4	$2,185,213.21	$2,176,877.61	-24.27 %	-24.21 %
⊞ 2015	$3,510,948.73	$3,510,948.73	60.67 %	60.67 %
⊞ 2016			-100.00 %	-100.00 %

Figure 12-4. Testing the filtered measures

Create the Dashboard

To create the dashboard, insert a new Excel sheet. Name the sheet Reseller Sales and add a column chart that shows Sales by Month and Business Type using the filtered monthly sales. Add a slicer to the report that controls the calendar year displayed by the chart. Your report should look similar to Figure 12-5.

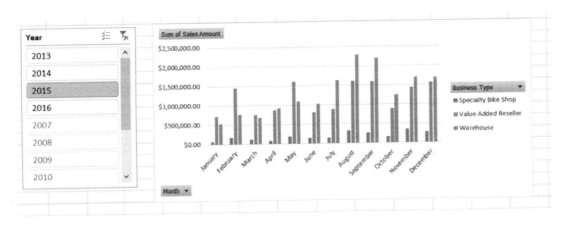

Figure 12-5. The Reseller Sales report

You now want to make another reseller analysis to find the best monthly sales for the month, quarter, and year. To do this, you need to add a new measure to the model. This measure uses the VALUES and the MAXX functions to find the maximum reseller monthly sales:

```
Max Reseller Sales:=MAXX(VALUES(Reseller[ResellerKey]),[Month Sales])
```

Once you have the new measure in the model, add another column chart to the Excel sheet that shows the maximum reseller sales for each month. Make sure you update the year slicer so that it filters both charts (see Figure 12-6).

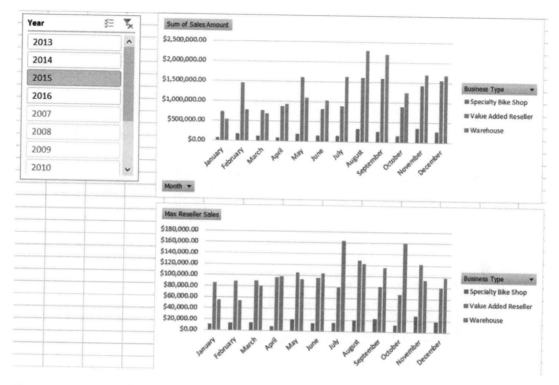

Figure 12-6. *Adding the Max Reseller Sales chart*

To take this one step further, let's say you want the name of the reseller who has the maximum monthly sales for the period. To accomplish this, you can use the TOPN function to find the top reseller for the month:

```
TOPN(1,Reseller,ResellerSales[Month Sales],DESC)
```

Because TOPN returns a table of values that could include more than one row for ties, you need to concatenate the results into a single string value. You can use the CANCATENATEX function for this. The final result is as follows:

```
Top Monthly Reseller:=CONCATENATEX(TOPN(1,Reseller,ResellerSales[Month
Sales],DESC),Reseller[Reseller Name],", ")
```

Add a new Excel worksheet named Max Resellers. Add a pivot table that shows the maximum reseller sales and reseller name for each month. Also include a slicer for the year, one for the business type, and one for the country. Your dashboard should look similar to Figure 12-7.

Year		
2014		
2015		
2016		
2017		

Business Type		
Specialty Bike Shop		
Value Added Reseller		
Warehouse		

EnglishCountryRe...		
Australia		
Canada		
France		
Germany		
United Kingdom		
United States		

Row Labels	Max Reseller Sales	Top Monthly Reseller
January	$46,261.87	Fitness Toy Store
February	$48,743.27	Closeout Boutique
March	$80,564.85	Outdoor Equipment Store
April	$97,791.62	Fitness Toy Store
May	$59,836.48	Closeout Boutique
June	$104,482.96	Outdoor Equipment Store
July	$163,930.39	Westside Plaza
August	$101,609.29	Closeout Boutique
September	$106,929.55	Extraordinary Bike Works
October	$160,378.39	Westside Plaza
November	$73,114.15	Permanent Finish Products
December	$77,475.23	Safe Cycles Shop

Figure 12-7. The final dashboard in an Excel worksheet

After completing and experimenting with the dashboards, save and close Excel.

Use Case 2: Sales Quota Analysis

For this scenario, you will use the sales data for the sales team of the same company from Use Case 1. This time, using Power BI Desktop, you need to create a dashboard that allows the sales manager to track the performance of the sales team. You will compare actual sales to the sales quotas for the sales team.

Load the Data

Create a new Power BI Desktop file named SalesRepAnalysis.pbix. In the Chapter12Labs folder is a folder named UseCase2; this folder contains a SalesRepAnalysis.accdb Access database with sales data extracted from the sales data warehouse. Using this as a data source, import the data tables and columns listed in Table 12-3.

Table 12-3. *Tables and Columns to Import*

Source Table	Query Name	Fields
Employee	Rep	EmployeeKey, EmployeeNationalID, FirstName, LastName, MiddleName, Title
SalesTerritory	Territory	SalesTerritoryKey, SalesTerritoryRegion, SalesTerritoryCountry, SalesTerritoryGroup
ResellerSales	Sales	OrderDateKey, EmployeeKey, SalesTerritoryKey, SalesAmount

Filter the Employee table to only include salespeople. Add a Name Column that combines the FirstName and Last Name columns. In the Sales table, use the OrderDateKey to create an OrderDate column. Because the OrderDateKey is in the format YYYYMMDD, you can use the Date.FromText() function to create an OrderDate column. Once you have the OrderDate column, you can use this to create a Year and a Quarter column. Then group the SaleAmount by EmployeeKey, SalesTeritory, OrderYear, and Quarter. Add a leading Q to the quarter numbers. Create a TimePeriod column that concatenates the Year and Quarter columns. After creating the TimePeriod Column, you can delete the Year and Quarter columns. The final result should be similar to Figure 12-8.

	1^2_3 EmployeeKey	1^2_3 SalesTerritoryKey	1.2 Sales Amount	ABC 123 TimePeriod
1	285	5	544530.0264	2013Q3
2	288	6	428607.3466	2013Q3
3	282	4	302271.1838	2013Q3
4	286	1	191328.4939	2013Q3
5	289	1	203348.2389	2013Q3
6	283	3	239893.6352	2013Q3
7	281	3	52539.7917	2013Q3
8	281	2	217470.9457	2013Q3
9	281	5	34744.8652	2013Q3
10	284	6	207335.5039	2013Q3
11	287	4	278285.4919	2013Q3
12	283	4	215191.6908	2013Q3
13	272	1	20544.7015	2013Q3
14	282	1	113907.9411	2013Q3

Figure 12-8. *The final Sales query data*

The sales quotas are kept in an Excel workbook called SalesQuotas.xlsx in the UseCase2 folder. Import the data using the Excel source and select the sheets for each year. Once the data is imported, you should see a query for each year. You need to add the year column to each query. Now you can combine the queries into a new query called Quotas. Rearrange the column order to SalesPerson, Year, Q1, Q2, Q3, Q4. Select the SalesPerson and Year columns. Unpivot the other columns. Rename the resulting Attribute column to Quarter and the Value column to Quota. Add a TimePeriod column that concatenates the year and quarter. After adding the TimePeriod, remove the Year and Quarter columns. The final result should look similar to Figure 12-9.

#	ABC Sales Person	1.2 Quota	ABC 123 TimePeriod
1	David Campbell	180800	2013Q3
2	David Campbell	282400	2013Q4
3	Garrett Vargas	195200	2013Q3
4	Garrett Vargas	284800	2013Q4
5	Jillian Carson	452000	2013Q3
6	Jillian Carson	697600	2013Q4
7	José Saraiva	420000	2013Q3
8	José Saraiva	613600	2013Q4
9	Linda Mitchell	509600	2013Q3
10	Linda Mitchell	624800	2013Q4

Figure 12-9. *The final Quotas query data*

Right-click each of the year queries and uncheck the Enable Load option (see Figure 12-10).

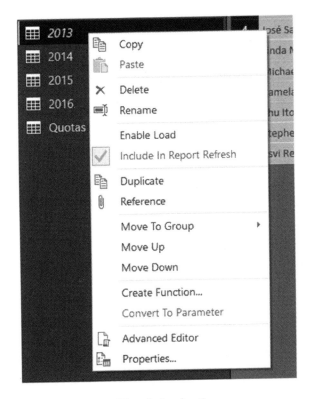

Figure 12-10. *Disabling the load option*

To create the appropriate relationships between the tables, you need to create a Period table that contains the calendar year and quarter. To get this table, right-click the Quotas query and select Duplicate. Rename the query to Period. Delete the step that removed the Year and Quarter columns. Remove the SalesPerson and Quota columns. On the Home tab, click the Remove Rows drop-down and choose Remove Duplicates. Finally, reorder the columns and order the rows by Time Period. The final results should look like Figure 12-11.

	TimePeriod	Year	Quarter
1	2013Q3	2013	Q3
2	2013Q4	2013	Q4
3	2014Q1	2014	Q1
4	2014Q2	2014	Q2
5	2014Q3	2014	Q3
6	2014Q4	2014	Q4
7	2015Q1	2015	Q1
8	2015Q2	2015	Q2
9	2015Q3	2015	Q3
10	2015Q4	2015	Q4
11	2016Q1	2016	Q1
12	2016Q2	2016	Q2

Figure 12-11. *The results of the* Period *query.*

Click Close & Apply to load the data into the model. You are now ready to create the data model.

Create the Model

After importing the tables, rename the table columns and show or hide the columns from client tools according to the information listed in Table 12-4.

Table 12-4. *Table and Column Property Settings*

Table	Column	New Name	Hide in Report View
Sales Rep	EmployeeKey	—	X
	EmployeeNationalID	Employee ID	
	FirstName	First Name	
	LastName	Last Name	
	MiddleName	Middle Name	
	Name	Sales Person	
Territory	SalesTerritoryKey	—	X
	SalesTerritoryRegion	Region	
	SalesTerritoryCountry	Country	
	SalesTerritoryGroup	Group	
	SalesTerritoryImage	Territory Image	
Quota	TimePeriod	—	X
	SalesPerson	Sales Person	
	EmployeeKey	—	X
	SalesTerritoryKey	—	X
	TimePeriod	-	X
	SalesAmount	Sales Amount	X

After renaming and hiding the key fields, format the Sales Amount and quota columns as currency. The next step is to verify the table relationships in the model. Figure 12-12 shows what the model should look like.

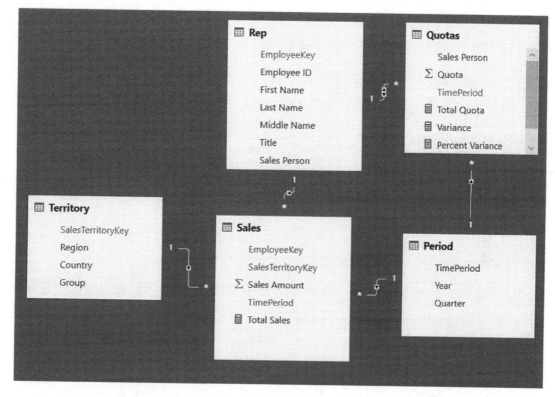

Figure 12-12. *The Sales Rep Analysis model with relationships defined*

You are now ready to add some measures to the model.

Create Measures

Add the following measure to the Sales table:

```
Total Sales = Sum(Sales[Sales Amount])
```

Add the following measures to the Quota table:

```
Total Quota = Sum(Quotas[Quota])
```

```
Variance = Sales[Total Sales] -Quotas[Total Quota]
```

```
Percent Variance = DIVIDE(Quotas[Variance],Quotas[Total Quota],BLANK())
```

Make sure you format the measures appropriately.

Create the Report

Create a report for analyzing sales person performance on Page 1 of the Report Designer by adding the following visuals:

- Slicer using the year from the Period table
- Stacked column chart that shows Total Sales by Country and Quarter
- Multi-row card showing Total Sales and Total Quota
- Multi-row card showing Variance and Percent Variance
- Clustered column chart showing Total Sales and Total Sales by Sales Person
- Text box for the title

Your final report page should look similar to Figure 12-13.

Figure 12-13. *The final Sales Person performance report*

Add another page to the report and add the following visuals to the page:

- Slicer with the Year field from the Period table

- Slicer with the Sales Person field from the Rep table

- Two tables with the Sales Person, Total Sales, Total Quota, and Percent Variance fields

- A line chart showing Total Sales and Total Quota by TimePeriod

Filter the tables so that one shows the top five Sales Persons by Percent Variance and the other shows the bottom five Sales Persons by Percent Variance. Edit the visual interactions so that the Year slicer affects the tables but not the line chart. The Sales Person slicer should affect the line chart but not the tables. The final report page should look similar to Figure 12-14.

Figure 12-14. The final report, Page 2

After completing and experimenting with the report, close and save the desktop file.

Use Case 3: Sensor Analysis

For this scenario, you work for a power company that monitors equipment using sensors. The sensors monitor various power readings, including power interruptions and voltage spikes. When the sensor senses a problem, it triggers an alarm signal that is recorded. You need to create a map that allows analysts to view and compare power interruptions and voltage spikes over time.

Load the Data

The data you will need is in several text files. Open the folder called UseCase3 in the Chapter12Labs folder. This folder has four files that contain the sensor data and the related data you need to complete the analysis. Create a new Power BI Desktop file named PowerAnalysis.pbix. Connect to the Alarms.csv file in the UseCase3 folder. You should have the following columns: PREMISE_NUMBER, METER_NUMBER, OP_CENTER, Type, and DateKey. Add a second query, AlarmType, which gets the alarm type data from the AlarmType.txt file.

Reopen the Alarms query and merge it with the AlarmType query using the appropriate keys (see Figure 12-15).

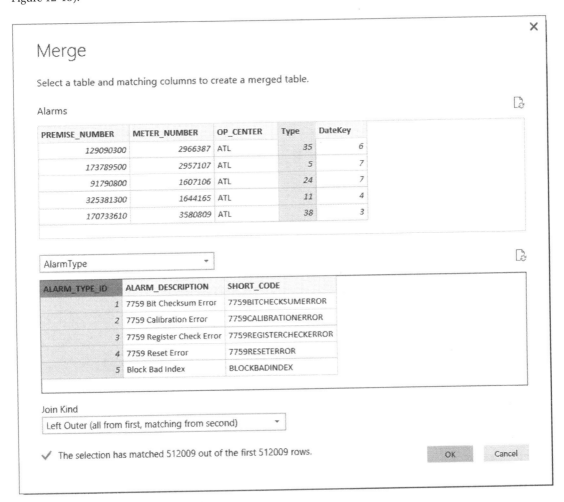

Figure 12-15. *Merging the* AlarmType *query with the* Alarms *query*

Expand the new column and select the ALARM_DESCRIPTION column. Rename this column to Alarm Type.

Repeat the previous procedures to replace the DateKey column with the dates in the Date.csv file. Use the Locations.txt file to add the longitude and latitude values to the Alarms query based on the OP_CENTER. You can rename the columns so that they use the same naming convention. Your alarm query data should look similar to Figure 12-16.

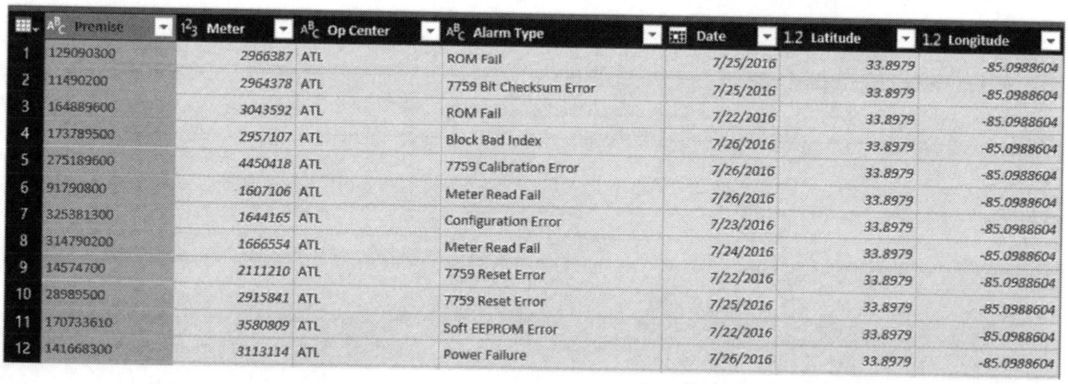

	Premise	Meter	Op Center	Alarm Type	Date	Latitude	Longitude
1	129090300	2966387	ATL	ROM Fail	7/25/2016	33.8979	-85.0988604
2	11490200	2964378	ATL	7759 Bit Checksum Error	7/25/2016	33.8979	-85.0988604
3	164889600	3043592	ATL	ROM Fail	7/22/2016	33.8979	-85.0988604
4	173789500	2957107	ATL	Block Bad Index	7/26/2016	33.8979	-85.0988604
5	275189600	4450418	ATL	7759 Calibration Error	7/26/2016	33.8979	-85.0988604
6	91790800	1607106	ATL	Meter Read Fail	7/26/2016	33.8979	-85.0988604
7	325381300	1644165	ATL	Configuration Error	7/23/2016	33.8979	-85.0988604
8	314790200	1666554	ATL	Meter Read Fail	7/24/2016	33.8979	-85.0988604
9	14574700	2111210	ATL	7759 Reset Error	7/22/2016	33.8979	-85.0988604
10	28985500	2915841	ATL	7759 Reset Error	7/25/2016	33.8979	-85.0988604
11	170733610	3580809	ATL	Soft EEPROM Error	7/22/2016	33.8979	-85.0988604
12	141668300	3113114	ATL	Power Failure	7/26/2016	33.8979	-85.0988604

Figure 12-16. The `Alarm` query with Latitude and Longitude data added

Next, filter the data to limit it to alarm types of power failure and high AC volts. Now you can aggregate the alarm counts grouping by the Date, Op Center, Alarm Type, Longitude, and Latitude (see Figure 12-17).

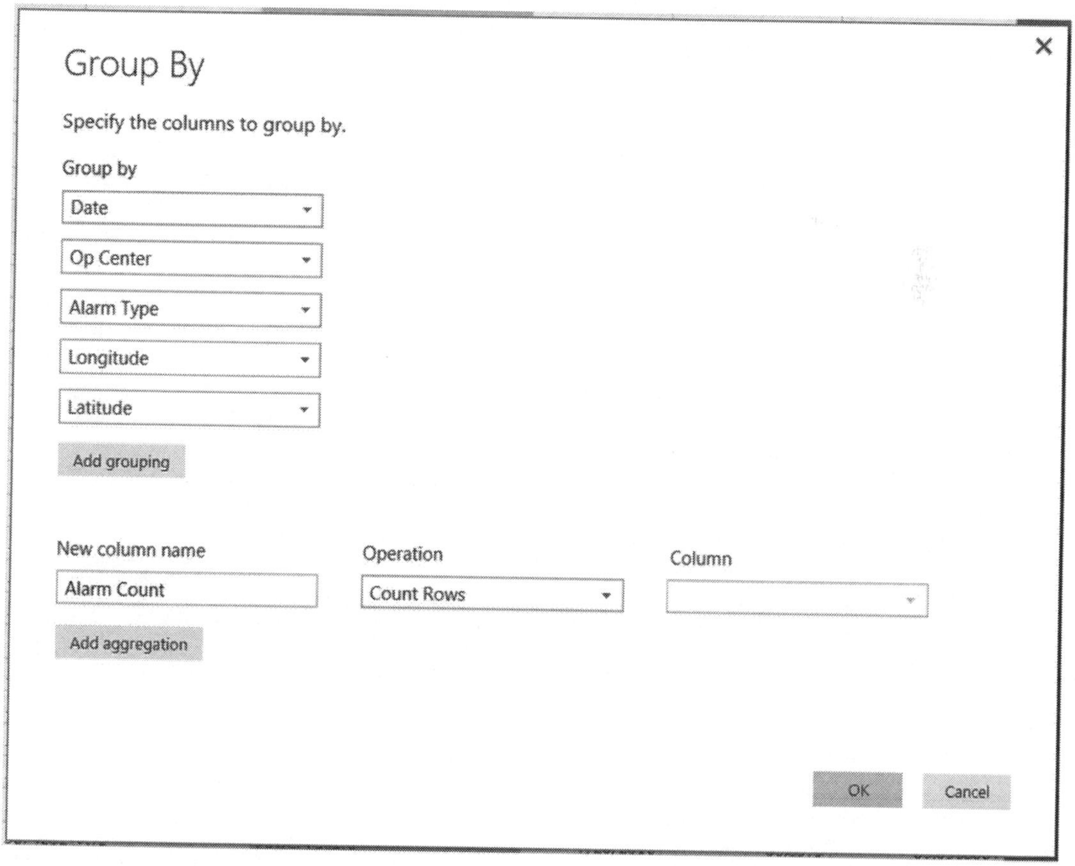

Figure 12-17. Aggregating and grouping the alarm data

After aggregating the data, disable the load for the `AlarmType`, `Date`, and `Locations` queries (see Figure 12-10). Select Close & Apply to load the data into the model.

On Page 1 of the report add a Map visual. Add the longitude and latitude values to the map. Add the Alarm Count to the Size and the Op Center as the legend. Next add a line chart to the report page. Use the Date as the Axis, the Op Center as the Legend, and the Alarm Count as the Values. The report should look similar to Figure 12-18.

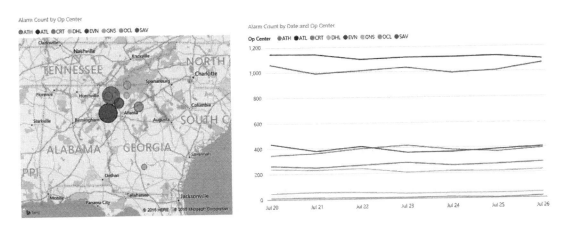

Figure 12-18

Notice that clicking a bubble on the map will filter the line chart. After exploring the alarm data in Power BI Desktop, save and close the file.

Summary

This chapter provided you with some use cases to help you gauge your mastery of the topics in the rest of the book. The goal of this book has been to expose you to the various tools in Microsoft's self-service BI stack. I hope you have gained enough confidence and experience with these tools to start using them to analyze and gain insight into your own data.

Now that you have a firm understanding of how to use these tools, you should be comfortable tackling more complex topics. The next two chapters are optional advanced chapters that contain topics I think you will find useful. In addition, there are many good resources available that cover various techniques and patterns that can be used to analyze your data. Microsoft's Power BI site (`www.microsoft.com/en-us/powerbi/default.aspx`), Bill Jelen's site (`www.mrexcel.com`), and Rob Collie's Power Pivot Pro site (`www.powerpivotpro.com`) are excellent resources. For more advanced topics, check out Chris Webb's BI Blog at `https://blog.crossjoin.co.uk/` and Marco Russo's and Alberto Ferrari's SQLBI site at `www.sqlbi.com`.

CHAPTER 13

■ ■ ■

Advanced Topics in Power Query

When you build queries using the Power Query designer, the designer creates the query using the M query
language. Although you can create robust queries using just the visual interface, there is a lot of useful processing
that you can only complete by writing M code. This chapter goes beyond the basics and explores some of the
advanced functionality in Power Query, including the M query language, parameters, and functions.

After completing this chapter, you will be able to

- Write queries with the M query language.

- Create and use parameters.

- Create and use functions.

Writing Queries with M

When you build queries using Power Query, each step you add inserts a line of M query code. If you select
the View tab in the designer and click the Advanced Editor button, you can edit the M code directly (see
Figure 13-1).

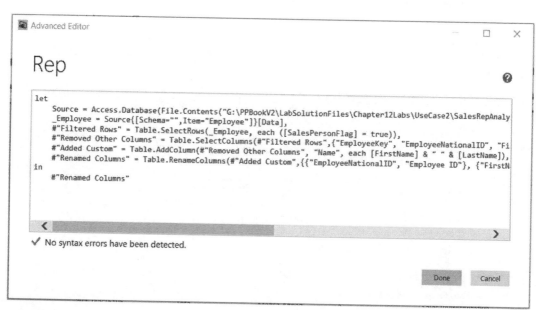

Figure 13-1. *Viewing the M code*

© Dan Clark 2017
D. Clark, *Beginning Power BI*, DOI 10.1007/978-1-4842-2577-6_13

Each line of code represents the steps applied in the designer (see Figure 13-2).

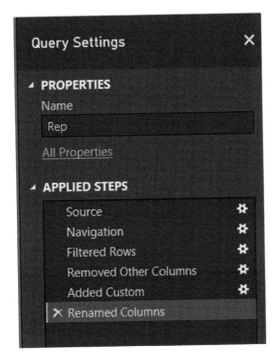

Figure 13-2. *Viewing the applied steps for a query*

The query starts with the key word `let` followed by the steps in the query and ends with the key word `in` followed by the name of the final table, list, or value:

```
let
        ... steps
in
        Table
```

The first step in most queries is to connect to a source. In this case, the code is connecting to an Access database file:

```
Source = Access.Database(File.Contents("G:\SalesRepAnalysis.accdb"),
    [CreateNavigationProperties=true]),
```

The next step is to navigate to the Employee table in the database:

```
_Employee = Source{[Schema="",Item="Employee"]}[Data],
```

The data is then filtered to only include rows where the SalesPersonFlag field is true:

```
#"Filtered Rows" = Table.SelectRows(_Employee,
    each ([SalesPersonFlag] = true)),
```

The each key word indicates that the query will loop through each row, and Table.SelectRows will select the rows where the condition is true. The next step uses the Table.SelectColumns function to narrow down the number of columns selected:

```
#"Removed Other Columns" = Table.SelectColumns(#"Filtered Rows",{"EmployeeKey",
    "EmployeeNationalID", "FirstName", "LastName", "MiddleName", "Title"}),
```

Next, a custom column is created by concatenating the FirstName and LastName columns:

```
#"Added Custom" = Table.AddColumn(#"Removed Other Columns", "Name",
    each [FirstName] & " " & [LastName]),
```

The final step is to use the Table.RenameColumns function to change the column names:

```
#"Renamed Columns" = Table.RenameColumns(#"Added Custom",
    {{"EmployeeNationalID", "Employee ID"}, {"FirstName", "First Name"},
    {"LastName", "Last Name"}, {"MiddleName", "Middle Name"},
    {"Name", "Sales Person"}})
```

Note that each step in the query references the table in the previous step. Also the steps have a comma at the end of the line, except for the last step.

There are many useful functions in the M query language. For example, there are text, number, date, and time functions. The following code uses the Text.PositionOf function to find the colon in a text column named ProductNumber:

```
Text.PositionOf([ProductNumber],":")
```

An example of a date function is the Date.EndOfMonth function, which returns the date of the last day of the month of a date. For example, the following code returns the end of the month date for an OrderDate column:

```
Date.EndOfMonth([OrderDate])
```

Some other useful function categories are the splitter, combiner, and replacer functions. For example, you can combine or split text by delimiters, lengths, and positions. The following code is used to combine a list of text values using a comma:

```
Combiner.CombineTextByDelimiter(", ")
```

▓ **Note**   For a full list of M functions, refer to the Power Query Formula Reverence in the MSDN library (https://msdn.microsoft.com/en-us/library/mt211003.aspx).

As you gain experience with M code, you will be able to build complex queries that go beyond what you can do with just the visual designer.

Creating and Using Parameters

The ability to use parameters in your queries is a very useful feature of Power BI Desktop. Using parameters is an easy way to update parts of your queries without having to alter the code. For example, you can create a file path using a parameter. When you share the Power BI Desktop file with a colleague, they can update the path without having to alter the query.

To create a parameter in Power BI Desktop, launch the query editor. On the Home tab, click the Manage Parameters drop-down and select New Parameter (see Figure 13-3).

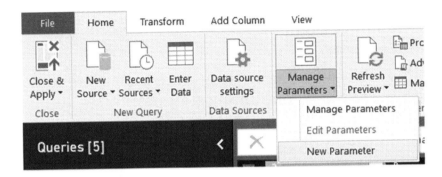

Figure 13-3. *Adding a new parameter*

This launches a window in which you can define the parameter properties (see Figure 13-4).

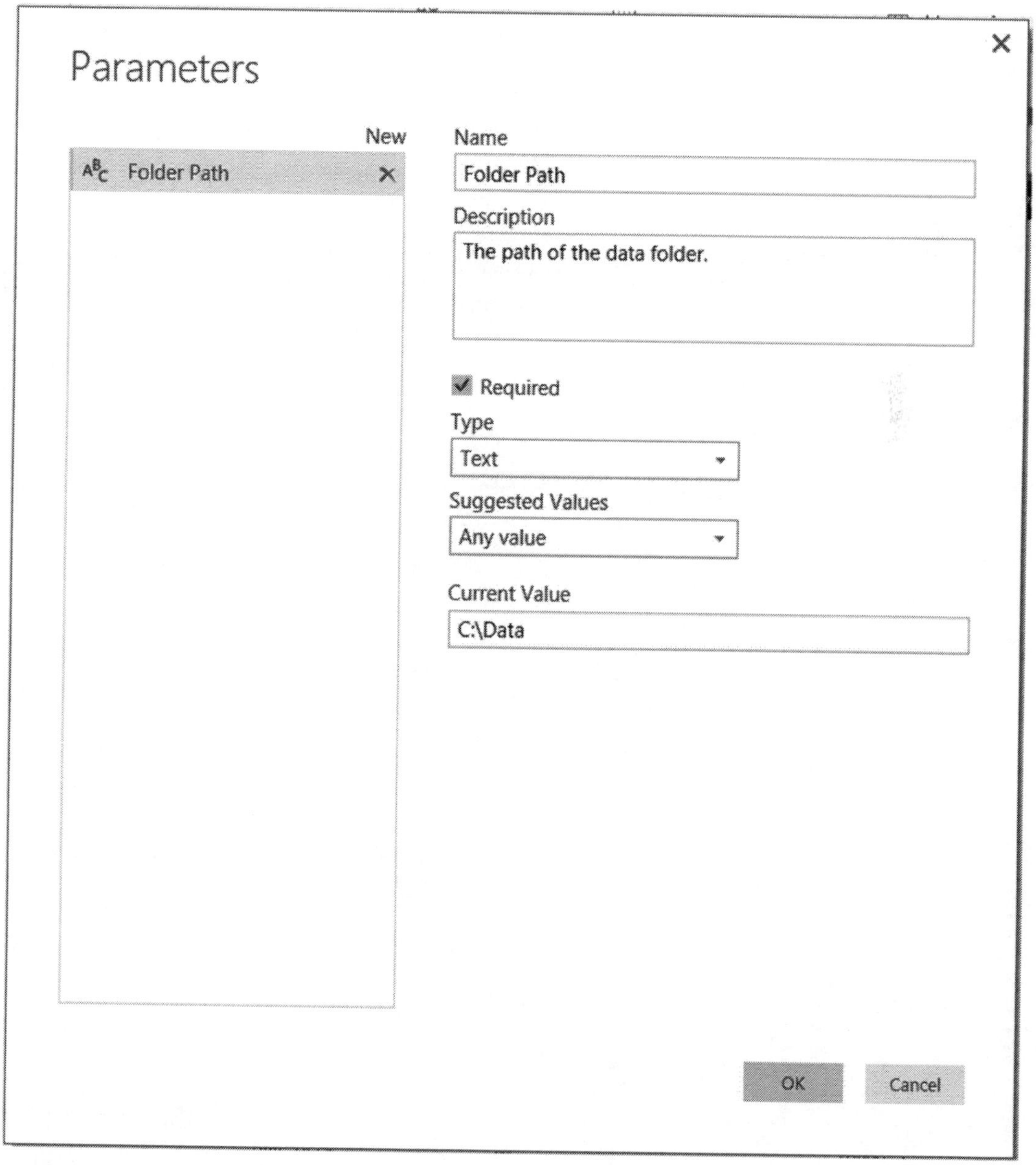

Parameters

	New	Name
ᴬᴮᴄ Folder Path	✕	

Name

Folder Path

Description

The path of the data folder.

☑ Required

Type

Text ▾

Suggested Values

Any value ▾

Current Value

C:\Data

OK   Cancel

Figure 13-4. *Defining a parameter*

The type can be any type supported by Power Query, such as text, date, or decimal. The value can be any value or be restricted to a list of values. The list of values can be entered manually (see Figure 13-5) or come from a query that returns a list.

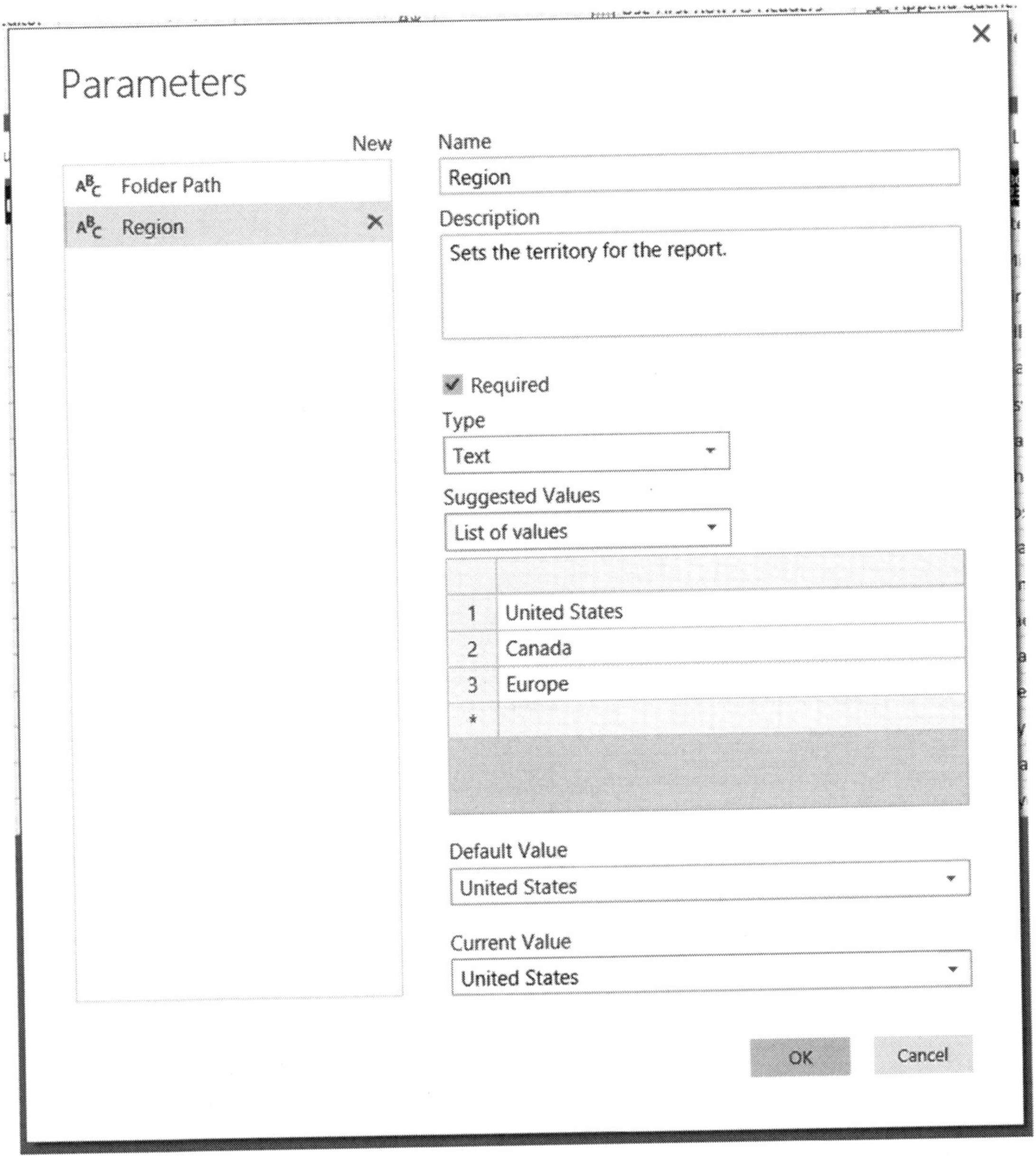

Figure 13-5. Defining a list of values for a parameter

To use the parameter in your queries, you just replace the hard-coded value with the name of the parameter. For example, the following filter statement

```
Table.SelectRows(#"Removed Other Columns",
    each ([SalesTerritoryRegion] = "Canada"))
```

becomes

```
Table.SelectRows(#"Removed Other Columns",
    each ([SalesTerritoryRegion] = Region))
```

Once you create a parameter, you can edit the parameter in the Home tab of Power BI Desktop under the Edit Queries drop-down (see Figure 13-6).

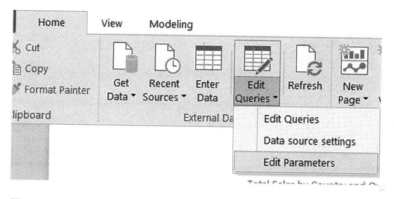

Figure 13-6. *Editing parameters*

This launches a window where uses can edit the parameter values (see Figure 13-7).

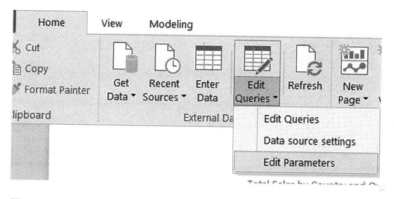

Figure 13-7. *Setting parameter values*

Unfortunately, parameters are not available in Excel at the time of this writing, but there is an easy workaround for this. First, create a table on one of the Excel sheets called Parameters. This should have two columns—one with the parameter name, and the other with the value (see Figure 13-8).

Parameter	Value
StartDate	10/28/2016
EndDate	12/24/2016
ProjectCode	BBRS004

Figure 13-8. *Creating a parameters table in Excel*

After creating the parameter table, select the table and then on the Data tab under the Get & Transform section, click the From Table button (see Figure 13-9).

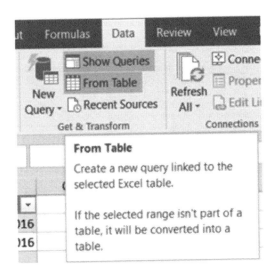

Figure 13-9. *Creating a query from the parameter table*

In the query editor, rename the query to the parameter you are interested in. Then filter the rows to only show that parameter. Next, use the Record.Field function to get the value from the Value column. The M code for getting the value of a parameter called ProjectCode is as follows:

```
let
    Source = Excel.CurrentWorkbook(){[Name="Parameters"]}[Content],
    #"Changed Type" = Table.TransformColumnTypes
        (Source,{{"Parameter", type text}, {"Value", type any}}),
    #"Filtered Rows" = Table.SelectRows
        (#"Changed Type", each ([Parameter] = "ProjectCode")),
    Value = #"Filtered Rows"{0}[Value]
in
    Value
```

Now you can use this value just like a parameter in your queries by using the query name. For example, you can filter by the ProjectCode as follows:

```
Table.SelectRows(#"Changed Type1", each [ProjectCode] = ProjectCode)
```

To change the filtering for a different project code, a user just has to update the value in the parameters table and refresh the queries.

Creating and Using Functions

One of the powerful features of Power Query is the ability to create functions using M code. Once a function is created, you can call it from other queries. For example, I have a set of dates for fire drills at a school and I need to determine the school year it belongs to. I need to check the date against a reference table that contains the school year, the start date, and the end date (see Figure 13-10).

SchoolYear	StartDate	EndDate
2016	9/7/2016	6/20/2017
2015	9/8/2015	6/22/2016
2014	9/9/2014	6/23/2015
2013	9/10/2013	6/20/2014
2012	9/6/2012	6/21/2013

Figure 13-10. *School year look-up table*

Say you have a date, 1/15/2015, and you need to filter this table so that the StartDate is less than or equal to the date, and the EndDate is greater than or equal to the date. This will leave one row in the table, and from that row you need to select the SchoolYear value. The M code to create this query is as follows:

```
let
    Source = Excel.CurrentWorkbook(){[Name="YearLookUp"]}[Content],
    #"Changed Type" = Table.TransformColumnTypes
        (Source,{{"SchoolYear", Int64.Type}, {"StartDate", type date},
        {"EndDate", type date}}),
    #"Filtered Rows" = Table.SelectRows
        (#"Changed Type", each [StartDate] <= #date(2014, 10, 10)),
    #"Filtered Rows1" = Table.SelectRows
        (#"Filtered Rows", each [EndDate] >= #datetime(2014, 10, 10)),
    SchoolYear1 = #"Filtered Rows1"{0}[SchoolYear]
in
    SchoolYear1
```

To convert this query into a function, you need to wrap the query into another let statement:

```
let
    LookUpSchoolYear = () =>
    [Original query]
in
    LookUpSchoolYear
```

The next step is to replace the hard-coded date in the query with a parameter you can pass in. The final query looks like the following:

```
let
    LookUpSchoolYear = (dt as date) =>
let
    Source = Excel.CurrentWorkbook(){[Name="YearLookUp"]}[Content],
    #"Changed Type" = Table.TransformColumnTypes(Source,
        {{"SchoolYear", Int64.Type}, {"StartDate", type datetime},
        {"EndDate", type datetime}}),
    #"Filtered Rows" = Table.SelectRows
        (#"Changed Type", each [StartDate] <= dt),
    #"Filtered Rows1" = Table.SelectRows
        (#"Filtered Rows", each [EndDate] >= dt),
    SchoolYear1 = #"Filtered Rows1"{0}[SchoolYear]
in
    SchoolYear1
in
    LookUpSchoolYear
```

Once you save the function, you can test it by clicking the Invoke button and entering a value for the parameter (see Figure 13-11).

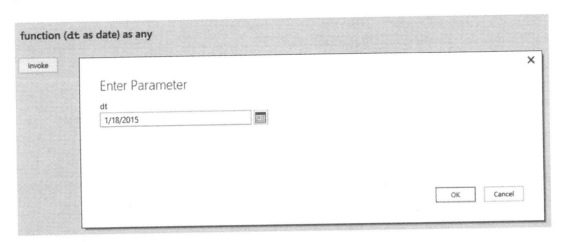

Figure 13-11. *Testing the function*

After testing the function, you can now invoke it from within another query. Figure 13-12 shows how you can use the function to create a new column called SchoolYear by passing the Date field to the function for each row.

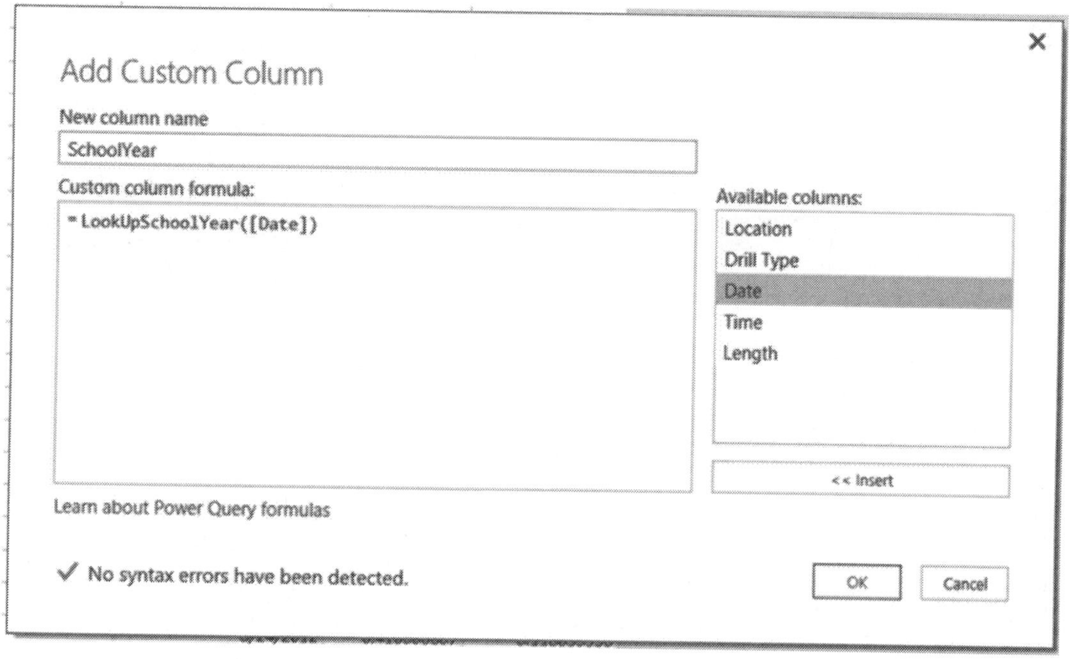

Add Custom Column

New column name

SchoolYear

Custom column formula:

= LookUpSchoolYear([Date])

Available columns:

Location
Drill Type
Date
Time
Length

<< Insert

Learn about Power Query formulas

✓ No syntax errors have been detected.

OK   Cancel

Figure 13-12. Using the function in a custom column

As another example of a function, you have data in the form of the table shown in Figure 13-13.

Location	Drill Type	Date	Time	Length	Year
CE	Fire	8/23/2012	12/31/1899 1:30:00 PM	12/31/1899 2:00:00 AM	2012
AA	Fire	8/24/2012	12/31/1899 9:45:00 AM	12/31/1899 3:00:00 AM	2012
BIS	Fire	8/24/2012	12/31/1899 9:15:00 AM	12/31/1899 3:00:00 AM	2012
MSS	Fire	8/24/2012	12/31/1899 10:10:00 AM	12/31/1899 2:33:00 AM	2012
CSE	Fire	8/24/2012	12/31/1899 10:35:00 AM	12/31/1899 1:38:00 AM	2012
BE	Fire	8/24/2012	12/31/1899 8:05:00 AM	12/31/1899 4:00:00 AM	2012
SAE	Fire	8/23/2012	12/31/1899 1:50:00 PM	12/31/1899 1:30:00 AM	2012
PHE	Fire	8/24/2012	12/31/1899 9:00:00 AM	12/31/1899 1:28:00 AM	2012
BH	Fire	8/24/2012	12/31/1899 9:50:00 AM	12/31/1899 2:42:00 AM	2012
GE	Fire	8/24/2012	12/31/1899 1:00:00 PM	12/31/1899 5:00:00 AM	2012
OFE	Fire	8/23/2012	12/31/1899 2:05:00 PM	12/31/1899 2:31:00 AM	2012

Figure 13-13. Initial drill data

You need to transform the data to show a list of dates for the drills grouped by location, drill type, and year, as shown in Figure 13-14.

	Location	Drill Type	Year	Dates
1	AA	Duck Cover	2012	1/31/2013, 11/2/2012
2	AA	Duck Cover	2013	2/6/2014, 9/13/2013
3	AA	Duck Cover	2014	2/6/2015, 9/5/2014
4	AA	Fire	2012	5/3/2013, 4/5/2013, 3/5/2013, 2/4/2013, 1/4/2013, 12/4/2012, 11/2/2012, 10/5/201...
5	AA	Fire	2013	4/1/2014, 12/20/2013, 11/20/2013, 10/25/2013, 9/30/2013, 8/29/2013, 8/23/2013
6	AA	Fire	2014	4/13/2015, 3/9/2015, 11/24/2014, 9/5/2014, 8/22/2014
7	AA	Fire	2015	8/28/2015, 8/25/2015
8	AA	Lockdown	2012	1/31/2013, 9/5/2012
9	AA	Lockdown	2013	2/6/2014, 9/13/2013
10	AA	Lockdown	2014	2/6/2015, 9/15/2014

Figure 13-14. Summarized drill data

To do this, you first want to remove the Time and Length columns. Then rearrange the columns and sort the Location, Drill Type, and Year columns ascending, and the Date column descending (see Figure 13-15).

	Location	Drill Type	Year	Date
1	AA	Duck Cover	2012	1/31/2013
2	AA	Duck Cover	2012	11/2/2012
3	AA	Duck Cover	2013	2/6/2014
4	AA	Duck Cover	2013	9/13/2013
5	AA	Duck Cover	2014	2/6/2015
6	AA	Duck Cover	2014	9/5/2014
7	AA	Fire	2012	5/3/2013
8	AA	Fire	2012	4/5/2013
9	AA	Fire	2012	3/5/2013
10	AA	Fire	2012	2/4/2013
11	AA	Fire	2012	1/4/2013
12	AA	Fire	2012	12/4/2012
13	AA	Fire	2012	11/2/2012
14	AA	Fire	2012	10/5/2012
15	AA	Fire	2012	9/5/2012
16	AA	Fire	2012	8/24/2012

Figure 13-15. Preparing the data

Next you create a step to group the data using the following code:

```
Table.Group(#"Changed Type", {"Location", "Drill Type", "Year"},
    {{"Dates", each fCombine([Date]), type text}})
```

Instead of aggregating the data, you pass the list of date values for each group to the fCombine function. This returns a text value with the dates concatenated together. The fCombine function in M code is as follows:

```
let
    Source = Combiner.CombineTextByDelimiter(", ")
in
    Source
```

Now that you are familiar with writing M code, you are ready to gain some hands on experience with the following lab.

HANDS-ON LAB: ADVANCED QUERY BUILDING WITH POWER QUERY

In the following lab you will

- Create and use a parameter.

- Alter a query using M code.

- Create and use a function.

1. In the LabStarterFiles\Chapter13Lab1 folder, open the Drills.xlsx file. This file contains data on drills for the various schools in a school district. Each tab in the workbook contains data for a different school year. After reviewing the data, close the file.

2. Create a new Power BI Desktop file called Chapter13Lab1.pbix. In Chapter 12, you loaded each worksheet as a separate query and appended the queries together. You can automate this using M code so that you don't have to update the query as more worksheets are added to the workbook.

3. On the Home tab, select Get Data from a Blank Query. In the Power Query Editor, Change the name to Drills.

4. In the Source step, add the following code to the formula bar. Make sure you use the path to where you saved the lab files. You should see each sheet in the file (see Figure 13-16).

   ```
   = Excel.Workbook(File.Contents
     ("C:\LabStarterFiles\Chapter13Lab1\Drills.xlsx"))
   ```

= Excel.Workbook(File.Contents("[redacted]\Chapter13Lab1\Drills.xlsx"))

	Name	Data	Item	Kind	Hidden
1	2012	Table	2012	Sheet	FALSE
2	2013	Table	2013	Sheet	FALSE
3	2014	Table	2014	Sheet	FALSE

Figure 13-16. *Loading Excel worksheets*

5. Keep the Name and the Data columns and remove the rest.
6. Add a custom column called TableWithHeaders and add the following code:

```
=Table.PromoteHeaders([Data])
```

7. Remove the original Data column and expand the TableWithHeaders column. Your data should look similar to Figure 13-17.

	Name	School	Drill Type	Date	Time
1	2012	CE	Fire	8/23/2012	12/31/1899 1:30:00 PM
2	2012	AA	Fire	8/24/2012	12/31/1899 9:45:00 AM
3	2012	BIS	Fire	8/24/2012	12/31/1899 9:15:00 AM
4	2012	MSS	Fire	8/24/2012	12/31/1899 10:10:00 AM
5	2012	CSE	Fire	8/24/2012	12/31/1899 10:35:00 AM
6	2012	BE	Fire	8/24/2012	12/31/1899 8:05:00 AM
7	2012	SAE	Fire	8/23/2012	12/31/1899 1:50:00 PM
8	2012	PHE	Fire	8/24/2012	12/31/1899 9:00:00 AM
9	2012	BH	Fire	8/24/2012	12/31/1899 9:50:00 AM
10	2012	GE	Fire	8/24/2012	12/31/1899 1:00:00 PM

Figure 13-17. *Data after expanding the TableWithHeaders column*

8. Rename the Name column to SchoolYear and change the Date and Time columns' data types to date and time.
9. Now you want to add a parameter that allows users to easily change the path to the source file. On the Home tab under the Manage Parameters drop-down, select the New Parameter option. Add a text parameter called `FilePath` that has a current value that matches the file path you used in step 4.
10. Alter the Source step in the `Drills` query to use the `FilePath` variable.

```
= Excel.Workbook(File.Contents(FilePath))
```

11. Select Close & Apply on the Home tab to close the query editor.

12. To test the parameter, move the Drills.xlsx file to a subfolder called Data. In the Power BI Desktop, click the Refresh button on the Home tab. You should get an error saying that it could not find the file.

13. Select the Edit Parameters option under the Edit Queries drop-down on the Home tab. Update the `FilePath`. You should now be able to refresh the data.

14. Select the Edit Queries option on the Home tab. In the query editor, right-click the `Drills` query and select Duplicate. Rename the new query `DrillTypeList`.

15. Remove the last two steps and edit the Expanded TableWithHeaders step so that it only selects the Drill Type column.

16. Remove the Name column and remove duplicates from the Drill Type column.

17. To convert the column to a list, right-click on the header and select Drill Down (see Figure 13-18).

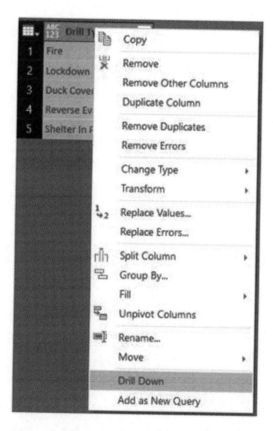

Figure 13-18. *Converting a column to a list*

18. Add a new parameter called `DrillType` that uses the list you just created as a source (see Figure 13-19).

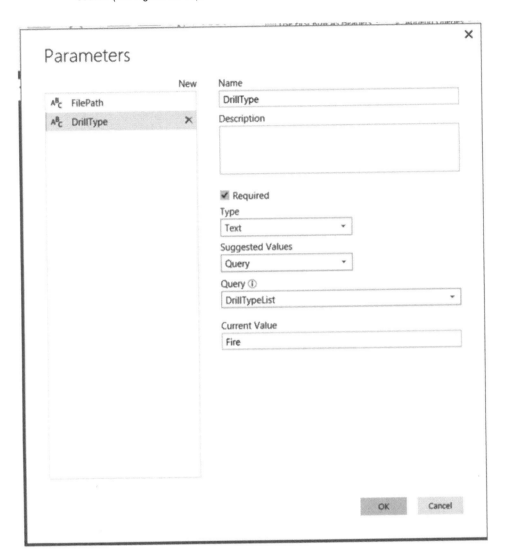

Figure 13-19. Using a list as a parameter source

19. In the `Drills` query, add a step that filters it by the `DrillType` parameter:

```
= Table.SelectRows(#"Renamed Columns", each ([Drill Type] = DrillType))
```

20. Close and apply the changes in the query editor. Test the parameter by updating it in Power BI Desktop and refreshing the data.

21. Launch the query editor and create a new blank query named CombineList. You are going to create a function that takes a list of text values and concatenates them together.

22. Open the advanced editor and add the following code:

```
let
    Source = Combiner.CombineTextByDelimiter(", ")
in
    Source
```

23. Close the advanced editor.

24. Make a duplicate of the Drills query and rename it DrillsSummary.

25. Add a step to sort by the SchoolYear, School, Drill Type, and Date columns.

26. Remove the Time column and change the Date column to a text data type.

27. Open the advanced editor and add a grouping step using the following highlighted code:

```
#"Changed Type1" = Table.TransformColumnTypes(#"Sorted Rows",
    {{"Date", type text}}),
#"Grouped Rows" = Table.Group(#"Changed Type1", {"SchoolYear", "School",
    "Drill Type"}, {{"Dates", each CombineList([Date]), type text}})
in
    #"Grouped Rows"
```

28. Close the advanced editor. The data after grouping the rows should look similar to Figure 13-20.

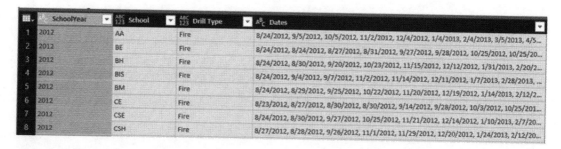

	SchoolYear	School	Drill Type	Dates
1	2012	AA	Fire	8/24/2012, 9/5/2012, 10/5/2012, 11/2/2012, 12/4/2012, 1/4/2013, 2/4/2013, 3/5/2013, 4/5...
2	2012	BE	Fire	8/24/2012, 8/24/2012, 8/27/2012, 8/31/2012, 9/27/2012, 9/28/2012, 10/25/2012, 10/25/20...
3	2012	BH	Fire	8/24/2012, 8/30/2012, 9/20/2012, 10/23/2012, 11/15/2012, 12/12/2012, 1/31/2012, 2/20/2...
4	2012	BIS	Fire	8/24/2012, 9/4/2012, 9/7/2012, 11/2/2012, 11/14/2012, 12/11/2012, 1/7/2013, 2/28/2013, ...
5	2012	BM	Fire	8/24/2012, 8/29/2012, 9/25/2012, 10/22/2012, 11/20/2012, 12/19/2012, 1/14/2013, 2/12/2...
6	2012	CE	Fire	8/23/2012, 8/27/2012, 8/30/2012, 8/30/2012, 9/14/2012, 9/28/2012, 10/3/2012, 10/25/201...
7	2012	CSE	Fire	8/24/2012, 8/30/2012, 9/27/2012, 10/25/2012, 11/21/2012, 12/14/2012, 1/10/2013, 2/7/20...
8	2012	CSH	Fire	8/27/2012, 8/28/2012, 9/26/2012, 11/1/2012, 11/29/2012, 12/20/2012, 1/24/2013, 2/12/20...

Figure 13-20. The final grouped data

29. When you're done, save and close Power BI Desktop.

Summary

Power Query is a very powerful tool used to transform data before it is loaded into the Power Pivot data model. Although a lot of functionality is exposed by the visual designer, even more functionality is exposed by the M query language. This chapter went beyond the basics and explored some of the advanced functionality in Power Query, including the M query language, parameters, and functions. This chapter only scratched the surface of advanced querying with M. If you want to learn more, I strongly recommend *Power Query for Power BI and Excel* by Chris Webb (Apress, 2014).

The next chapter covers some advanced topics in Power BI that I think you may find useful, including using custom visuals, advanced mapping, row-based security, and templates.

CHAPTER 14

■ ■ ■

Advanced Topics in Power BI

This chapter covers some advanced topics in Power BI that I think you may find useful. It includes using custom visuals, advanced mapping, row-based security, templates, and content packs.

After completing this chapter, you will be able to

- Use custom visuals.

- Implement geo-spatial analysis.

- Implement row-based security.

- Create templates and content packs.

Using Custom Visuals

Although Power BI includes an impressive set of visuals out of the box, there are times when they might not fit your needs. The great thing is that Microsoft has provided the source code for the visuals it ships and have provided an open source framework so that developers can create their own visuals. Although you probably won't create your own visuals, there is an active developer community creating and sharing their visuals. You can download and import these into Power BI Desktop for use in your own reports. To view the available visuals, go to the Visuals Gallery at `http://app.powerbi.com/visuals` (see Figure 14-1).

© Dan Clark 2017
D. Clark, *Beginning Power BI*, DOI 10.1007/978-1-4842-2577-6_14

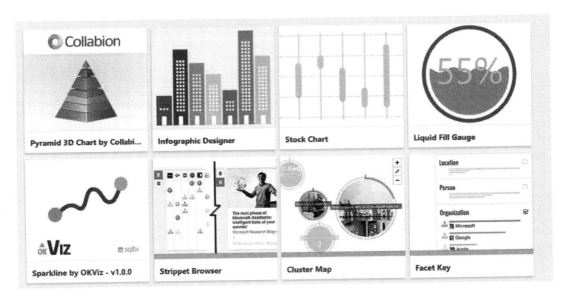

Figure 14-1. Some of the custom visuals available

If you click a visual in the gallery, you can download the visual and a sample Power BI Desktop file that shows how it is used (see Figure 14-2).

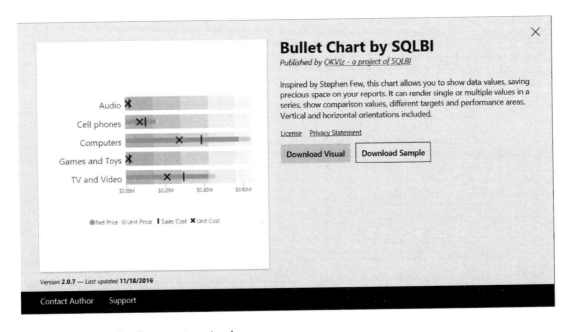

Figure 14-2. Downloading a custom visual

The custom visual is contained in a file with a pbiviz extension. After downloading the file, open an instance of Power BI Desktop. At the lower right corner of the Visualizations toolbox, click the ellipses (see Figure 14-3). This will give you the option of adding or removing a custom visual.

Figure 14-3. *Adding a custom visual*

To add the visual, you just import the pbiviz file. After importing the visual, you will see a new visual icon in the toolbox.

It's a good idea to download and experiment with the demo file. They usually give you hints on using the visual and explain the various properties. Figure 14-4 shows the Bullet Chart in a demo report.

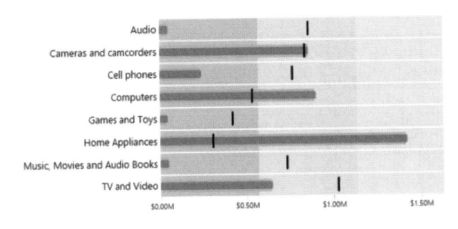

Figure 14-4. *The Bullet Chart in a demo report*

Another place to get some interesting visuals is at the OKViz website at `http://okviz.com`. They have a Synoptic Panel visual that allows you to create areas on images and assign colors and display information driven by your data. For example, you can create a map of a warehouse and display the number of parts in stock (see Figure 14-5). The color indicates how close you are to the safety stock level.

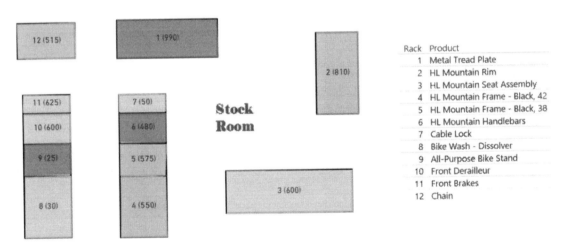

Figure 14-5. *Using the Synoptic Panel custom visual*

I definitely recommend that you investigate the custom visuals available. There are many visuals you will find beneficial to displaying and analyzing your data.

Implementing Geo-spatial Analysis

If the data you are analyzing has a location component, displaying the data on a map is a powerful way to gain insight and analyze the data. There are many different options available when mapping data in Power BI. You can use the built-in map, filled map, or shape map. You can also use custom visuals such as the Synoptic Panel and the Globe Map. There is also an Esri ArcGIS for Power BI. Selecting the right map comes down to how you want to display the data, whether you neep to incude custom maps, and whether you need to include multiple map layering.

The map is a good choice if you want to show data based on location such as latitude and longitude, street address, or city. For example, Figure 14-6 shows sales for cities in England. The bigger the buble, the larger the sales.

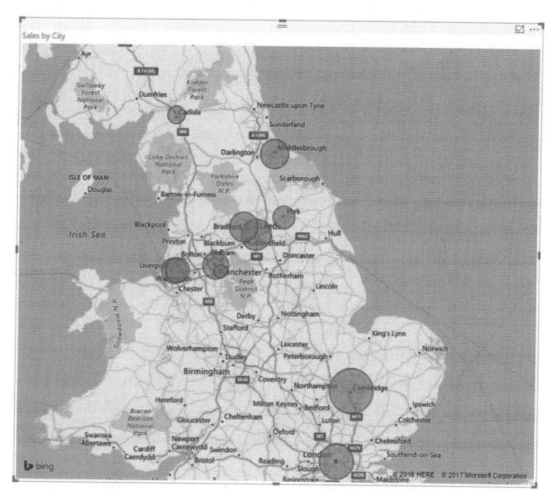

Figure 14-6. *Sales by city*

Along with associating the size of the bubble to a measure, you can adjust the color and color saturation. Figure 14-7 shows the location of potholes using latitude and longitude as well as indicating the priority by color.

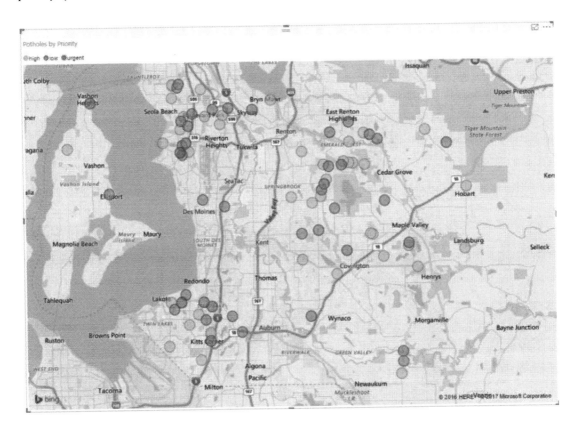

Figure 14-7. Using colors to display categorical values on a map

A filled map is useful to show how a value varies across a geographic area. For example, you may want to compare demographic data such as population, median age, or life expectancy. Figure 14-8 shows a filled map comparing the number of seats in the House of Representatives by state.

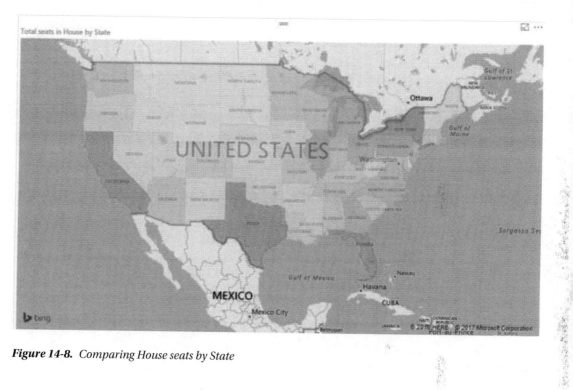

Figure 14-8. *Comparing House seats by State*

If you need to create your own custom maps, you can use the shape map. Using the shape map, you can load a map file in the TopoJSON format. To create the map file, you can use an online tool such as Map Shaper (`http://mapshaper.org`). Figure 14-9 shows San Francisco neighborhoods where the darker the shape, the more 311 calls were reported.

Figure 14-9. *Number of 311 calls for San Francisco neighborhoods*

If you need advance mapping capabilities such as clustering, heat maps, filtering, and multiple layers, Esri has released an ArcGIS Map visual for Power BI (www.esri.com/software/arcgis/arcgis-maps-for-power-bi). Figure 14-10 shows an ArcGIS Map depicting pothole locations imposed over a map layer showing population density.

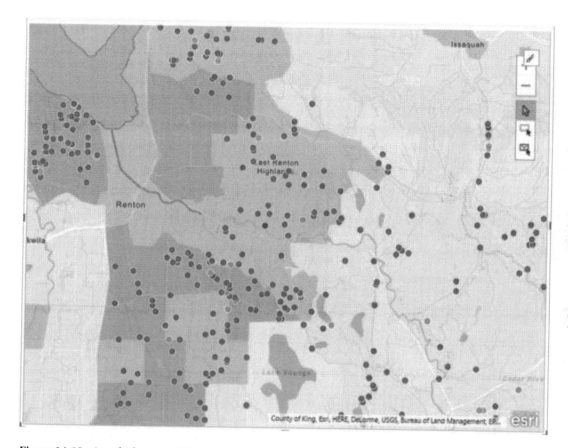

Figure 14-10. *A multi-layer ArcGIS Map*

As you can see you have many options when considering geospatial analysis using Power BI. If you just need basic mapping, the native map visuals are very capable. If you need more powerful features such as multi-layering, clustering, and map-based filtering, the ArcGIS map provided by Esri is definetly up to the task.

Implementing Row-Based Security

Security is an important aspect of any reporting system. It is critical that users only see data that they are authorized to see. To implement security in Power BI, you set up roles and use DAX to enforce data access rules. For example, you can create a role for USA Sales and authorize them to see sales for stores in the United States (see Figure 14-11).

Figure 14-11. Creating roles and DAX filters

Once you set up the roles and rules, you can test the security by viewing the reports as a member of the role would (see Figure 14-12).

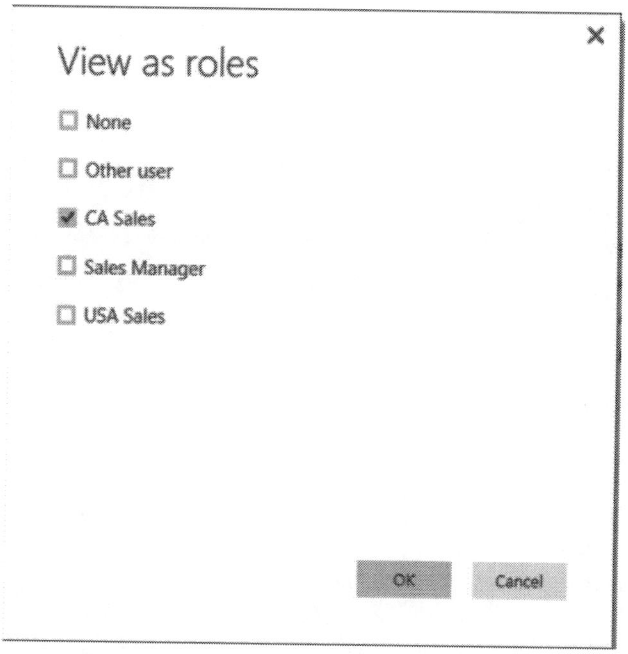

Figure 14-12. *Testing the role security*

Once you deploy the Power BI Desktop file to the Power BI Service, you can assign users and groups to the roles (see Figure 14-13).

Row-Level Security

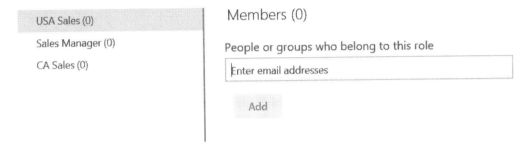

Figure 14-13. *Assigning users and groups to a role*

Being able to secure your data is crucial to any successful enterprise reporting/analytics solution. Using row-level security is a great way to ensure that data is only exposed to users authorized to see it.

■ **Note**   In order to implement row-level security, you need to have a Power BI Pro license.

Creating Templates and Content Packs

When sharing your Power BI Desktop files, you can make a copy of the pbix file, but this also contains the data. A better way is to create a template file based on the Power BI Desktop and share that. The template doesn't contain the data but does contain all definitions of the data model, reports, queries and parameters. When you import the template, you are prompted for any parameters defined in the file. This is very useful when the file is moved to a new enviorment. For example, when you share a file with a colleague, they can easily specify the file path to a local data source.

To create a template file, click File ➤ Export in Power BI Desktop and choose the Power BI Template (see Figure 14-14).

Figure 14-14. *Creating a Power BI Desktop template file*

Once you save the file, it will have a pbit extension. When a user opens the template file, they are asked to provide any parameter values (see Figure 14-15).

Figure 14-15. Providing parameter values

When the user saves the file, it becomes a Power BI Desktop file with the pbix extension.

Although using templates is a great way to share Power BI Desktop files, if you want to package up a complete solution for deployment to the Power BI Service, content packs are the way to go. With content packs for Power BI, you can package up your dashboards and reports for your colleagues to use. Once you create the content pack, you publish it to the Content Pack Library on the Power BI Service, where you can expose it to the entire organization or members of a security group. If you restrict the content pack to a specific group, only members of the group will be able to see it in the library. Members of the group have read-only access to the data, reports, and dashboards. The content pack creator can modify and republish the content pack. Users of the content pack will automatically see the updates.

To create a content pack, deploy the Power BI Desktop file to the Power BI Service and create a dashboard. In the upper right corner of the portal, click the cog icon and the Create content pack option (see Figure 14-16).

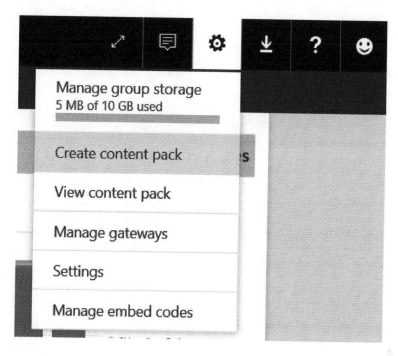

Figure 14-16. *Creating a content pack*

In the Create Content Pack window, choose whether you want to publish it to the organization or to specific groups. If you select specific groups, enter the emails of the groups. Add a title and description for the content pack. You can also add a logo for it (see Figure 14-17).

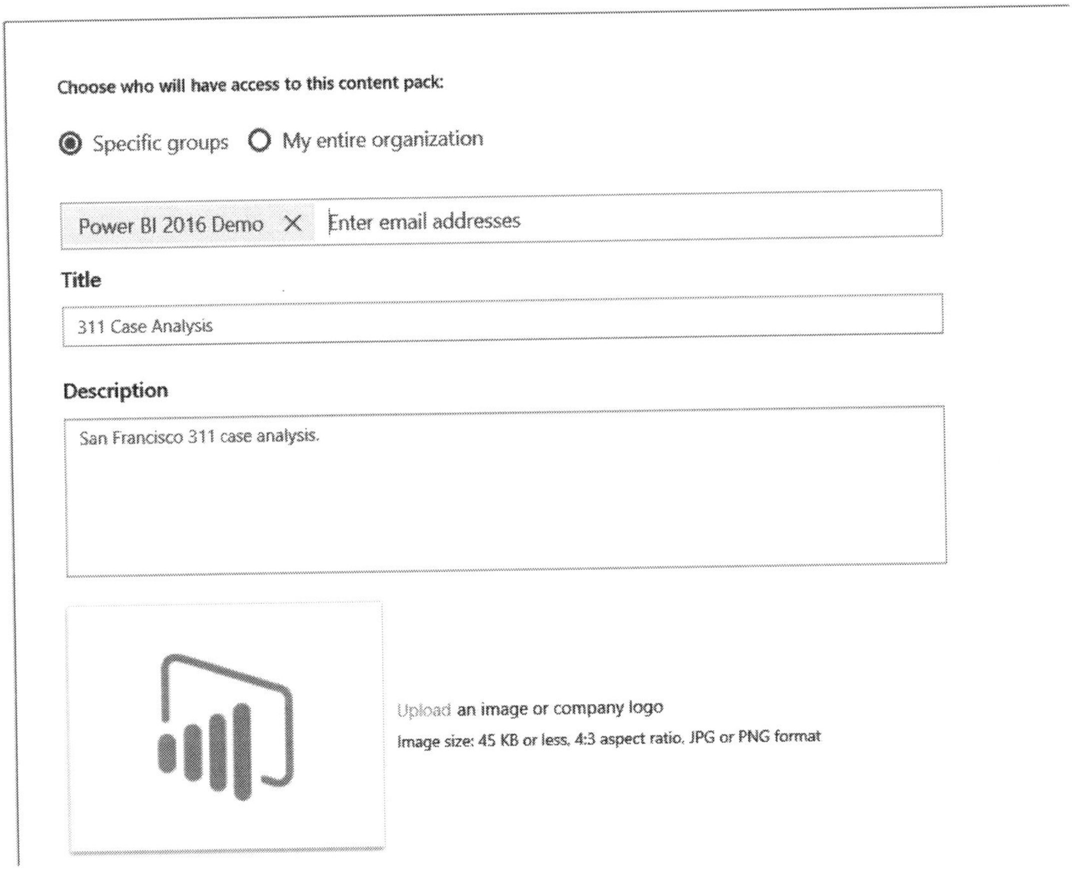

Choose who will have access to this content pack:

◉ Specific groups   ○ My entire organization

| Power BI 2016 Demo   ✕ | Enter email addresses |

Title

311 Case Analysis

Description

San Francisco 311 case analysis.

Upload an image or company logo
Image size: 45 KB or less, 4:3 aspect ratio. JPG or PNG format

Figure 14-17. Adding a title and description to a content pack

Next, select the items you want to include in the content pack (see Figure 14-18).

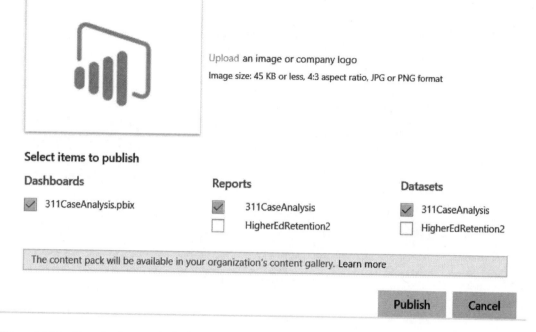

Figure 14-18. *Choosing items to include in the content pack*

Once the content pack is published, members of the group can import the content pack by clicking the Get Data link in the navigation pane and then selecting the My organization tab (see Figure 14-19).

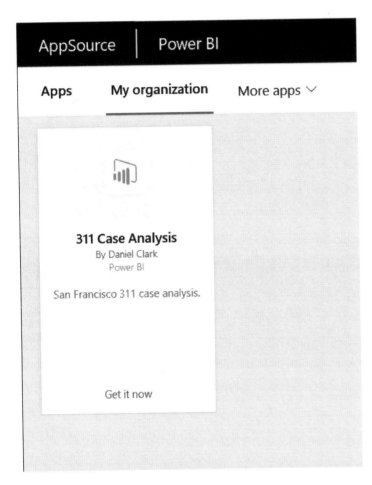

Figure 14-19. *Importing an organizational content pack*

In addition to your organizational content packs, many app-based content packs are available (see Figure 14-20). For example, there are content packs for Salesforce, CRM, and Azure Audit Logs. These allow you to get up and running quickly and deploy dashboards related to the service.

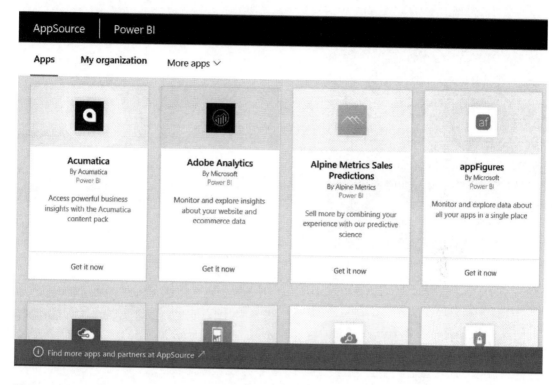

Figure 14-20. Selecting an app-based content pack

■ **Note** To create content packs, you need to have a Power BI Pro license.

Now that you are familiar with some advanced features of Power BI, you are ready to gain some hands-on experience with these features in the following lab.

HANDS-ON LAB: ADVANCED TOPICS IN POWER BI

In the following lab you will

- Use some custom visuals.
- Implement row-level security.
- Create a Power BI template.

1. In the LabStarterFiles\Chapter14Lab1 folder, open the CustomVisuals.pbix file. This file contains data on sales and quotas for sales reps.

2. In the LabStarterFiles\Chapter14Lab1 folder, there is a Visuals folder that contains several custom visual pbviz files. Add these visuals to the Visualizations toolbox in Power BI Desktop. After importing the visuals, you should see the new icons in the toolbox (see Figure 14-21).

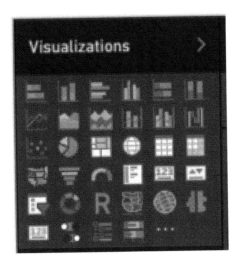

Figure 14-21. Adding custom visuals to the toolbox

3.   Add the following visuals and fields to the wells, as indicated in Table 14-1.

Table 14-1. Adding Visuals and Fields to the Wells

Visual	Well	Fields
HierarchySlicer	Fields	Period.Year
		Period.Quarter
CardWithStates	Field	Sales.TotalSales
	State Value	Sales.TotalSales
	State 1 Max	Quota.NinetyPercentQuota
	State 2 Min	Quota.NinetyPercentQuota
	State 2 Max	Quota.Quota
	State 3 Min	Quota.Quota
	State 3 Max	Quota.MaxQuota
BulletChart	Categort	Rep.LastName
	Value	Sales.TotalSales
	TargetValue	Quota.Quota
	Minimum	Quota.SeventyPercentQuota
	Satisfactory	Quota.NinetyPercentQuota
	VeryGood	Quota.Quota

4. The final report page should be similar to Figure 14-22. Investigate the different formatting available in the visuals.

Figure 14-22. Report, Page 1, with custom visuals

5. Add a second page to the report and add the visuals and fields to the wells as shown in Table 14-2.

Table 14-2. Adding Page 2 Visuals and Fields to the Wells

Visual	Well	Fields
Tornado	Group	Territory.Region
	Values	Sales.Sales2015Q1
		Sales.Sales2016Q1
GapAnalysis	Statement	GapAnalysis.Region
	Groups to Compare	GapAnalysis.TimePeriod
	Values	GapAnalysis.SalesAmount

6. The final report page should be similar to Figure 14-23. Take some time to investigate the different formatting available in the visuals. Close and save the file when finished.

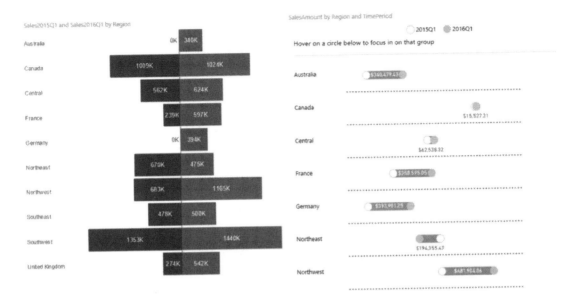

Figure 14-23. *Report, Page 2, with custom visuals*

7. In the LabStarterFiles\Chapter14Lab1 folder, open the RowLevelSecurity.pbix file.

8. On the Modeling tab, select Manage Roles. Add the NorthAmericanSales, PacificSales, and EuropeanSales roles.

9. Using a DAX filter, restrict the territories they can see. Figure 14-24 shows the DAX filter for the PacificSales role.

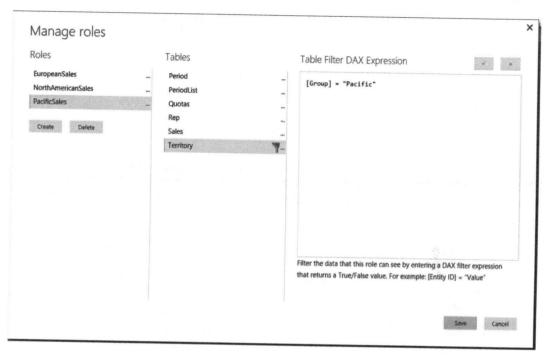

Figure 14-24. Setting role-based filters

10. Test the filter by selecting the View As Roles. If you view Page 1 of the report as the EuropeanSales role, you should only see France, Germany, and United Kingdom data (see Figure 14-25).

Figure 14-25. Testing the EuropeanSales role

11. Once done testing the roles, save the file. On the File tab, click Export and export the file as a Power BI Template file. Add a template description and save the file as TemplateDemo.pbit.

12. Close Power BI Desktop and double-click the template file. This should launch Power BI Desktop and ask you for the folder path. Provide the path to the data folder and click Load.

13. After the data loads, save the file as TemplateDemo.pbix.

14. Close Power BI Desktop and compare the size of the template file with the original pbix file. The template file doesn't contain data, so it should be much smaller.

Summary

This chapter covered some advanced topics in Power BI, including using custom visuals, advanced mapping, row-based security, and templates.

As I mentioned at the end of Chapter 12, the goal of this book has been to expose you to the various tools in Microsoft's self-service BI stack. I hope you have gained enough confidence and experience with these tools to start using them to analyze and gain insight into your own data. I also encourage you to take advantage of the many excellent resources available on the Internet. Microsoft's Power BI site (www.microsoft.com/en-us/powerbi/default.aspx), Bill Jelen's site (www.mrexcel.com), and Rob Collie's Power Pivot Pro site (www.powerpivotpro.com) are excellent resources. For more advanced topics, check out Chris Webb's BI Blog at https://blog.crossjoin.co.uk/ and Marco Russo's and Alberto Ferrari's SQLBI site at www.sqlbi.com.

Index

Get the eBook for only $4.99!

Why limit yourself?

Now you can take the weightless companion with you wherever you go and access your content on your PC, phone, tablet, or reader.

Since you've purchased this print book, we are happy to offer you the eBook for just $4.99.

Convenient and fully searchable, the PDF version enables you to easily find and copy code—or perform examples by quickly toggling between instructions and applications.

To learn more, go to http://www.apress.com/us/shop/companion or contact support@apress.com.

Apress®
THE EXPERT'S VOICE™